Carpetbagging America's Public Schools

Carpetbagging America's Public Schools

The Radical Reconstruction of Public Education

Curtis J. Cardine

ROWMAN & LITTLEFIELD
Lanham • Boulder • New York • London

Published by Rowman & Littlefield
A wholly owned subsidiary of The Rowman & Littlefield Publishing Group, Inc.
4501 Forbes Boulevard, Suite 200, Lanham, Maryland 20706
www.rowman.com

Unit A, Whitacre Mews, 26–34 Stannary Street, London SE11 4AB

British Library Cataloguing in Publication Information Available

Library of Congress Cataloging-in-Publication Data Available

ISBN: 978-1-4758-4019-3 (cloth: alk. paper)
ISBN: 978-1-4758-4020-9 (pbk. : alk. paper)
ISBN: 978-1-4758-4021-6 (electronic)

♾️™ The paper used in this publication meets the minimum requirements of American National Standard for Information Sciences—Permanence of Paper for Printed Library Materials, ANSI/NISO Z39.48–1992.

Printed in the United States of America

Dedicated to all of the teachers who have made a difference in the lives of children whether in sectarian, public, charter or private schools.

We owe them our best efforts, they know we can do better if only we will apply ourselves!

What the best and wisest parent wants for his child, that must we want for all the children of the community. Anything less is unlovely, and left unchecked, destroys our democracy.

—John Dewey

Contents

Contents

Introduction

THE CARPETBAGGING OF THE GREAT AMERICAN PUBLIC SCHOOL SYSTEM

Carpetbagger: 1. A Northerner in the South after the American Civil War usually seeking private gain under the reconstruction governments in the South.
2. Outsider; especially a nonresident or new resident who seeks private gain from an area. Often by meddling in its business or politics.

A hostile takeover of the American Public School System is currently under way. Like the carpetbaggers and scalawags who were protected and enabled by the Radical Reconstruction Laws passed by Congress after the American Civil War, a new wave of free market opportunists and their minions have raided the financial and governance systems that fund and oversee public education. The raiders have been enabled by deregulating legislation from the state and federal levels. This is occurring in an ethically and morally neutralized financial marketplace where,

> "the only social responsibility" of the "public" charter or private school business is to use its resources and engage in activities designed to increase its profits.
> —Paraphrasing Milton Friedman

The carpetbaggers who invaded the old South used the Radical Reconstruction laws to commandeer valuable real estate and assets. They operated under the protection of those laws. Modern carpetbaggers and scalawags have ensured they are working in a deregulated marketplace through carefully crafted legislative actions. The new rules, "freeing charters from the

1

rules and regulations governing public school funding, spending, and governance," ensure that the newcomers are operating with limited liability for their actions. The legislative process used to "deregulate" what was once a locally controlled community-governed public education is pervasive and expanding.

The premise of the economic theory of action behind this corporate takeover is that the current governance system for public schools is antiquated and immune to change. The proposed cure is innovation and entrepreneurship led by CEOs and corporate boards. This "free market" approach is supposed to transform the educational marketplace. This in turn will provide "consumers" of educational services the freedom to choose from a market filled with choices.

Authorized Carpetbagging

Unlike other free market enterprises, state charter laws and federal mandates protect the carpetbaggers and scalawags raiding the public education system from financial harm. The legislation enacted facilitates this real estate acquisition by granting the ownership of all property and assets accumulated by the charter school owners. After granting that ownership, the carefully worded laws release charter authorizers, their officers, and their corporate boards from liability for their actions related to debts or financial obligations from their "good faith" actions.

Often the owner is all three components of the charter's structure: owner, officer, and corporate board president—a recipe for what normally would be termed "fiscal malaise." Charter laws are an intentionally crafted deregulation of public education. Part of that crafting ensures that the laws free the charter authorizers, officers, and corporate board members from fiscal liability—the antithesis of what happens in a real capitalist business world.

Great freedom has been given without the attendant great responsibility that a true free market calls for. As a consequence, a financial disaster similar to the one caused by the deregulation of banking and mortgage lending is brewing. Charter and private school financial failures are pervasive in the data.

During the reconstruction period, there were agents who were in the South on a mission of goodwill and rebirth. These were the honest players who did their best to provide assistance consistent with what Lincoln, citing Shakespeare, termed "the better angels of our nature." The charter and private school owners in 23 percent of the cases studied behave in an ethical and fiscally sound manner. They are in the educational market with an educational purpose. They are exemplars of integrity and honor in the charter and private school ranks.

A View from 30,000 Feet

The "Free Markets" Are Neither Free nor Open

The protections afforded to charter schools in law are a tell[1] that this "free market" is neither free nor is it an open marketplace. Charter laws represent a radical reconstruction, through deregulation, of the funding and governance systems designed to protect the American Public Education System. The market that has emerged is rigged, by law, in favor of the owners, their agents, and their corporate boards. A "free market" rigged in the same way that the deregulated mortgage, hedge fund, and junk bond markets were prior to their collapse.

An egregious proliferation of related party transactions,[2] a form of self-dealing with "for-profit" subsidiary companies, owned by the same owner and corporate board, has created a financial time bomb in our systems for funding public education. After twenty plus years, a critical mass of charter holders are in financially precarious positions. The quasi-public debt funding these companies is similar in structure and composition to the debt that caused the mortgage and securities crisis in 2007.

Subsidiary "for-profit" companies organized as adjunct firms controlled by the owners and boards of nonprofit charter schools are the preferred tool for this financial manipulation. For-profit subsidiaries control and stage-manage the finances of the related nonprofit charter schools in this scenario.

What is revealed in the data is a rampant and implicitly condoned practice of financial situational ethics embedded in the "free market" choice world. The model described represents the modus operandi of 77 percent of the charters studied, a critical mass. The data set used in the meta-analysis informing this work was all of the charter schools in Arizona since 1994. Related data from other states was also extensively researched and analyzed as a part of this work.

Excessive debt has led to an over-leveraging of charter "properties and assets." This debt load leads to critically stressed financial positions where the bulk of educational funding is going to management and debt rather than children. At present, fully one-third of the charters in Arizona *do not meet* the Arizona State Board for Charter Schools Financial Performance Standards. 138 charter corporations are not meeting the Arizona State Board for Charter Schools Performance Standard. The charter board's rating system for financial performance is a standard devised by that board.

The measure understates the problem. There is another group of 90 charter groups, beyond the 138, that have not met the cash flow performance standard. Cash flow is a "tell" in business financials. There is also evidence that the financials are being manipulated to reflect better financial performances than the real numbers indicate. The national data on charter schools mirrors these results.

The underlying financial issues are manifest in charter bankruptcies and financial collapses under copious, over-leveraged, unsustainable debt. Statistically 65 percent of charter and private school failures nationally are caused by mismanagement and financial collapse. The failure rates of these schools stand at 40 to 50 percent depending on the type of charter held by the organization (non-profit or for profit). The failure rate in the "for-profit" category is 50 percent.

This work looks at the financial and governance effects of the free market economic theories espoused and acted upon as charters developed in Arizona and nationally. The theories of action used by charter and private school corporations in day-to-day operations. Essential questions were asked and answered using a forensic accounting method to analyze the meta data.

Real estate acquisition loans in these private ventures are being financed and guaranteed by government payments from the state and federal government to the charters' owners. The guaranteed equalization payment for student population counts used to disperse funding to the schools (Arizona Equalization Payments) is the primary state source of funding for charters. Similar "backpacks full of cash"[3] follow students in other states.

This educational paradigm shift has resulted in a redirection of funds that originally were court-ordered corrections designed to equalize the state's payments to districts, that is, the money states use to finance public education in a fair and equitable manner. This funding source was the result of lawsuits filed to ensure equitable funding of educational opportunity across the state. Students in towns *where there was little or no equalization funding have reaped the benefit of state aid for their placement in private and charter schools.* An example is the city of Scottsdale, a mecca for charter and private schools. Scottsdale is one geographical area that received limited funding from the state of Arizona under equalization of funding. Millions are now going to fund those students outside of the system that Scottsdale residents fund with their property taxes.

The resulting facility debt load at those charters is "insured" ("guaranteed" is the term used on audits) by those "backpacks full of cash." The debt structure on those facilities is a house of cards. It relies on exponential growth in the number of students being served: the premise of a Ponzi scheme. The student numbers *are not keeping up with the expenditures and debt.*

The real estate loans involved in charter finances are often from governmental agencies, county, and municipal bonds. Industrial Development Loans (IDA) are the preferred financing tool. These bonds in turn are purchased by Wall Street investors in the government bonds market. Balloon payments on these loans are premised on the idea that the indebted school will renegotiate the loans within five years rather than be on the hook for the balloon payments.[4] Bankruptcies and financial collapses from mismanagement are the predictable outcomes from these schemes.

The failure rate is currently 42 percent of all charters between 1994 and 2016. This rate is well beyond the foreclosure rate at the hardest-hit state during the mortgage crisis, California, which had a *one-year* foreclosure rate of 9.1 percent in 2008.

In Arizona, the state has recently *directly backed* the expansion of charter schools. State-backed securities are being used to fast-track charter real estate expansion. Like the mortgages backed by junk bonds in the 2007 financial crash, the backers of these loans are often junk bond and hedge fund professionals keen on cashing in on a deregulated marketplace of $800 billion. The "private" former government agencies behind many of those loans in 2007 were Fannie Mae and Freddie Mac.

Freedom to Choose

The general public has been provided local public common schools since the early part of the 1920s. Massachusetts had mandatory public education in 1852. Early Catholic and private schools predate the revolution and mandatory education laws. The funding of public schools has always been at issue in the long history of education.

Parents *have always had a choice* regarding where to send their children to school. These choices included public, sectarian, homeschooling, or private placements. In the past, two of those choices required a financial decision and a financial commitment by the parents. This was another way of saying "financial responsibility" for a personal choice. Choice always required an accompanying personal financial commitment. Parents could also opt to home school. In the past, this too was a choice that did not seek public financing for a personal choice.

We are making another choice when we choose "choice." The choice of abandoning the neighborhood schools that are provided for the citizens in a municipality often means unintentionally (or intentionally) resegregating ourselves and our future citizens from one another. A polite term for this is isolating ourselves from "the other." We are choosing to separate our children from their neighbors.

Robert Putnam refers to this type of loss as a loss of social capital. This loss of social capital is a result of this deliberate detachment from our common community enterprises and our neighbors. Putnam's term "bowling alone," which decried the loss of social capital throughout our country, has morphed into "schooling alone."

It is not a coincidence that the first efforts to establish vouchers and charters occurred after federal rulings by the Supreme Court ended the practice of "separate but equal" education. An intentional act of some in school-choice leadership has been a trend toward resegregation by social class, political bent, religion, and academic ability. While the promoters of choice insist this separation is unintentional, it is real. This is the nature of polarities. Choice for some leads to no choice for others. Who chooses, who loses?

On the monetary side, the results are mixed. Financial mismanagement and profiteering at the expense of our children occurs at 77 percent of the schools analyzed. It is an ongoing phenomenon. This statistic is a cause for alarm.

On the other hand, if 23 percent of charters are not profiteering and running their academically performing charters with ethically sound business decisions, they are a sign of hope for the charter movement. A common denominator of the 23 percent is their universal acceptance of all students and their deliberate involvement with their communities. Charters can work.

This literary reflection seeks to inform the public, especially parents who are contemplating where they want to place their child. A choice needs to be an informed decision. It is also designed to assist decision makers at charters and in the legislatures as they move to pass legislation to expand "choice."

This work is intended to demystify some of the financial and governance practices that have been shrouded in mystery since charters were introduced in 1994. The financial consequences of ignoring the fiscal and governance issues identified will ultimately cause a financial collapse of our public funding system for public education. That failure is as certain as the last financial crash. It threatens our entire system of public educational finances.

Financial collapses harm everyone. Everyone was impacted by the financial collapse in 2007. Our children's educational future depends on clear thinking and vigilance regarding who is controlling the decision making regarding our taxpayer-funded investments in public education. We are giving up local control and community input when we choose to isolate ourselves from one another. The great charter schools in the mix know this, and they work to keep the public involved in their public charter schools. A look at the political and social implications of choice is embedded in this story.

Financing charter and private schools with county and municipal IDA loans on over-leveraged properties is dangerously akin to the mortgage-backed security losses in the last financial failure. That failure as noted consisted of loans backed by Fannie Mae and Freddie Mac along with junk bonds sold as AAA-rated securities. It appears that a heist of our educational tax dollars is in progress. The Ponzi scheme survives by expanding its base of students. That expansion is not keeping up with the debt being incurred.

A common question from people interviewed for this work was, "How are they paying for all those new buildings?" The answers are in the story.

This Ponzi scheme is being sold as an educational innovation freed from the regulations that "hamstring" districts. The target of this scheme is the $800 billion dollar educational market.[5] The warning signs are in the data collated and evaluated for this story. We have been sold a product that "frees" us from the cumbersome democratic process[6] represented by public school boards and publicly owned district schools. Buyers beware.

NOTES

1. For non-poker players, a tell is a motion or sign in a card player's behavior that signals what they are holding in their hidden hand.

2. Related party transactions are those financial transactions that are carried out with relatives or related companies (i.e., for-profit subsidiary companies with the same ownership and corporate board membership). Former "charter owners" are included in the IRS definition of related parties.

3. The term "backpacks full of cash" is used by the charter industry to describe state funding following the student to a private or charter school.

4. Many homeowners engaged in this type of mortgage practice prior to the economic collapse in 2007. Balloon payments were part of the foreclosure surge as desperate homeowners were unable to refinance after the collapse. The foreclosure rate in 2008 was up by 81 percent over the norm. California's rate was 9.1 percent.

5. For a discussion on this topic from both sides of the spectrum, see: *The Prize: Who's in Charge of America's Schools?* (Russakoff, 2016).

6. Democracy is always messy. Will the next cumbersome process eliminated by "reform" be other elected positions?

Chapter 1

Perspective

Education is always and inevitably a personal and a social process. For communities and their children, going to school isn't about raising national test scores or the merits of core standards. It's about social aspirations and personal opportunity, public hopes and private fears.

—Sir Ken Robertson, October 2013

This work is not intended nor meant to disparage the concept of charter schools. Nor is it designed to debate about the educational value of charter and private schools. Charter and private schools can and do serve a vital educational need in our communities good for those who do this type of vital work in a fiscally sound, moral, and ethical manner.

There are models of these types of charter and private schools in this work and in the schools celebrated in Sam Chaltain's *American Schools* and in his follow-on book *Our School*. The titles of these works that focus on successful charters and district schools speak volumes about what an American Education should be about. Schools need to be our American schools.

The Arizona Agribusiness and Equine Centers are exemplary charter organizations in Arizona. The leadership and corporate board at that charter group gets this balance of ethical and financial business practices right. This charter school group is highlighted along with other schools in the 23 percent of charters that get it right. Charters in Arizona that have developed to serve autistic children, deaf students, homeless populations, Montessori programs, and organizations like the Florence Crittenton charter school for young women stand out in the data. They are exemplars of what is right in the Arizona charter world. There are comparable charters in other states.

As a democratic republic, we need to be educating our citizens to be Americans. The schools that we finance for this purpose need to be *our* schools centered and governed by people in our communities. We are educating Americans. Sometimes we lose sight of that.

Dr. Robertson, who is quoted in the first part of this chapter, also wrote the Foreword of *Our Schools* where he noted, "Effective systems of finance, organization, and accountability *do matter*. But they are not what education is or what it is for."

This work focuses on following the money. The organizational structure and financial accountability of charters matter. While effective systems of finance are not what education is for, they do constitute a major factor in a charter or district's viability. Carpetbaggers and scalawags should have no place in the discussion and solutions to our educational models. The underlying economic model for charters and privatization is a fault.

An economic theory of action that states that "the only social responsibility" of the "public" charter or private school business is to use its resources and engage in activities designed to increase its profits appears to be guiding the operational principles in use at a majority of charter schools. While the charter mission statements read for this report express altruistic goals, it is apparent in the data that "money talks." Business decisions trump educational decisions in the majority of the schools looked at. Profit motives overshadow mission statement ideals.

When a profit motive drives the train of reform, a conflict of interest will quickly develop. The data indicates that educational decisions in some 77 percent of charters are being trumped by business decisions affecting the owner's bottom line. These business and governance decisions are moderated by only one thing, *situational ethics*. Situational business ethics rule in too many of those decisions. Lax charter laws regarding finances and governance have created an opening for educational opportunists to profiteer in the education marketplace.

This opportunism is justified in this quote from a pro-charter advocacy group praising Arizona's charter laws, "The law is silent on related party transactions and bidding rules."

The law is silent. The resulting malaise is deafening.

Educational opportunity based on school choice has been promised to the public. Educational opportunism has been delivered in its place in 77 percent of the cases. A disregard for financial ethics or morality seems to be the modus operandi concerning taking public money for personal and corporate financial gain at these businesses. The statistics gleaned regarding how money is actually being spent verify that public education is an afterthought for these opportunists. Actions speak louder than their words regarding their charter's stated "mission statement."

This opportunism is manifest in administrative costs running at *20.5 percent* of total charter costs in fiscal year 2015. The average is actually higher,

22.2 percent[1] or $239,706,913. This figure represents over $1,500 per student as an average cost for administration at charters when the data excludes the university, district, and municipal charters from the mix. The same figure for districts is $774. Districts in Arizona spent *10.33 percent* on administrative costs in 2014–2015 (Staff 2015). This data is reflective of administrative costs across the country.

Opportunism shows up in classroom instruction spending statistics of *45.3 percent of expenditures versus* districts in Arizona at *51.88 percent* for classroom instruction.[2] This disparity in classroom spending is embedded in ten years of data; the difference between district and charter spending on the classroom is consistent.

A deeper dig into the data reveals the charters that *are* spending more on classroom supplies are often buying those supplies from "for-profit" subsidiaries of the charter (related parties). Online schools that are buying their own software provide an example of this type of self-dealing. Both district and charters in Arizona need to improve on this spending pattern as the figure for classroom spending nationally is usually 60 percent of expenditures.

Teachers, a precious resource, are the ones suffering from this gap in classroom spending as the majority of the classroom spending figures represent teachers' salaries and benefits.

Primavera Inc., an online K–12 charter, is one example of the issue. During the 2014–2015 school year, Primavera spent $3,396,301 in the classroom spending category. That breaks down to $3,930 per child.

Under Student Support, the group spent another $695 per student and $305 per child for other support.[3] Using the prior year's statistic on expenses, $2,364 of those expenditures were spent paying American Virtual Academy, a subsidiary for-profit company of the same management group.

Were these large sums, which were sent to a for-profit subsidiary, appropriate? How strong is the curriculum? Is the expense justified relative to alternative options? Did anyone take an excessive income? None of these details are publicly accessible. It also appears no one in authority (the charter board) is asking these questions.

We don't know if that payment went only to classroom-related expenses. If it did it would represent more than half of their classroom-related expenses. However, the amount spent is three times what Mesa, Arizona, school officials estimate it costs to maintain their online curriculum and software. Mesa Distance Learning (MDL) is an online school in the public Mesa Unified School District. MDL paid $581,000 to develop software for their online program in 1998.[4]

Mesa pays for maintenance, improvements, and additions to their online courseware. Jim Hall of Arizonans for Charter School Accountability asked and found out from officials at Mesa Unified School District that it costs about $760,000 a year to maintain their online program and software. The estimate is based on the salaries for content specialists (developers), administrator, and programmer, and additional stipends paid to online teachers for curriculum development. Mesa Distance Learning offers a complete K–12 curriculum, though primarily serves high school students (Hall 2017). The data regarding Mesa's expenditures is public information.

By developing their own "online" learning program, Mesa School District is competing in this online arena. Another example of a competing online program is the Tucson School District's "Beyond Textbooks" initiative. Competition, an often-used word in the choice debates, is supposed to be one of the goals of "choice." These public school districts are competing in the online space. Their costs are a fraction of the other players in the "choice" arena.

Neither of these competitors is spending the $2,422,625 in advertising that Primavera spent in 2013–2014. They also did not accumulate $232,626 in travel expenses promoting their products in other states and countries.

THE NEW JUNK BONDS: CHARTER DEBT, A HIGH-YIELD INVESTMENT TOOL

Charter schools and the public money used to fund them have become the new mortgage, hedge fund, and junk bond marketplace of the free marketers on Wall Street. This is happening on the national stage as well as the state and local levels. This hostile takeover of public funding for school construction and capital should be a concern to the general public *and to the core group of charter operators and private schools that are doing the right thing with the structure that is in place. This kind of reckless financing should also shock and dismay fiscal conservatives to their core.*

By showcasing the charter exemplars that finance their debt with solid investing strategies, the author offers proof that the rhetoric regarding choice can match the results. *Twenty-three percent of charters* have personal financial integrity and sound business practices driving their practice. Others come close to this standard of practice. These charters consistently avoid the markets that finance schools with junk bonds.

Doing It Right: Thoughts from an Advocate

One of the schools selected as a notable American School in Sam Chaltain's American Schools was (and is) the Monadnock Community Connections School in Keene, New Hampshire. This charter school is part of the First Amendment School Network. The school was created by a district that the author led from 1999 through 2004. Charter schools can serve the public good that is public education by offering a real choice to the offerings at the local public schools. They do not have to withdraw from their communities to do so.

Denis Littky's Big Picture Schools are another example of a large-scale charter group whose reform of education produces informed and capable citizens. "One Student at a Time" means something at the schools this masterful innovator creates. Denis' work and that of Kim Carter at the QED foundation are bright beckons of light in the charter "marketplace." They and innovators like Deborah Meyers in New York are charter innovators who provide educational opportunity to their students.

Linda Proctor Dowling's Arizona Agribusiness and Equine Centers provide a unique charter choice. The board of this charter is filled with community members from the areas she serves. The school's emphasis, Agribusiness, is embedded in the name. Linda's schools continuously rate an academic score of "A."

American Leadership Academies provide a distinct learning environment while operating with financial integrity. They treat their professional staff with dignity and grace. Ethics trump profits at this school. They are one of the few charter schools providing transportation to their schools ensuring all students have a chance to attend. They lease from the owner of the land and facilities at a reasonable rate. This model is also used in their Utah sites.

The Rose Academies, a "for profit," takes on students who were struggling in their district schools. They should wear their "C" in academics with pride. They are doing the right thing with children who need what they offer. Big charter organizations can get educational priorities right.

The online school at the Edkey Group, Sequoia Choice, uses curriculum that the staff has developed themselves. Their academic results mirror this involvement of the staff with the content they teach. Students are brought into the home site when they need tutoring. That tutoring is provided by superior online teachers who care about each child. The staff works together and identifies issues with each child as they arise, not weeks later. Their academic data reflects their commitment to excellence.

Opportunity versus Opportunism

Educational opportunity is not the same thing as educational opportunism. The two are polar opposites.

This work and the research project underpinning the cited statistics focuses on the financing and governance of charters as they currently exist. *It is not a call to abandon the charter model.* The 23 percent of charters that are doing the job of providing an alternative to public school programs with sound financial and governance models are celebrated. They are a proof of concept. The rules of the game need to assure that they, the model charters, are emulated and replicated.

When "our community school" becomes "my company's school," charter and private schools separate themselves from the community at large. Social capital is lost as a casualty to the free market economics theories dominating the financial and governance practices at 77 percent of the charters studied. Community matters in a democratic republic.

Monadnock Community Connections, Surry Elementary Charter, and Sequoia's Pathway Academy in Maricopa, Arizona, are all successful charter schools that serve communities and their students. The "All Aboard" School in Arizona while having some related party expenses meets the ethical criteria for those expenses. Their name, All Aboard, is also reflected in their desire to work with children across the academic spectrum. They are a small charter in the 23 percent.

The financial and governance practices identified in this work are reporting out on the financial and governance issues as they currently exist. While some data is provided on academics, it is only used to counter academic prowess claims that have not panned out. The final chapter concludes with recommendations for change.

This work is informed by the author's work developing and promoting charter schools in New Hampshire and Arizona. The viewpoint is that of an informed research practitioner with experiences in business, public schools, and charter schools (district and independent charters).

CHARTER CEOs AT THEIR BEST

There are charter CEOs who understand what community schools and their obligation to those communities are. Ron Neil, a charter CEO (Edkey Inc.) who was trying to deal with the dark side of charter financial dealings, often spoke of "the moral imperative" for charter schools.

The carpetbaggers and scalawags in the business troubled this author and Mr. Neil. Ron demanded and produced charters that served their communities' needs. However, within months of Mr. Neil's passing, the frailties of the governance and financial oversight of charters re-emerged. To their credit, the charter corporate board at the organization fulfilled their governance role and reset the direction the company was going. Righting the ship required an independent charter corporate board. *This type of courageous, engaged corporate board is the exception. It needs to be the rule.*

For the author it was a time for a period of reflection and examination about what the data can tell us about charter school financial and governance models.

Models that rely on situational ethics to guide the owners and their corporate boards are not up to the challenges that human behavior often manifests itself as when it comes to money. If Edkey had a one-person board who was the owner, there would have been a different outcome.

Ron Neil knew that the machinations he witnessed and sought to correct could cause the financial collapse of a charter business. He also knew that this business was operating in a field that should be about public good. The world of publicly funded education requires "the better angels of our nature."

Charter and private school do have a moral imperative to our children and communities. They violate that imperative at their own financial peril. They delegitimize their existence as agents of positive innovation and change when they do so.

The Better Angels of Our Nature

Not all of the Northerners heading south after the Civil War were there as carpetbaggers. Every political leader left at the local level was not a scalawag. Historical evidence suggests that the good work done by reconstruction often outweighed the bad. The country learned from its Radical Reconstruction Period. An assessment of what is really happening with the finances and governance of charters is in order. "Starving the beast of public education," a term heard often during the research phase of this report and in the charter field, is neither constructive nor productive. The Teacher Wars[5] need to end. A truce to survey what choice has wrought is in order.

Leaders need to lead. It is up to our elected leaders to fix and amend the laws they created. It is up to the public to learn from twenty years plus of experience with charter schools and vouchers and to demand accountability from those legislative leaders.

Financing Matters

The precarious financing of charters is highly reliant on Industrial Development Loans,[6] Commercial Loans, and New Market Tax Credits. Financing charters with municipal, state, and federal government–backed securities and tax credits is a national issue.

A new mortgage bond crisis in over-valued, over-leveraged charter properties is creating a bubble that is starting to burst. There is quick money to be made by the same cast of characters that brought us previous national financial crises. Making money is not, nor should it ever be, the *primary purpose of public education*. New Market Tax Credits are about making money.

The New Markets Tax Credit and the Financial Markets

At the end of 2000, Congress passed a new tax credit tool known as the New Markets Tax Credit. The purpose of this credit was to "encourage" lending in new markets (i.e., traditionally risky areas). In reality the rich get richer under the pretext of helping poor communities.

Investors who put money into New Market Tax Credits are virtually guaranteed to double their investment in seven years using a 39 percent tax credit from the federal government. The New Market Tax Credits are a dream-come-true tool for hedge fund managers and junk bond dealers—high interest, low risks using government tax credits.

The same investors noted earlier then "lend" the money to charter schools in eligible zones. This lending takes place by the investor buying the property that the charter school is located on (and the buildings). A purchase scheme noted in the majority of large charter groups and small- to medium-sized operators. In New Market situations, the investor receives a 39 percent credit and the same investor gets to "lease" property purchased with the money they are getting a credit on at ever-increasing lease rates. When the charter "fails" financially, the lender becomes the owner of the property. All of the partial payments that were made with tax dollars are lost to the taxpayers.

This practice while it seems to benefit the charter movement is in fact a polarity. The fact is over-leveraged lending leads to the demise of charters that become victims of the parties (lenders) that own the junk bonds on the property. Those parties assume the foreclosed properties as collateral on the loan.

The practice also allows for interlocking relationships between boards, owners, and lenders as those types of interactions are not "illegal" under the current rules. For-profit subsidiaries of the nonprofit charter typically hold the property and assets of the school.

These financial instruments have become the new playground for hedge fund managers. The Harvard Club sponsored a symposium titled, "Bonds and Blackboards: Investing in Charter Schools." The sponsors: the Gates Foundation and the Walton Foundation. The topic, making money in charter schools by investing in the underlying bonds financing them.

In the data set, under the heading "Commitments," related party transactions and nonrelated party transactions have been delineated and collated. Built in "rent" or "lease" increases based on either time or student population are noted in these "Commitments"[7] as they are on the audits and were traceable using this method.

Leasing charter properties from for-profit subsidiaries is often accompanied by ever-increasing lease charges paid to the "for-profit" leasing company. Payments to ownership often occur at a 10 percent markup. Non-profit charters plan and set up for-profit subsidiaries to move money around in a private company setup to conceal the transactions from public scrutiny. A fee is captured from leases with related parties, leased employees, and management companies. The ownership and corporate boards of the non-profit schools are the same people operating the subsidiary for-profit firms.

There is virtually no educational purpose being served by these arrangements. The money earned *is not going back* to improve the educational outcomes at the schools. The motivation is profiteering from public funds designated for educating our children—a public good.

This type of lending and selling of employee services quickly turns into a drag on the charter school's cash flow as more and more money goes into the payments to the for-profit subsidiaries and to debt on over-leveraged assets. Profiteering replaces sound educational financial practices. Imagine your local school district leasing teachers from a "for profit" that the superintendent controlled with the school board. Outrage would follow. In charters, it is business as usual.

There is no other way to explain the practice of leasing employees from a for-profit subsidiary. The practice effectively shuts out the employees from the retirement system offered by the state, creating an immediate 11.1 percent return to the charter group. This saving is then captured by the fees charged[8] for "leasing" the teachers to the school—an example of carpetbagging.

NOTES

1. There were over seventy charters that had administrative costs greater than 30 percent with outliers topping more than double that percentage.

2. Source: Superintendent's Report January 2015.

3. The Annual Financial Report lists several categories for expenditures: Classroom Instruction, Classroom Supplies, Administration, Student Support, and Other Support.

4. TAPBI Auditor general Report, 2007, p. 23 at: https://www.azauditor.gov/sites/default/files/TAPBI.pdf.

5. *Teacher Wars* (Goldstein, 2015) is an excellent up-to-date short history of education in this country. For other sources, see Diana Ravitch and the multivolume works of Lawrence Cremin.

6. See chapter on IDA Loans.

7. On an audit, commitments are payments that are covered by a rental or lease agreement. A five-year guaranteed lease is common. Some for-profit companies lease their own properties, owned by another company with the same owners, back to the schools. The ADM at the school is used as a guarantee for the loan on the property. For links to more information regarding investing in charters, follow the link here. (Link is at Democracy Now.)

8. The 10 percent fee was often stated on the audits. When a fee was not listed, a calculation was performed that considered all of the employee costs on the audit and then compared that total to the amount sent to the for-profit leasing company. The amount "missing" was found to be 10–15 percent. When companies stopped listing their expenses on their audit in detail, this type of checking becomes difficult at best. This type of reporting is deliberately being done to hide the transactions.

Chapter 2

Carpetbagging

RADICAL RECONSTRUCTION

The radical deregulation and reconstruction of the nation's public schools' finance and governance rules has resulted in a real estate and public property transfer of epic proportions. Taxpayer funds once used to purchase and staff commonly held community schools are being drained by educational opportunists under the guise of free market choice and vouchers (empowerment scholarships as they are euphemistically called) for private school placements.

SOWING THE WIND

What has followed from deregulation and the charter laws replacing and bypassing sound educational financing regulations regarding bidding and related party transactions?

The result has been an open door for carpetbaggers and scalawags to gain access to an unfettered and deregulated national treasure. That treasure being the $800 billion dollar market monetary prize known as public education funding.

Schools that our communities owned, controlled, and cherished as centers of their civic life have been co-opted in a *carefully planned hostile business takeover*.

The corporate takeover of America's public schools has been a planned acquisition by the newcomers in what is falsely described as the educational free market. The deregulation granted by charter law and opportunity

18

scholarships only applies to charter schools and vouchers. A closed field of competition with different rules for the competitors is the result.

In Arizona, an additional funding source of $1,700 per student for charters allows those schools to continue their building acquisitions while the public school building funds are continually underfunded. This is what passes for "free market" competition. "Districts need not apply" is written into the laws. So much for equal opportunity lending (or sound) financial practices.

When the veneer is scratched off the facade of shiny new charter schools sprouting up across the country, a sense of déjà vu sets in. Unpeeling the onion reveals who is really controlling this supposed free market. It's not the parents or the community the school locates in.

The financial strings are controlled by Wall Street junk bond salesmen and hedge fund managers who manipulate government-backed and sponsored loans. These risky loans are backed by the same government entities that the Goldwater Institute critiqued in an investigative report in 2012 entitled, "Debt and Taxes: Arizona Taxpayers on Hook for $66 Billion Tab Run up by State, Local Governments" (Slivinski, 2012).

While the Goldwater Report focused on "governmental debt" at the time, one cannot ignore the fact that there are now tens of millions of dollars of charter debts currently out in IDA Loans. The funds are also being used to fund projects that charters have in other states and countries, China being one of many. Our educational taxes are funding charter and private expansion projects outside of the state where the funds originated. As microeconomic teaches us that capital investment is lost to the local community.

The state of Arizona moved to guarantee more debt ($100 million) in April of 2017. A tactic that will be repeated in the debt funding for charter schools nationwide. A substantial portion of IDA debt was issued to failed charters including the most recent failure (October 2016) of Hillcrest Academy in Mesa in a scandal-ridden financial scheme involving junk bonds and alleged misappropriated funds from a client's trust fund to cover and hide the losses. At the same time, the public districts have had to sue the state for building and repair funding. An item in the budget that has been completely underfunded for years.

Governance and decisions about what type of education will be provided at the new schools occurs in the backrooms of the corporate office. Decisions that used to be made in the community based on what that community could afford based on property value.

The federal level picture isn't any better. Federal grant losses to fraud are estimated to be $216,000,000 as of 2016 according to the Center for Popular Democracy report of June 2016 (Staff, 2016). Under the guise of deregulation, no one is left minding the public till. The auditing of federal grants is insufficient to the task at hand.

Reaping the Whirlwind

What is revealed as one probes deeper into the financial data?

Who is holding the charter debt that is funding the financing and governance structures in place?

The multiple heists of our public funds are directed by the same cast of characters that brought us the mortgage and financial meltdowns in 2007, the savings and loan scandals in the 1990s, junk bond failures, pension fund raids, and the hedge fund industry. The financial tool of choice in this heist is government-backed securities on over-leveraged properties.

A Ponzi scheme is being played out utilizing our taxpayer-funded investments in our children's education and other government sponsored funding. The scheme relies on capturing ever-increasing numbers of students to pay off the debt. Continuously adding new investors is the definition of a Ponzi scheme. Shiny new buildings help sell the desirability of the choice option. At what cost?

One hundred and fifty-three charters in Arizona had a negative net result in 2015, over 25 percent of the charters in the study. This means their revenues *did not meet their expenditures*.

A disturbing involvement of elected officials in their roles as policy makers is seen in the data and in the weekly reporting on those elected officials by local media. What is cast into doubt by their involvement in the free markets they are supposed to be overseeing is the financial and governance integrity of the system of checks and balances. A republican version of Tammany Hall comes to mind as one reads the details of this self-serving political behavior in the news.

The failure rates at charters and private schools *are manifestations* of the deficient financial and governance theories in play. Over-leveraged properties are causing cash flow and solvency issues that are not being checked in time to prevent financial and management induced failures. The problem grows each year. It shows up in the red figures in the data. Negative net receipts at 144 charters in 2013–2014 are followed by 153 charter net losses in 2014–2015. These are usually in the same companies.[1] The amounts are going up overall, not down.

This work probes the financial and governance data vertically and looks at that data horizontally in an effort to demystify and expose the great "free market solution" lie that exists at the heart of charter and voucher legislation. The market is rigged.

A defective economic theory of action is being applied without the checks and balances necessary to prevent a financial collapse. After twenty years, the course corrections in law have been to widen the scope of the issue rather than to trust but verify. Surely, that type of trusting but verifying is a conservative view.

BAIT AND SWITCH

The academic mediocrity that pervades the charter and private industry is another telltale sign that we in the west have been taken in by snake oil salesmen again. The bait was supposed to be academic excellence the switch is alternative schools posing as "academies."

When academic standards were enforced with a grading system in Arizona, a total of 120 charter schools converted their status *from "Traditional School²" to "Alternative School."* This was in a group of 371 schools that went through a financial and academic rating in 2012.

The switch occurred when fully 32 percent of charters opted to *lower their academic standards for grading* by the charter board by switching to alternative status in 2013. This was a blatant attempt to save their academically underperforming businesses from academic closure by the monitoring authority.

Businesses are often forced into unpleasant business decisions like this. The fact that a business decision to reclassify their school, so they could survive trumped educational decisions is symptomatic of the kind of thinking that drives the decision making of those organizations.

As H. L. Mencken would say, "When someone says it's not about the money, it's about the money." Mismanagement, misrepresentation, and misuse of public money at charters is widespread. Counterbalancing this negative aspect in the data are the stories of charters that manage correctly, represent themselves honestly, and use public money for the public good. Charters like Northland Preparatory Academy in Flagstaff.

Management at Northland operates a true academy like program with great academic results, clean financial practices, well-paid staff, and fairly paid administrators. Northland Preparatory is an exemplar. They talk the talk and walk the walk.

Snake Oil

The public has been sold unproven economic theories from the 1960s as an innovative way to improve academic performance. A promised panacea that would produce a Lake Wobegon educational effect in our communities "where all the women will be strong, all the men good-looking, and all the children will be above average" has us waiting for superman. Like superman, this promised financial and academic result is mythical.

The economic theories postulated by charter advocates insist that open competition in an educational free market will lead to "savings" and competition. The economic theory underpinning this theory is fundamentally unsound. The promised savings have not materialized. Funds that were allocated for the classroom have been diverted to profits and fees to "for-profit" subsidiaries owned by the same owners and boards.

One manifestation of the problem is clear in the data on distributions at for-profit charter groups. Distributions, a form of dividends paid out of those for-profit subsidiaries to shareholders, *do not show up in the statistics regarding administrative costs.*

Practices that would be called deception and fraud in a district are touted as business management decisions by the CEOs in charters. A CEO whose salary is showing in the nonprofit charter school may be enhanced by distributions (and in some cases a second salary) to the same individual from a for-profit subsidiary owned by the same person and controlled by the same board. The market created is neither free, open, nor is it competitive. *It is lucrative.*

Efficiencies that we were told only CEOs and their ilk could deliver have not been delivered. The CEOs in 77 percent of all Arizona charters have done what business CEOs have always done, maximize their personal wealth and that of the company. This includes golden parachutes when the private properties acquired are sold by the owners. (Related party sales of property are also not subject to Capital Gains, another financial ploy used by owners selling their assets to related parties). These owners are usually one and the same as the CEOs. They are hurting the honest charter operators and the public schools with these deceptive opportunistic business practices. The preferred phrase used to describe this practice is, "We are running schools like a business."

The term "free markets" as applied to charters and private schools is a misnomer. The charter school and private school "free marketplace" that has evolved from deregulation is neither a free nor an open marketplace. It is monopolistic. Related party transactions with for-profit subsidiaries are one of the worst aspects of monopolies. Oligarchical management structures guarantee monopolistic practices.

The competition to charter "free market building sprees" is the underfinanced building and repair programs for public schools. Promising "A"- rated district schools are being operated in insufficiently maintained buildings. These crucial building and maintenance programs have been underfunded by the state for years.

The debt funding the charter properties is being funded by the IDA loan program in municipalities and counties. That debt is often on over-leveraged properties. Property acquisition by charters is being tacitly encouraged, even though the financial backing that lending are in trouble. Parents are lured into the charters "shiny new facilities" with promises of "traditional school" programs. In the Hillcrest Academy example, that large-scale facility now sits idle after one year of operation. In the meantime, the charter group adversely affected the local district and legitimate charter operators in the area.

The data in the research used for this report shows that there is debt load of 2 to 1 on the combined value of all the property and assets held by charters. This type of debt load is similar to owing $300,000 on your $150,000 house using the salary that you had when you bought the house at $150,000. A time when your $80,000 salary could cover your combined debt payments.

The financial stress shows up in the data. In 2014–2015, there were 153 charters out of 407 that ended the year in the red. The previous year the number was 144, an upward tick of 9. When this type of event (negative nets) happens in a district, there are consequences. Not in charters. The oversight system is not up to the challenge. A blind person could see the financial issues Hillcrest was struggling with two years ahead of its demise.

An oligarchy of related parties control and manipulate the "free" marketplace. Nationally, financial failure from mismanagement and bankruptcies are the cause of 65 percent of charter failures in the country. The rate of failure for private schools nationally is eerily close to those statistics.

The legislature and public need to ask a simple return on investment (ROI) financial question.

After twenty plus years what have the results of that deregulation been on our publicly financed educational systems?

Charter and private schools vouchers have existed for over twenty years. The public funding promise is found in the phrase: *"They receive public funding similarly to traditional schools. However, they have more freedom over their budgets, staffing, curricula and other operations. In exchange for this freedom, they must deliver academic results and there must be enough community demand for them to remain open."*

What have charter owners and corporate boards done with this freedom granted over their budgets, staffing, curricula, and other operations? For the answer, we need to probe vertically and see horizontally.

PROBING VERTICALLY, SEEING HORIZONTALLY

The research supporting this account took three years to complete. The answers gleaned from a forensic accounting look at the metadata[3] set have been documented in several published research papers. The data set is posted online.

This then is an effort to convey what is happening to the finances underpinning the public educational systems in this country. The approach used is purposefully designed to present this in a nontechnical manner.

Public schools are *our* schools, the real owners need to look out for our property and investments. The public is funding those over-leveraged loans. An understanding of what has transpired is a key to informed decision making. We control who we elect to represent our voices in our democracy. In short, an informed electorate needs to be expressing their wishes.

THE RULES FOR PUBLIC SCHOOL ADMINISTRATION AND GOVERNANCE

Districts schools and charter schools play by different rules as illustrated in table 2.1. Expenditures and oversight in public district schools face a far higher accountability bar than for public charter schools. Conflicts of interest that would not be allowed in a public district school setting, where the CEOs who receive financial benefits also make decisions that provide them those financial benefits, whether by salary or contracts. Corporate Boards of one, two, or three related people are a fairly normal occurrence in Arizona's charter schools.

Any property and asset purchases become the personal property of the charter operators—not the public—as with a public district school. Table 2.1 highlights those differences in the rules.

This table is designed to simplify the information being discussed in the rest of this book. A discussion in greater detail is presented in a later chapter.

Table 2.1.   Public Rules versus Charter Rules of Engagement

	Public District Schools	*Public Charter Schools*
Governance	School board (size of board set by district), conflict of interest not allowed (AZ Public School Laws), compensation of board member in AZ Law (limit of $500 by statute). Superintendent of schools is an agent of the board.	CEO, corporate board (may be one and the same), number of members is not stated (i.e., one member board is allowed), for profit or nonprofit allowed, payment of board members allowed (compensation for board members is not limited). A religiously affiliated group may operate and govern the charter.
Ownership of School Buildings and Assets of the District	Community and State of Arizona	Property of the charter holder, may be one person even in for profits. Sale of assets goes to charter holder(s). Sale of property is not in open market. This does not stop related party sales.

	Public District Schools	*Public Charter Schools*
Financial Controls	AZDOE, board and budget committee oversight and community input at public meetings, audits submitted to AZ Auditor General. Salary of superintendent is negotiated in public and published.	AZ charter board accepts audits, AZDOE accepts AFRs with limited power to question contents, AZDOE Refers Issues to AZCB for Oversight, corporate board votes on budgets, dealings with related parties are *supposed* to be included in Audit and IRS Form 990. Compensation of executives is unchecked. Charters can use any auditing firm, 38 currently used (this # includes out of state auditors [6]).
	Public District Schools	**Public Charter Schools**
Limitation on Financial Expenditures	Accounting books must be deficit free (although there is at least one district that is negative). This negative balance forced cuts at the district (Roosevelt Elementary District).	Allowed to run deficits and pay out distributions at for profits (distributions can occur even when the entity is in the red. this is true for several "for profits" studied.
Transportation	Student transportation must be provided. Limits to car provided for district employees and limits on its use. Travel expenses monitored by board.	Bus transportation is optional. Owner may buy cars and vehicles for their company vehicle (no limits on cost or type of vehicle). Travel accounts appear to be unregulated with some charters hitting over $1 million.
Special Education	Mandated special education responsibility. Title One required in schools with Title One populations identified.	Outsourcing may be used, parents can be counseled to pick another school, expenditures listed do not meet average costs normally associated with a Robust SPED Program.
Profit (Surplus)	Goes to either designated reserve funds or back to funding source to reduce property taxes.	May go to either shareholders in for profit (distributions) or to asset balance (equity).
Debt	May not exceed capacity of the district to support the resulting bonds issued.	Allowed to exist with excessive debt to income ratios, limited power to close charter is given to AZCB.
Hiring of Relatives	Not allowed (nepotism policy).	Allowed (and prevalent) especially at management level. Majority of charters have related parties working for and/or managing on the board of their charter.
Student Choice	Must accept all students.	May use lottery if oversubscribed. All students are supposed to be allowed to enroll. Testing out is allowed.

A Theory of Justice: If you read something that contains a statement about an organization or a different ethnic group than your own try substituting your own ethnic group or organization into the statement. If the resulting transposition of nouns makes for troubling reading, then you have put yourself in a place where Rawls' Theory of Justice[4] suggests we place ourselves when deciding whether the theory or rule we are reading about is just (Rawls, 2005).

Suggested Focus: After looking at the "rules" differences, the reader is invited to use this "substitution method" to judge the justice of the practice being discussed.

NOTES

1. In some cases, new debt (refinancing) supplied enough cash to move the company into the black in the following year. The strategy may work for one year but is doomed to failure in the long run.

2. The use of the term "traditional elementary or high school" for charters seems to suggest that at one time the district schools were ideal. After all they were the traditional schools at the time.

3. Metadata defined: The data set collected for this work is over 12,000 lines deep. It includes all of the audits, annual financial reports, and IRS 990 information on every charter in Arizona. The data set is over 150 columns wide. A link to those sources is provided in the Addendum.

4. See Rawls, John: *A Theory of Justice.*

Chapter 3

Rise of the Petty Academies

"Petty academies," a term from post–Revolutionary War times, are resurgent. They have morphed and reappeared as charter and private schools pretending to be academies of learning.

Widespread use of the word "academies" in the charter and private school markets are designed to give the impression that these schools are institutions of learning akin to Phillips Exeter and Andover Academy. Charters and private schools that play at being a school are petty academies at best. They are Ponzi schemes and snake oil salesmen at their worst.

The founders would be appalled to discover that we have allowed people with a mind-set that includes a belief that the universe is 6,000 years old to run some of our publicly financed schools. Jefferson and Adams voiced concerns over handing over education of our children to people with a limited and biased mathematical and scientific background. We need standards.

The value of a liberal arts education was one of the few things these particular founding fathers agreed on.

> When sobered by experience I hope our successors will turn their attention to the value of education. I mean education on the broad scale, and not that of the petty academies, as they call themselves, which are starting up in every neighborhood, and where one or two men, possessing Latin, and sometimes Greek, a knowledge of the globes, and the first six books of Euclid, imagine and communicate this as the sum of science. They commit their pupils to the theatre of the world with just taste enough of learning to be alienated from industrious pursuits, and not enough to do service to the ranks of science.
> —Correspondence between John Adams and Thomas Jefferson

Vouchers and taxpayer credits for private schools are designed to aid and abet schools whose primary mission is the promulgation of a religious belief system. What about "a wall of separation between the church and the state" is unclear to these "conservatives"?

BUILDING THE WALL

The phrase "wall of separation between the church and the state" was used by Thomas Jefferson in a letter written to the Danbury Baptists on January 1, 1802. Historians and scholars of constitutional law note that "his (Jefferson's) purpose in this letter was to assuage *the fears of the Danbury, Connecticut Baptists,* and so he told them that this *wall had been erected to protect them.*"

The wall referred to in Jefferson's letter protected the Danbury Baptists, not the state. Public funds used for religious indoctrination damage both the state's interest and the independence of those churches from the state. There are growing numbers of church leaders who are speaking out against vouchers and the public funding of private religious schools. They understand the issue.

"Conservative" and liberal families who chose Catholic Schools or private schools in the past knew that free religious choice required sacrifice. They did not feel *entitled* to take money from public funds to do so. This is called *putting your objections aside and doing what is best for your community*, a tenet that was taught in *civics classes*[1] at the time.

Parents like those of the author exercised their freedom to choose a religious school. They knew that along with that great freedom of choice came its counterpart, great responsibility. How do you protect your religious freedom while taking money from a public source?

The rise of Catholic Schools in the United States was in response to the openly anti-Catholic textbooks used in New York City and other parts of the country.[2] Are we supposed to believe that private religious schools are not going to promote their religion's dogma to their students?

COUNTERPOINT

"Conservative" pundits of this time period will argue that at that time, the 1800s, most of the schools in the country were being run by protestant boards and educators. Those writers often write as if this meant that the schools were de facto religious, Protestant. The literature on the topic is rife with claims that the Blaine Amendment of the time is being misinterpreted. It isn't.

James B. Blaine, who was the son of a Catholic mother, was generally viewed as an unbiased Speaker of the House. His political ambition led him to cater to and appease prejudiced voters of the time. In 1875 Blaine proposed an amendment to the U.S. Constitution to permanently block "sectarian" (Catholic) institutions from enjoying equal treatment.

Blaine's amendment failed to pass at the federal level, but *Protestant majorities in state legislatures wrote similar clauses into most state constitutions.* The word "sectarian" as it was used at that time is often misunderstood. Legal scholars, lawyers, and courts normally interpret sectarian to mean "religious." That is a mistaken interpretation when the time period is considered. Sectarian at the time meant Roman Catholic. These scholars argue that the public schools receiving state aid at the time were religious (Protestant). So, therefore, the state *was* giving money to a religion. That premise is a stretch. We have better evidence in current practice that this bias toward one religion over another is a problem.

The problem manifests itself immediately in states that have gone the "Christian Scholarships" route. This redirecting of public funding to a religious group is done through tax credits and entitlement payments for empowerment scholarships. The scholarships are funded with taxpayer funds through tax credits.

The amount of money that is being diverted to this type of tax-funded scheme has hit $1 billion annually in the United States (Pudelski, 2017). As of 2017, seventeen states have these tax-funded scholarships available as tax credits[3] (versus tax deductions). Federal legislation is currently being ushered through that does not even cap the amount of funds that could be redirected from the treasury into unaccountable, nonprofit organizations supplementing tuition at private schools.

PARADOXES IN PRACTICE

One of the first groups to organize their collection of tuition tax credits was organized by Arizona's State Senate President, Steve Yarborough. Mr. Yarborough's organization runs the Arizona Christian School Tuition Organization out of his law office. Their website claims that they have issued $150 million in scholarships to 28,500 students. Details regarding what Senator Yarborough "charges" for this service are provided in another chapter.

DEFINING CHRISTIAN TO EXCLUDE CATHOLIC

The Arizona Christian School Tuition Organization only serves Protestant private schools. If one wishes to pursue the "public scholarships" (financed by tax credits) being offered and they want to go to a Catholic or Jewish School, then they need to go to either the Catholic or Jewish organizations that cater to those faiths. There are currently fifty groups involved in the "scholarship" market in Arizona. Most take a piece of the donations collected as payment for their services. The same is true for the vast fundraising arms of many of the charters. They have paid fundraisers.

Evidently "Catholic" and perhaps even "Mormon" are not included in the "Christian School" definition. The lone exception at ACSTO is a Greek Orthodox School. This exempting of other Christian faiths accessing a Christian scholarship fund speaks volumes about the problems inherent in using public funding for scholarships to a religious school.

SOBERING UP

We are acting like we have not been sobered by our national experience regarding what constitutes a free and appropriate education. The separation of church and state was not only an issue for the founding fathers. Using public funding for religious schools is contrary to the admonition in the New Testament, "Render therefore unto Caesar the things which are Caesar's; and unto God the things that are God's." If your church tithes at 10 percent, should the government take 10 percent of that tithing? Of course not. Why open that door by comingling public funds with tithed collections?

To be sobered by our twenty plus years of charter experience, we have to look at the results of our experiments with charters and private school vouchers with a clear and open mind. Direct payments to parents for private schools force all taxpayer to fund these private placements. The payments are not well monitored, allowing misappropriations to flourish without accountability. Who choses and who loses?

We cannot act soberly if we have the delusional view that is present when *known* financial issues and sham "governance" is rampant in the existing charter and private school models. The current laws by allowing unrestricted scholarships to organizations that promote specific religions are de facto promoting those religions.

In the case of nonsectarian charters, we are supporting cronyism at best and oligarchies at worst at 77 percent of these "private businesses." This cronyism is protected by the law's silence on related party transactions. When the related party is a pastor, priest, rabbi, imam, or bishop moving funds between the church involved with the school and the school itself, there is a good chance public funds are supporting a religion. In the data, there were pastors involved with schools who were collecting salaries as religious leaders at their church *and* as CEO of their charter school. The properties used were adjoining facilities.

Leases for charter school properties on properties owned by a religious organization are suspect. A not so "benign" neglect of our public funds is in play. The transgressions laid out in countless studies on the issue are being ignored by the agencies overseeing the charter schools because as they say, "It is legal" under the rules.

Legislator/charter owners who don't abstain from votes affecting their charter related businesses have a conflict of interest. Their answer to this conflict issue, "It's legal under the law."

This was literally the answer of several charter "advocacy" leaders when presented evidence of financial and management misbehavior. When queried about the issue, one state senator, a charter school owner, replied, "That's how we meant it to work. The market will take care of the issues."

The neglect and outright refusal to provide sound financial oversight is not benign. Charter financial and mismanagement failures account for 65 percent of all charter closures nationally. The loss of property and assets to the public assets paid and in many cases financed by bonds that use taxpayer dollars. A *conservative accounting* of the amount of charter property has been lost through financial failures in Arizona is $400,000,000 since 1994. (Source: Data analysis of 2013–2014 audit declarations on Property and Equipment.)

"What are the financial and governance results of two decades of charters in Arizona?" The facts *are* sobering.

CONSERVATIVE DATA SETS

The approach used to calculate failure rates in Arizona did not count the public school attempts to establish district charters. Statistically the failure rate of charters in Arizona is 42.79 percent for individual charter schools[4] and 40.11 percent for charter companies. Adding in the district charters that closed would cause the rate to surpass 60 percent.

Failure in this context means that 42.79 percent of all *charter school facilities* that opened since 1994 have been closed mostly due to financial and mismanagement issues. Looking at the data on charter organizations (i.e., the charter level organizational failure, not just a school in the organization's portfolio), the percentage is 40.11 percent.

The statistics used *do not* include schools that were reopened by another company or charters that were assumed by other charter companies. The statistics also do not include university-run charter schools or schools managed by local government entities.

Failure in this case also means the loss of all of the property and equipment that were purchased with dollars designated for public education. The additional funding for charters, currently $1,700 per ADM, is supposed to be used for transportation, repairs, building expenses, and other purposes.

How did charters spend that extra money?

In fiscal year 2013–2014 charters spent:

- 1.69 percent of their total expenditures providing access to their programs by offering students transportation. In contrast, districts must provide transportation past a certain distance.
- 14.8 percent on maintenance (often to related parties)
- 22.2 percent on administration

    ○ Of the total 84.06 percent spent on administration, $107,599,645 went to administrative purchased services.

        – This means the payments for administrative purchased services went to management groups and related for-profit entities. Districts spend very little in this area of the budget as the services are provided by paid employees of the district.

Reasons for the Failure Rates

The reason for charter and private school failures are myriad and include the following:

- Over-leveraging of property and assets.

    ○ This is often because the property was overpriced during the "sale" of the property to a new (related party) owners.

        – This type of sale price is sometimes "backed up" in the financials as an inflated "good will"[5] estimate built into the assets statement.

- The over-compensation of the management companies involved in mega-charters and small scale charters alike.

    ○ Including: management salaries, teacher leasing fees, distributions in the for-profit subsidiaries, and management fees.

- Inappropriate uses of funds meant to educate our children (travel for staff and kickbacks to related party subsidies paid out as distributions or salaries in related for-profits subsidiaries). Excessive fees for managing building projects are one manifestation of this type of spending with related parties.
- An unelected governance system that provides limited, if any, governance over the owners of the charter.

Table 3.1.   Related Party Dealings for All Charters

# Dealing with Related Party	Small or No Dealings with a Related Party
309	91
Percentage Dealing with Related Parties	Percentage NOT Dealing with Related Parties
77%	23%

- ○ In many cases, the one-person corporate board is the owner. District charters are not counted in the statistics on charter failure rates for a reason. It would be unfair to count the closures against the charter governing body, the Arizona State Board for Charter Schools. The second reason is that the property and equipment purchased by district charters that closed reverted to the districts (state). In 2011, the legislature effectively cut off districts from starting charter school. This is what passes for open free market competition.

The practices noted were not present in the financial data of the 23 percent of ethically run charters. Ownership at the majority of those charters is commonly held in the community they serve.

CRITERIA USED ON DEALINGS WITH RELATED PARTIES

The criteria used to determine whether a charter was using ethical practices was devised and used for this analysis. The results in table 3.1 illustrate the findings.

Charters were counted as a charter entity if they were an independent charter. This negated the consolidation effect of consolidated audits. The statistics revealed a total of 101 charters with either no related party transactions or related party transactions that fit the criteria, "Related Party expenditures can be a way to save money through efficiency."

Why 91 rather than 101?

- While 101 Charters met the stated criteria, charters that had not passed the AZCB financials or their academics were D or less were taken out of the count. Thus the number 91 in the statistics.
- Forty-three of the 101 met the criteria, "Related Party expenditures can be a way to save money through efficiency."
- Fifty-eight avoided any conflict of interest by heeding standard district protocols regarding related party transactions. They didn't have any related party transactions.

- Seventy-four of the 101 had diverse corporate boards with community representation on those boards.

A plan to eventually "offer vouchers to every public-school student in Arizona" passed in the Arizona Legislature and was signed by the republican governor in April 2017. In a separate piece of legislation, they suggested privatizing oversight of the public money given to parents to pay private-school tuition and other expenses. One wonders which related party crony will start a business overseeing those funds for a fee, 10 percent sounds about right.

These tax-payer-funded scholarships are euphemistically known as Empowerment Scholarship Accounts, ESAs. ESAs are currently used to provide "scholarships" for religious schools using tax credits and outright donations to those organizations. There are fifty agencies raising funds under Empowerment Scholarship Accounts. Most take a cut for the money they raise others charge and operational cost to the scholarship funds. It is often 10 percent of the gross.

This is on top of the myriad fund raising wings of many charter schools. In addition, some of the larger charters have "suggested" donations of $1,500 per student per year. The results of this fundraising are reflected in the audits. The audits were replete with "fundraising" events where the cost to run the event exceeded the net taken in or represented more than 50 percent.

Paid fundraisers were the norm in the data. They were paid even when the amount netted was less than their salary and benefits. When a fundraising account shows $51 K raised and expenses of $35 K, the netted sum of $16 K is cause for an auditing of the event.[6]

The pretext for all of this fund raising and scholarship activity is that this provides choice and freedom to parents. In reality, the law provides money for people to segregate their children from the common schools provided for all of our citizens. A *right* that they had prior to this legislation. The difference is they didn't get a subsidy from the government to segregate themselves in the past.

The right "choosing" parents did not have prior to the legislation was the right to an *entitlement to public money* for their choice of a separate educational experience for their child. This entitlement is presented to the public as a "conservative" measure. This type of "conservative" mind-set was not present at the real Boston Tea Party during the time period that Adams and Jefferson were alive.

The original Boston Tea Party attendants were protesting taxation without representation. The taxpayers have no representation on charter corporate boards. They are appointed. We, the taxpayers are not represented on the boards passing out the scholarship funds. Funds we provided from tax revenues.

TORIES

The correct Revolutionary War term for this type of "fiscal" conservative is "Tory." A person whose conservative bent supported the existing oligarchies and by extension the schools the oligarch's of the time choose to send their children to attend. They did not want to be going to school with the locals. Universal common schools were not established at the time. Tories supported the lords and monarchies having ancestral rights. They didn't worry about the commoners going to school.

REAL CONSERVATIVES CONSERVE TRADITIONS

The term used in New England to describe an old time Republican conservative is "Yankee." Yankees, once they agree to a political proposition are true to their word. A Yankee's word means something. If the voters vote for a proposition and it passes by one vote, Yankees carry out the will of the people.

When we have legislative actions that override popular vote intentions, there is something wrong with the legislative process. State and federal meddling in how municipalities run their schools is the antithesis of local community control through elected local boards. Is democracy messy and inefficient? Yes. It always has been and always will be.

PROPOSITIONING THE VOTERS

Arizona's Proposition 100 was a ballot initiative move to raise the sales tax in the state from 5.6 percent to 6.6 percent. The expressed purpose was to raise money for education and public safety. The critics of this proposal included the "Tea Party" and the National Federation of Independent Businesses.

When Proposition 100 was passed, the legislature circumvented the voters' wishes and used part of the funding for other purposes. This included business tax relief.

A true conservative, a Yankee, would have gritted their teeth and abided by the will of the voters. In Arizona, a common reply to this type of legislative overreach is "the people elected us to represent them, therefore we can do what we decide to do with the money."

How did we get here?

NOTES

1. Civics need to be a part of all our educational programs, public, charter, and private. Civics are part of the overall program at "First Amendment Schools."

2. The public schools of the nineteenth century were deeply imbued with Protestant teachings and practices. Diane Ravitch wrote about the battle between Protestants and Catholics in her history of the New York City public schools (*The Great School Wars*). The arrival of large numbers of Irish immigrants in the 1840s, mostly Catholic, concurred with the beginnings of public school systems in urban areas.

3. A tax credit comes off the amount the taxpayer owes to the state. A tax credit is a deduction that normally nets a savings relative to one's tax rate.

4. A charter school is an individual site. A charter is the organization that owns that school. There can be many schools "replicated" under one charter. Likewise, the company may opt to have a separate charter for each school. These nuances are explained throughout this work.

5. Good will is used on financials to inflate the asset value of the firm. The amounts chosen and commented on here were arbitrary and capricious. As with the restaurant business, good will often disappears when the original owner leaves the business.

6. The event was noted on the audit of Montessori Academy Inc., a firm with many financial issues in their data including the fact that the company does not meet the Arizona Charter Boards Financial Performance Expectations. Using fundraising for day-to-day operational costs seems to be a pattern in the data. Closer review of these events needs to be done at the charter board level.

Chapter 4

Schools for the Adults

CORPORATE TAKEOVERS

A systematic and relentless attack on public education has opened the door for carpetbaggers and scalawags to enter into a publicly funded arena. Once legislatures passed laws freeing these "innovators" from regulation, they began to plunder the finances and governance structures of our nation's public school systems.

This was accomplished by writing laws that bypassed or superseded regulations designed to ensure fiscal and governance integrity.

The pride of America's greatest generation, public common schools for all of our citizens, was berated and scorned. The agents of the new agenda started by setting a stage that included coining the word "government schools." This was a first step to destroying the heart of our local communities, commonly held public common schools.

A common school system that was once the envy of the free world became a financial acquisition target. Where does the assault originate from?

Corporate, state, and federal initiatives to undercut local governance of our schools.

Who is really running the government sponsored schools if the funding and initiatives are from the state and federal government? Who are the real "big government schools" we have been told to be wary of?

HOSTILE TAKEOVER

The result of this hostile takeover is a system of financial and governance "rules" that benefits adults by diverting money from the classroom to the new

37

owners, stockholders, related party for-profit companies, and their shareholders and corporate boards.

The public has been sold a proposition. What was needed to solve the manufactured educational crisis was CEOs. The idea was promulgated and put into law by those most likely to benefit financially from this governance "innovation." Guess who became the CEOs?

The same public that watched their housing values, pensions, and savings disappear has let the same corporate raiders into their publicly held public schools. They have renamed *their* schools in honor of themselves and their companies. Most often, the chosen name of the school has no reference to the community it is located in. When the community's name is used, it usually follows the corporate name.

The same moves, using taxpayer money to partially fund stadiums that get named after corporations, have led to schools without real community ties. The same national Chamber of Commerce that decried the demise of main street retailing is an enthusiastic supporter of the privatization of local education. It's not "personalized education." It's business.

It is not coincidental that most charters have this naming convention in common. They name schools after the corporation, and they assign those schools with the moniker "academy."

The charter advocacy lobby and proponents of vouchers and tax credits for private school tuition have sold this "market solution to educational reform" using misrepresentation, misdirection, and the misstating of facts.

The three sisters of spin.

Chapter 5

The Road to Perdition

SETTING THE STAGE FOR DEREGULATION

There is a formula for declaring that an institution is broken beyond repair. The formula works whether the subject is public schooling, banking, pension funding, mortgages, the bond markets, or the savings and loans. Something is broke and it needs fixing.

Formulaic rhetoric prepares the public for the "need" for deregulation.

Another word for this politically and financially motivated activity is "propaganda."

The formula was applied to traduce[1] local community common schools in order to pave the way for what was being sold as freedom of "choice." Charter schools and vouchers were the answer to a manufactured crisis in public education.

MISS REPRESENT, MISS LEAD, AND MISS STATE

Spinning the data[2] about the institution that needs "reforming" is key to this type of deception and chicanery when you are setting the stage for deregulation. The "reformers" and free market economist theorists employed the "three sisters of spin" in their efforts to discredit community owned schools and the teachers who work in those schools.

There's nothing so absurd that if you repeat it often enough people will believe it.
—William James

39

The three sisters of spin along with social media and political activism by charter school proponents repeated things often enough and loud enough. The ruse worked. The public believed their sales pitch. The camel's nose was in the tent.

The derision and scorn generated toward public employees was extended to our neighbors who serve on local school boards. School board membership was once the gateway to public service as it demonstrated commitment to your community's well-being. Those school boards are locally elected positions, not appointed corporate boards. Corporate boards is the chosen name of the governing boards of charters. The result of this rhetoric?

The resulting legislation has been a loss of what Robert Putnam calls "social capital." We have gone from Putnam's "bowling alone" to "schooling alone."

We have taken the road to perdition. We are being encouraged to move away from social engagement and a commitment to public schools for all to private school vouchers and scholarships. Scholarships that are being used to separate us from our neighbors. These tools have become the new "entitlement" to public funds for a private education. They are voraciously sought after and promoted by so-called conservative activists.

It is sobering to note that legislative action is consistently used to pass charter and voucher laws. The ideas are never put to a public referendum vote. When it is put on the ballot, voters, as they did in Massachusetts in 2016, vote down the efforts to privatize their public schools. Legislative actions meant to further curtail our rights to petition our government are wending their way through the legislature at this writing. The First Amendment right to petition the government for a redress of grievances is being removed from local decision making. A triumph of the will of the corporate raiders has been achieved.

The method used is a formulaic attack on public schools, school boards, and teachers.

THE FORMULA FOR MISREPRESENTING, MISLEADING, AND MISSTATING INFORMATION

1. Declare the status quo whether it is banking, mortgage loans, public schools, regulations on financing, the viability of pension funds, etc., is broken beyond repair.

   a. Repeat phrases like "public schools are bureaucratic," "the federal government is telling us what to do," "public schools are government schools," and "the public schools are monopolistic."

   Employ Sister 1 in this effort: Miss Represent.

2. Establish "think tanks" and foundations that preach the "free market" and "choice" gospel. This includes loading colleges and universities with like-minded professors of economics, education, and government studies: Miss Lead

   a. Use donated money from corporations, family run charities and foundations, charter foundations, and investors that will benefit financially from "deregulation." Direct this largesse to the academic institutions as "gifts" to establish these university positions.
   b. Promote your ideas at the universities and college level. Hire experts in academia that will validate your thesis: "The institution(s) you are attacking is/are failing[3]. Use the "research based" data they publish to validate your theory: Miss Represent

3. Promote the premise that public "government" schools are broken and beyond repair and need to be replaced by a "free market" deregulated system."

   a. Success in *selling the ideas* is the important thing. The rhetoric need not be lovely or theoretically correct. The point of the rhetoric is to persuade people of what the free market theorists and their minions think is the *right* solution. Refer to those who disagree with you as liberal leftists.

4. Ensure the election of like-minded political leaders to key positions in state and local government using "dark money" sources.

   a. Gain a political lock on the legislative process including local school boards.
   b. Refuse to put the issue to a ballot vote.
   c. Control what comes before the legislature for a vote.
   d. Complain loudly when the NEA, AFT (or any labor organization) and the School Board's Associations speak up. Repeat the phrases, "Those groups are representing 'vested interest' in the status quo." "They want to run schools for the adults."
   e. Ensure your "rules" allow the representatives in government positions a share of the new free market they have helped create. This is a form of what used to be termed, *Graft*,[4] under the old regulations. The new rules make it "legal." If it's legal, then it's not graft. Situational ethics define what is right and wrong.
   f. Design new laws limiting the rights of the public to put referendums on the ballot. Ignore the intent of the articles the public managed to get on the ballot in prior years.

5. Promote the experts you have injected into the profession you are assailing to leadership positions in the organizations you set up and charged

with "fixing the manufactured problem." This includes think tanks run by like-minded organizations, loading the appointed oversight boards with charter school advocates and owners, and the keeping the Department of Education in your state at bay.

a. Advocacy groups that push for "choice" while paying themselves and their "Choice Advocacy Centers" premium wages and consulting fees are examples of this process. Pahara Institute[5] in California is a prime example.

The salary and other payments of $420 K plus for the "director" at Pahara is not an atypical amount in the charter advocacy world as most were listed at $200 K to a high of $970 K.

i. Do we really need to be reminded of who was charged with fixing the financial markets and fallout from the collapse of the market in 2008? The same people who are now pushing for new "deregulation" of the financial markets.

6. Deregulate. Propose to fix the identified problems by getting rid of regulations regarding financial controls, certification (professional standards), and governance first.

a. Pass laws that do just that!

The result, in Arizona:

i. You do not need any certification or educational pedigree to be a principal or CEO of a charter school.
ii. "CEOs" who do not have an education *or business* degree.
iii. Practicing principals with a high school diploma as their vitae's highest educational attainment.

7. Point to and advertise your successes and hide your failures.

a. It is not a matter of what is right or wrong, true or false, it is a matter of what is believed. There are multiple charters claiming they are the best charter school in Arizona on their webpages. Who's right?

Sister 2: Miss Lead.

8. Make your financial practices as complicated and convoluted as you can.

a. Allow charters to pick any auditor they want in state or out of state.

i. Allow large charter groups to "Consolidate" their audits so they can hide financial weaknesses of individual charters in the group.
ii. Allow audits that count the net and net Assets of their other non-school properties to "count" as property held by the school.
iii. Allow generalized rather than specific accounting of expenditures and revenues sources.[6]

b. Discredit the voices speaking up. Finance professional "plants" trolling news related to charters. Have them write "replies" to editors, social media, and news professionals to misinform the reader and discredit critics.

9. Avoid transparency in your financial reporting so that the public can't follow the money. Sister 3: Miss State, especially your financials.
10. Repeat the process.

Imagine this process applied to our public police, fire departments, and parks.

After all isn't the crime rate too high? Shouldn't we get a tax credit if we have to hire a private security firm? How about to pay for my home security system? In Alabama, this type of question is currently being decided by the courts. A mega-church is seeking to hire a police force with the same powers as the public police force. Evidently, they believe they are akin to Vatican City.

SPECIAL NEEDS AT CHARTERS

One of the ploys used to push through educational opportunity scholarships was to allow special-needs children to go to programs designed for them. So how did the charter movement help these children out when they had the chance during the last twenty years?

The Arizona Department of Education report entitled *10/1/2009 Federal Child Count by PEA (Public Education Agency) updated as of 2/1/2010* indicated that nearly *93 percent of all special-needs students in the state are enrolled in traditional public schools*. Using a *simple* average expenditure per student, traditional schools will average a *higher cost per student than charters because they are getting more dollars for the special-needs students*. If the distribution of special-needs students in traditional versus charter public schools was more even, one would expect the simple per-pupil average to be nearer to that of traditional schools.

What's next? In Pennsylvania, the "home district" of the charter student can be forced to pay up to $40,000 to the charter for taking a special-needs student. The district is financially responsible literally because of the laws that the charters could exempt themselves from via deregulating. Public Law 94.142 provides parents with a procedure to obtain a private "least restrictive environment" already. The legislature did not need a new program of scholarships to solve this issue. They did need to ensure that "placed" special education children really need that placement.

What are the economic theories in use that allow this kind of thinking and behavior?

NOTES

1. The word is chosen for its precise meaning: Traduce is a verb that means to speak badly of or tell lies about (someone or some institution) so as to damage their reputation. Synonyms include misrepresent and vilify among others.

2. For books and counterpoints to this rhetoric, see any of the works of Diane Ravitch or the works of Dr. Gerald Bracey debunking the "crisis" in American Public Education.

3. The hiring of academic experts was explored in the work *Inside Job*, a film narrated by Matt Damon. This documentary exposes the academic leaders whose "theories of action" were implicated in the financial failures of 2007–2008.

4. Graft: A form of political corruption, being the unscrupulous use of a politician's authority for personal gain. The term has its origins in the medical procedure whereby tissue is removed from one location and attached to another for which it was not originally intended.

5. See, Pahara Institute link here, http://www.guidestar.org/FinDocuments/2015/455/141/2015-455141625-0cb0fb57-9.pdf, for detailed Form 990 report.

6. Instead of breaking expenses up in recognizable pieces like salaries, books, benefits, a charter can have a category called charter school expenses and another called management. They provide only two numbers. There is only one reason for this tactic. Deception.

Chapter 6

Economic Theories in Use

THEORIES IN USE VERSUS ESPOUSED THEORIES OF ACTION

Theories in practice (use) should align with the theory that was espoused when adherents of the theory were promoting and selling their free market "solutions" to public school "problems." A mismatch between one's theory in use and their espoused theory destroys the credibility of the original thesis. It disproves it. Alignment matters.

The credibility of charter school advocates' economic theories is being tested and questioned here. If the theory is correct financial and governance data that validates the economic theories behind deregulation, benefits should show up in significant measurable ways in that data.

After twenty plus years of charter experimentation in Arizona and thirty years nationally, there is little to no match between what was sold to the public and what is being delivered. Schools like the Painted Pony Ranch Charter in Prescott, an exemplary small charter, are harmed when we don't expect all charters to run their finances for the benefit of their students, not the owners.

National data in most of the forty-two states with charter laws on the books is also bleak.

The Emperor Has No Clothes

Rather than deal with the problem, the research and the facts on financial malaise are ignored. A loud defense throws up irrelevant responses to any data that contradicts the party line. Critics and whistleblowers are mocked and dismissed as naysayers. The public is told to look at outlier success stories rather than look at the industry as a whole. Success stories are trotted out to counteract overwhelming factual data. No one is arguing that there aren't some successes. However, a 23 percent success rate is not acceptable.

We have been sold a bill of goods that does not reflect what is happening in real time in the real world. There are twenty plus years of data to prove this assertion.

Although the source data on charter schools is convoluted and difficult to come by, forensic accounting can and has been used to decipher and illustrate trends and issues. The process took three years and is part of the academic paper this book draws its statistical information from.

Statistically, the financial and governance theories in use at *77 percent* of charters do not match the efficiency and competition theories espoused by the promoters of the model when they were "selling" their version of the economic free market theories espoused by Dr. Friedman[1] and Dr. Hayek.

Releasing charters from the "regulations" regarding sales and contracts with related parties[2] (relatives, board members, former charter owners, friends, and family) played out in the charter audit data from 2013–2014. In that year 144 out of 407 charters ended the year in the red. The following year was even worse with another nine charters finishing the year in the red (153).

Malaise shows up in statistics showing total related party contracts at all charters of $374,181,560. In addition, the related party leases and rent commitments totaled another $478,717,233. We are told that this is a way charters save money. It isn't.

Over 90 percent of Arizona's charter schools have sought and obtained waivers from exemptions regarding bidding and related party transactions (Source: Edreform). De facto 100 percent can use this opting out of laws designed to prevent nepotism and cronyism in the publicly financed arena of public schools. There is little to no evidence that anyone is calling out the practitioners on these expenses.

CRIME AND PUNISHMENT

What about district malaise? Barbara Byrd-Bennett, former top administrator (CEO) in the nation's third-largest school district, Chicago, was sentenced to four-and-half years for rigging bids for services to her schools (Smith, 2015). The amount involved was $2.3 million. She was also sued by the district. *This is how accountability should work.*

NO HARM, NO FOUL

Related party sales, which are legal in the charter sector, go unpunished. Why? It's not a violation of charter laws to do what Ms. Byrd-Bennett did.

The difference, she did it in a district, where it is illegal and not a charter, where it is not illegal.

The reason the Chicago School Chief was caught because the public could see what was going on in the financials at a district school. You can't see the spending in for-profit subsidiaries of charter schools. They designed it that way.

RELATED PARTY TRANSACTIONS DO NOT "SAVE MONEY"

The antithesis of this premise, a theory of savings and efficiency gained by competitiveness, is what is really happening in Arizona. Here we have a charter and private school system where savings and efficiency claims mask insider dealings. There are exceptions, but they are just that, *exceptions*.

The lease and rent amounts cited represent commitments[3] to pay *that are contractual*. That means the lease is not able to be broken. There is little to no chance of that happening. Why?

Why would you break a lease or rental agreement you are counting on to pay your subsidiary "for-profit" company's debt on the property? A subsidiary with the same ownership and the same corporate board. All of the related companies are being dragged down by the financial manipulations going on among the "for-profit" subsidiary companies.

It gets worse. The statistics cited on the related party transactions did not include family members hired as teachers or administrators salaries and benefits in its calculations. The resulting number would have inflated the related party expenses dramatically. Family members and payments for salaries in the subsidiaries are not subject to the auditing rules that the "schools" are. They are hidden in "for-profit" subsidiaries transactions.

The rhetoric of the language regarding the desired outcomes of deregulation does not match what has actually transpired. This is a mismatch between charter and voucher promoters' "talk" and their walk.

VOUCHER SIDESHOWS

Poor children in underperforming schools are not using vouchers to escape those schools. Evidently, neither are handicapped children as 93 percent of these children are still in the districts.

We know this instinctively. Giving a poor or even a middle-class consumer a coupon to go to Saks Fifth Avenue does not mean they will come in to the store and purchase an expensive item. The store isn't even located in their neighborhood. Saks Fifth Avenue, like boutique charters and private schools, locate in neighborhoods where wealthy, well-healed, consumers live. This type of transaction is the rule, not the exception.

VOUCHERS: A "WHITE CHIP" IN THE POKER GAME OF CHOICE

In the film *My Little Chickadee*, W.C. Fields sits down at a poker game in a high-end salon and announces his presence by throwing out a one hundred dollar bill.

Without breaking stride the dealer says, "Give him a white chip."

Vouchers are a white chip.[4] When we pretend that giving a voucher to an impoverished person changes their ability to attend a private school, it is a cruel charade. We know who chooses and we know who loses. Citing an "example" as proof that this works is as pernicious as it gets.

A white chip does not change the choice game for a middle-class or poor person. The assertion that it does is patently false.

Nassim Taleb said it well in *Anti-Fragile, "If you see fraud and do not say fraud you are a fraud."* Vouchers are being fraudulently sold as solutions that allow children to "exit" underperforming schools. Private schools are not swarming with escapees from underperforming schools even though those types of private schools have always offered scholarships. Can we please stop pretending this really works?

Private is private. When the wall comes down separating private from public, it harms the private sector's private schools. The scholarships at those schools rightfully come from endowments from their alumni. They are designated for the type of student the school is looking to help. Using taxpayer money to allow someone to enter a private school harms both the private and public sector. Applying does not mean you can get in even for the well-healed applicants.

Twenty plus years on, the talk regarding what charters' freedom from regulation would bring to educational academic, financial and governance performance has not matched the "walk." The footprints of this mismatch are in the data and the unacceptable financial failure rates due to mismanagement and financial malaise.

Milton Friedman, one of the economist founding fathers of the voucher movement, wrote of this need for rules in his early writings. His economic theories are replete with cautionary advice regarding "the rules of the game":

> The existence of a free market does not of course eliminate the need for government. On the contrary, government is essential both as a forum for determining the "rules of the game" and as an umpire to interpret and enforce the rules decided on. What the market does to reduce greatly the range of issues that must be decided through political means and thereby to minimize the extent to which government need participate directly in the game. The characteristic features of action through political channels is that it tends to require or enforce

substantial conformity. The great advantage of the market, on the other hand, is that it permits wide diversity.

—Capitalism and Freedom 1962: 15

Please note that the follow-on statement was provided in the quote above. That statement is the one so often cited by charter and voucher proponents (the quote is often used without the first sentences). The limited rules of the game *even Dr. Friedman described* are being ignored. The umpires, the Department of Education, and the State Board for Charter Schools *have no real authority* to enforce the limited financial rules that are in place.

While the State Board for Charter School has closed charters for academic reasons, it has limited authority in financial and property transactions. Over-leveraging of property is one of the biggest issues in the charter financial failure. Proper oversight of charter sales and sale prices could eliminate the issue.

The agency charged with oversight, the Arizona State Board for Charter Schools has identified 138 of 409 charters listed as *not meeting* Financial Performance Recommendations. Ninety more charter organizations meet the requirements overall but do not meet the performance standard for cash flow. Playing the audit by manipulating the data allows other charters to squeak by and pass the standards. *The numbers used here are conservative.*

The charter board is also basing those financial ratings on information that does not capture the problems in a timely manner. That is, before financial failure is imminent. The "check engine" light is on, and the driver (charter owner) is ignoring it. The car company (the charter board) knows about the flaw that is causing the light to come on, but they decide fixing the problem would cost too much. They say, "We don't want to over-regulate the drivers. That would be burdensome." The result, financial crashes.

How have these economic theories played out in the arena of private ownership of public schooling?

Twenty years on, the social and economic theory experiment of privatization, through charter schools and tax credits for vouchers to private schools continues to grow without adequate oversight.

There is a decided lack of transparency regarding how the public's money is being spent. That problem, *transparency*, exists in most of the other states that have charter schools, private school scholarships, and vouchers.

Private ownership of publicly paid for assets, a hallmark of the charter and private schools, is being rushed to expansion nationally. We are being legislated into throwing good money after bad. The foxes are in charge of the henhouse.

In Arizona, that push includes "tuition scholarships" for private placement in private schools. Legislative efforts to access even more public funds and facilities through thinly veiled legislation to aid and abet the privatization of Arizona's public schools. The 2017 legislation signed expanding "vouchers" went into law in April. We are past the tip of the spear in this move to privatize public education. The spear is in and its barbed head is being twisted into our public schools' core.

"The rules of this game" are rigged.

Allies of the three sisters of spin are spinning the rule making to their financial advantage. They are doing this in a "market" that is supposed to be providing a public good.

What has evolved from a theory of economics applied to public education is the good, the bad, and the ugly present in the current educational "marketplace." The bad and the ugly of this self-dealing represent *77 percent* of the players. The good are a mere 23 percent.[5]

Legislators and governors have been influenced and pushed by the charter school advocacy groups. Private sector businesses with an interest in the market and their lobbyists have continued to push legislators to enact laws that benefit the "inside job people" involved in charter school finances. They have created laws that allow "new rules" for the governance and management of charter schools. The rules allow those same legislators to own charter schools. A conflict of interest.

The rules being replaced were the result of this country's long history of funding and governing "common schools." Rules that were designed to protect all citizens' rights to a free and appropriate public education. Those rules have been jettisoned for the newcomers' empty promises.

The same governing parties (state legislatures) have been moving to eliminate the rule-making authority of towns and cities. In Arizona, the legislative assault is also being carried out against Arizona citizen's rights to petition the state, a First Amendment right. This is an assault on local rule and choice disguised as a procedural change. It is an assault on the social capital of municipalities. Enough already.

Historic Context: Why We Have Regulations

There are reasons why public school boards and superintendents need the financial guidelines that are in place. The system that was in place was designed by the citizens of the republic to prevent nepotism, cronyism, and "sweetheart" deals from occurring. The rules we have are largely the result of the greatest generation's effort to provide the country with future generations of civic-minded citizens. That generation's "rule-making" was what and is under attack in the 1960s and today. Shame on us.

THE GREATEST GENERATION'S WISDOM

Creating and Supporting Common Schools

The wisdom of the greatest generation's community building and citizen developing public schools was reflected and demonstrated in 2001. The latest generation's 2001 responses to the 9–11 attacks reminded us of why *united we stand* is such an important ideal. Children who were a product of our public schools volunteered and continue to volunteer to serve their country. A generation that we can be proud of came out of those "failed" public schools, just like their great-grandparents[6] before them. The public schools of that generation were berated in the 1930s in a similar manner. Critics at the time cited Germany and Japan as school systems that worked well. Really?

This berating of the "outcome" of our public schools has been going without reflection on what has been accomplished by our common schools. Those common schools produced citizens who put their own safety and concerns aside for what was best for their community. By constantly comparing our schools to other nations, we are ignoring the fact that our schools are designed to produce American citizens who can pursue happiness. Happiness is not guaranteed. Your ability as a citizen to pursue it is.

Twenty years on the social experiment of charter schools in America, they continue to grow without adequate monitoring on how the public's money is being spent. We have replaced social capital and common schools for all with capitalist profits and segregation from the community for the few.

We are doing this at the expense of our sense of community and the social good that comes from attending a truly public school with our neighbors. There are charter schools that get this right. They are in that 23 percent in the data.

Those charters are a vital part of their community and the pride of their neighbors. They are being harmed by inaction on financial and governance issues as much as the public district schools in those neighborhoods.

At the twilight of his life Mark Twain was asked, "What is it that we should all live for?"

His answer was, "The good opinion of our neighbors."

Common community schools matter to the republic's continued viability. Neighbors in a democratic republic should value the good opinion of their fellow citizens. Great charters and private schools care about their community and their impact on that community. Public schools belong to the public.

Carol Burris, a nationally recognized outstanding educator recently wrote,

What the privatizers never talk about is that every dollar that goes to school choice is taken away from public schools. To adjust for the loss of revenue, public schools have to lay off teachers and close down programs. As a result the great majority of students are injured so a few can attend a charter or use a voucher.

Voucher programs almost always begin small—targeted at poor children, or children with disabilities, or foster children, or military children—but then expand to apply to all students. Sometimes the privatizers admit that they are pursuing a camel's nose-under-the-tent strategy, but usually they claim to want "only this small program."

Unaccountable, unsupervised privately-managed schools waste taxpayers' dollars with bloated administrative salaries and overhead. In these conditions, without public oversight, fraud and corruption go undetected, and when a whistleblower complains, we learn that hundreds of thousands or millions of dollars were squandered or stolen.

When we turn our backs on our public schools, we turn our backs on our most profound American values. We are not embracing conservatism; we are embracing consumerism. It is as simple and sad as that.

I would put it somewhat differently. I would say that the privatizers' goal is not only to destroy public education but to encourage us to think as consumers, not as citizens. As citizens, we support public services that are for everyone, even if we don't use those services.

At many charter conferences, the idea of "consumers of educational services" is used to describe choice. As an attendee at over forty public and charter conferences, the words "consumer choice" were often heard. The vendors at the choice events tend to be looking to construct new schools, finance them, or provide financial services. A justification for what is occurring is being wrapped up in a mantra of consumer choice.

We have public schooling because we are interested in an educated citizenry for our republic. Anything less is unlovely. It is a threat to our democracy.

The charters in the 23 percent are producing citizens, not consumers. They are true public charter schools. An overheard conversation informed the author about the mind-set of some charter owners. The event was the National Charter School Conference in Las Vegas, Nevada.

NOTES

1. Dr. Friedman's work includes warnings related to free market businesses that commit suicide by seeking government subsidies and exceptions. See: Friedman, 1999.

2. A related party can be a relative, business associate, a former owner, or a company that has the same owners and board as the company they are doing business with.

3. Commitments are listed in audits as an obligation for present and future payments. Future because they are contractually bound agreements.

4. A white chip is the chip with the lowest value in a poker game.

5. This is statistically close to the percentage of actors in the Milgram experiments who chose to disregard a directive that conflicted with their sense of ethical behavior. This experiment involved assigning people to be teachers and instructing them to give electric shocks to students when they answered incorrectly. The majority of people kept giving out the electric shocks even when the "student" was screaming for them to stop.

6. A generation that was also berated when they were in high school in the 1930s (Bracey, 1997).

Chapter 7

Mind-Sets about Public Schools

OVERHEARD IN LAS VEGAS

This charter school administrator had spent that morning searching. The search had been a long drawn out affair with a great deal of walking around searching for the workshop that he had intended to attend. While pondering his participation in this National Conference on Charter Schools, he couldn't help seeing the irony of this conference's location. A new casino in Las Vegas.

A query at the main desk confirmed his suspicion that he had missed Carol Dweck's morning session, a discussion about her book, *Mind Sets*. Rather than continue on to the continental breakfast provided for convention goers, he opted for a Las Vegas breakfast at the hotel restaurant. The host sat him at a table in the middle of a crowded room filled with convention goers, that is, charter school owners.

That's when it happened.

He couldn't help overhear a vociferous conversation at the table behind him. Three men were seated at a comfortable wicker dining set that reflected the motif of the restaurant. Each one of the individuals was affiliated with their own charter school in their separate home cities. The schools were all located, as they say, "somewhere in Ohio":

As they awaited the arrival of a fourth friend, their conversation centered on berating and bemoaning the public school system in their area. All of the clichés that those who traduce the educators in the nation of "government" common schools use to cast aspersions on the "competition" were invoked by each speaker in turn. Each, "school leader," engaged their friends in this tirade. Each nodding agreement as they spoke about avoiding accepting special-needs children into their "highly performing schools" and sending those parents on to the local public schools.

"I tell them we don't accept federal funds for title one so if they want that service for their child, we don't have it," noted one.

"Just before mandatory testing we encourage certain students to leave," chimed in another. This is a ploy referred to as "cut day" by teachers in his charters. "We use AP testing to 'test' them out," said another. Hearty laughter followed each ploy for eliminating "problem" children.

That's when the tide turned.

The conversation turned to the subject of their missing friend; "Fred and I played football with Tom," declared the speaker. This triggered a new focus for the conversation. The group spent the next half hour regaling one another with fond common memories they had of their high school days (academically and athletically). This went on for the next half hour. When "Fred" showed up, the conversation continued in an amplified and animated manner for another twenty minutes.

It was evident from the affection in their voices as they spoke about their "alma mater" that the public high school they went to must have been a vital part of their lives. Surely, this must have been an aberration. It certainly wasn't like the schools they described earlier in their diatribes regarding "government" schools.

They wondered out loud about whether "coach" was still at that high school. "Yes, he is still there," one of the group announced, "My wife and I sat with him and Mrs. Jones at the reunion dinner. Couldn't believe it was 20 years ago."

As they got up to leave high fives and former high school related chants and sayings were the last pieces of the conversation that the man listening had heard. They left the room heading to the conference with warm memories regarding their commonly held childhood experiences, the times shared at their public high school.

IRONY PERSONIFIED

As this writer's civics teacher, Mr. McHugh, said about the "revolutionaries" in the book *Animal Farm*, this conversation had been *irony* personified. "All animals are equal, but some animals are more equal in Culture."[1]

The degree to which these charter school leaders connected as citizens and human beings via their common experience in a public high school was evident to anyone overhearing their conversation.

What was troubling and disturbing was they did not see or consider what their efforts, running several charters in competition and isolation from the local high school, were doing to the social fabric of their community and to a greater extent the ideals of a "republican" educational experience as described by the founding leaders of this country.

When your charter high school goes out of business, as 40 percent have, where do you go to for a reunion?

We have moved toward schooling alone.

NOTE

1. *Animal Farm* (Block and Orwell 1961, Orwell 1971).

Chapter 8

Schooling Alone

Robert Putnam, the author of *Bowling Alone, The Collapse and Revival of American Community,* talks about the significance of social connectedness and just how pervasive its effects are on the fabric of our public life in a republic.

> We are not talking here simply about nostalgia for the 1950s. *School perfor-mance*, public health, crime rates, clinical depression, tax compliance, philan-thropy, race relations, community development, census returns, teen suicide, economic productivity, campaign finance, even simple human happiness—*all are demonstrably affected by how (and whether) we connect with our family and friends and neighbors and co-workers.*
>
> And most Americans instinctively recognize that we need to reconnect with one another. Figuring out how to reconcile the competing obligations of work and family and community is the ultimate "kitchen table" issue. As practical solutions to the problem become clearer—a radical expansion of the Family and Medical Leave Act is my current favorite—the latent public support for addressing the underlying issue will become an irresistible "market" for ambi-tious political candidates."
>
> —Robert Putnam, Atlantic Unbound interview, 2000

In another discussion, Mr. Putnam continued the discourse regarding the "preconditions for democracy":

> The concept of a "civil society" has played a central role in the global debate about the preconditions for democracy and democratization. In the newer democracies this phrase has properly focused attention on the need to foster a vibrant civic life in soils traditionally inhospitable to self-government.
>
> In the established democracies, ironically, growing numbers of citizens are questioning the effectiveness of their public institutions at the very moment

when liberal democracy has swept the battlefield, both ideologically and geo-
politically. In America, at least, there is reason to suspect that this democratic
disarray may be linked to a broad and continuing erosion of civic engagement
that began a quarter-century ago.

    High on our scholarly agenda should be the question of whether a comparable
erosion of social capital may be under way in other advanced democracies,
perhaps in different institutional and behavioral guises. High on America's
agenda should be the question of how to reverse these adverse trends in social
connectedness, thus restoring civic engagement and civic trust.

                                                                —Putnam 2000: 77

"Schooling Alone" destroys social capital.

    Separate but equal is not equal. We are not "more equal in American cul-
ture" because we opt to go to a private school. That is a status that the pigs
claimed in *Animal Farm*. We are "less equal in culture" when we isolate our
children from that culturally binding experience of public schools. Social
capital is lost when we separate ourselves into groups.

    There is something inherently destructive and obscene about using public
money to do so.

    It is unlovely. It is a threat to our democracy.

    In order to build, social capital charters and districts need to work together.
Great charters do this. Students in the public charter schools created in New
Hampshire remained a part of their home school community. Sports, music,
the arts, clubs, and all of the socializing aspects so vital to the communities
that public schools serve were a part of the public charters that the community
asked for and built.

    Our citizens expect that "a public school" is a locally owned and controlled
part of the American educational experience. Our local public schools are for
producing *American citizens*. Citizens who are entrepreneurial, independent free
thinkers. This starts with a connection to the community you live in, not a with-
drawal from that community. Our children have become segmented by social
class, religious affiliation, and race. It is unlovely. It is a threat to our democracy.

    This separation of community is the opposite of what we were working
toward in the past, *unity*. In the 1940s towns like Swanzey, New Hampshire,
closed their small, one-room school houses in each section of town and created two main elementary schools to serve all of their children. This was the
town's way of uniting the community that had been segmented by distance
when horses and carriages were the norm. The town had several sections,
West Swanzey, East Swanzey, Swanzey Center, and Westport. Swanzey is a
small town of 7,230 people. Town meetings and direct votes by the citizens
of the town are the norm to this day. Community still matters in rural New
Hampshire.

The purpose of developing common schools in this nation was to develop citizens for the republic who had the skills to participate, *with their fellow citizens*, in this great experiment in a republican form of government. The public school system of governance was debated over many years and designed to keep decisions about what type of schools to provide and how to pay for them at the local level. We have failed our culture by not passing these ideas down in civics classes. By our actions, we are teaching the antithesis of civic involvement.

We should applaud and emulate the efforts of people like Richard Dreyfus as they work to bring civics[1] back to all of our schools. During a recent television interview, Mr. Dreyfus went on to explain the significance of this historical shift away from mandatory civics instruction in American educational priorities:

- Many members of Congress never studied in detail the Constitution and Bill of Rights during their K–12 education.
- He asked an open question: "Wouldn't it make sense to teach children how to run the country before it's their turn to take the reins?"

What are we saying about our local community's role when the federal government or state legislature policymakers mandate that we will have separate types of schooling experiences?

What does it say to our children when formerly publicly held institutions move into private hands? The Civics Initiative decries the loss of civics education.

First Amendment Charter Schools promote the ideals of civic education every day.

Critics of research such as this often suggest that the researcher look at the reasons why the public is drawn to charter schools and private vouchers. By initiating charters that focused on citizenship and encouraging the public schools to reintroduce civics, the author acknowledges some of the reasons why the public has been led down this path so easily. We failed to ensure that there is a public for public schools.

As a result of that neglect, those public assets are rapidly moving into private ownership. The support groups for this real estate transfer are often highly paid lobbyist for the charter industry. We can do better.

NOTE

1. Mr. Dreyfus heads the organization known as The Civics Initiative. A movement to bring back the teaching of civics in all of our schools.

Chapter 9

Private Ownership of Public Assets

There are states that prohibit charter owners from owning the public spaces they conduct business in. In general, private ownership of publicly paid for assets are the norm. Buildings, capital purchases, and materials that are privately held remain a hallmark of the charter school network and a fact of the private school industry.

The charter schools started in New Hampshire are still in existence. They are operated by certified trained educators. Those school use public spaces rented from unrelated parties. They cost less money to run and offer an alternative to the programs offered at the local public schools. They are named using their communities' name. Monadnock Community Connections is one of these charters. The other school is a K–8 elementary named for the town that it is located in Surry Elementary. The town runs their charter through a local board.

There are examples of this type of charter school in the data. Charter schools that serve the needs of autistic students are one manifestation of the type of work and ethical business practices of the 23 percent of Arizona charters that the study identified as exemplars.

These types of schools often seek to include their students in their local district school's sports and they actively promote civic involvement. Monadnock Community Connections, MC², is a member of the First Amendment Schools initiative. An organization that Arizona's Sandra Day O'Connor helped found. Civics is imbedded in the curriculum. The leadership at MC² founded the QED foundation a forum where they freely share their curriculum and ideas.

FREEDOM WITH RESPONSIBILITY

Schooling alone, whether in separate schools, home schooling, or online, should always be a choice in a free society. No one is arguing that the right of free association be curtailed. The argument is about who pays for a personal choice. Arguing that an individual can't speak about the public schools because they sent their children to private schools is counterproductive in the debate. You do have the right to choose a private school. However, you are not entitled to the public paying for that right. You choose. Expecting the public to fund that choice is an example of an entitlement mentality.

ENTITLED ISOLATIONISM

Expecting the community to pay for isolationism from the community and providing funds for the property used for that isolationist approach is not what is promised by the words, "provide a free and appropriate public education." The concept of isolating ourselves from one another is antithetical to a pluralistic society's premise.

By definition, a pluralistic society is a diverse one, where the people who are in that society believe all kinds of different things and tolerate each other's beliefs even when they do not match their own. E Pluribus Unum as a motto says much more than "Diversity Training" about who we are. Anything else than what the best and brightest of parents want for their child is as John Dewey reminded us "unlovely, and a danger to our democracy."

We have sacrificed too much for our common American heritage to abandon our common schools. This was struck home to the author on a recent visit to the Normandy region of France. The American Cemetery at Normandy has graves with one thing in common. They face eastward toward the United States. Officers, enlisted personnel, different service branches, and all faiths represented in that hallowed ground are all in the same plot of American soil in Europe. A piece of America that is lovingly maintained by the people of France.

It is not time to go back to "separate but equal." It is a threat to our democracy. We need to understand why we have common schools in the first place, and we need to cherish them.

The origins of Catholic schools in this country are rooted in the anti-Catholicism of the 1840s. While there were always Catholic Schools, the move to provide them at every local parish originated during this period of anti-immigrant fervor. This statement is not to suggest that people like the grandchildren of the author should not be allowed to choose to attend a Catholic school.

The promoters of the theory of action that suggest choice means being able to opt out of the public schools while taking the funding associated with that choice with you is the issue. These promoters and advocates are well-paid lobbyists who are engaged in seeking more public funding for private enterprises. There is a price to pay for this lobbying for choice. It is substantial and is reflected in IRS Form 990 filings for those "Nonprofits." The businesses and corporations that would profit from the law's deregulation financed the lobbying effort. A form 990 is a required filing for nationally approved nonprofits.

The salary figures at these lobbying firms tell a tale, $242,000 for the AZ Charter Association director in an organization that took in $2.5 M versus $156,000 for the Arizona School Boards Association in an organization that represents a far larger constituency with revenue of $3.8 M. The salary of $242,000 is also more than twice the payment that the director of the Arizona State Board for Charter Schools, *the oversight organization for charter schools receives*. The salary is also greater than any superintendent in the state. The membership fees are disproportional to the size of the organization.

Where Are the Priorities? Lobbying or Educating?

This fixation with money and profiting from education also shows up in the six and seven figure salaries paid out at mega-charter groups and in salaries for "choice" foundation directors. Salaries that often have nothing to do with the fiscal success of the company. We were outraged when bonuses were paid out to firms involved in the financial meltdown in 2007. We should be outraged by profiteers in charters raising salaries and paying bonuses for management in bad financial years.

What definition of charter schools and choice allowed this kind of scheme to come to be acceptable practice? What was the initial "promise"?

Chapter 10

Mission Failure: Academic Results

THE PROMISE IN THE PURPOSE

The purpose stated for charter schools reads: "Charter schools are publicly funded, privately managed and semi-autonomous schools of choice. They do not charge tuition. They must hold to the same academic accountability measures of traditional schools. They receive public funding similarly to traditional schools. However, they have more freedom over their budgets, staffing, curricula and other operations. In exchange for this freedom, *they must deliver academic results and there must be enough community demand for them to remain open.*"

This purpose statement sounds innocuous.

It isn't.

Generous and extensive uses of the word "freedom" are embedded here as in most discussions regarding charter school financial and governance practices. "Freedom" from the district model is used to describe charters "unencumbered" governance by the replacement oversight structure, CEOs, and corporate boards.

The word "choice" is another favorite word of the charter and private school voucher crowd. This is a word selected to imply that we have no choice with our public schools. Even though, as some defenders of the current public schools assert, we choose where we live.

In their groundbreaking look at charter schools, *Who Chooses? Who Loses? Culture, Institutions and the Unequal Effects of School Choice,* Bruce Fuller and Richard F. Elmore explored the issues raised by vouchers and charter school expansion several years into Milwaukee's and other city and state experiments with "deregulation and innovation."

A democratic, free society needs to ensure that choosing does not result in its most vulnerable constituencies losing. Often the "losing" referred to in *Who Chooses: Who Loses* occurs as an unintentional consequence of ideas that appear at first blush to be right and democratically sound. The "ideals" in the definition are often co-opted by human nature and the real world mechanics of the "free market."

Polarities

Polarities are a well-known phenomenon. *Polarities between what is idealized in the rhetoric and what is occurring play out in the data.*

* Insistence on freedom of choice for one group leads to no choice for others.
* Freedom without responsibility is not true freedom.

Who can argue with the idea that we should have choice or freedom of choice?

Freedom and choice are used to describe charter schools and private placements as a way of selling their presumed virtues. There is an assumption that "privately managed and semi-autonomous schools of choice" will work because free markets always work. Right?

The premise is false. Human nature where money is concerned is purposefully left out of the logic equations of free marketers. In this war against America's public schools, the battle plans and espoused theories went out the window once the first shot was fired. It is folly to slavishly follow an ideology when twenty years of data proves it is not working as its advocates promised.

The words "choice" and "freedom" have connotations that have been used and played upon to manipulate public perceptions regarding charter schools.

If one group, charters and vouchers, is freedom and choice, then the other group, district schools, must be no choice and no freedom.[1]

Academic Underperformance Instead of Academic Results

The impetus behind expanded school choice in Arizona and nationally has been improving academic performance based on the assumption that parents would choose the best school for their children. Likewise, public district schools are supposed to also improve since they must now compete for students to retain funding. Consequently, since charter enrollments have grown faster than public district schools, due to parents choosing, one would expect that for equivalent students that charters would be outperforming public district schools.

Two recent comprehensive studies have used publicly available student data to evaluate the performance of Arizona's charter schools. The Center for Research on Educational Outcomes (CREDO) at Stanford University has done nationwide analyses by state to evaluate charter performance relative to traditional public schools, overall, in urban areas and for online schools. At the behest of the Goldwater Institute, the leading advocate of school choice in Arizona, the Brookings Institution also evaluated Arizona's charter schools. Both studies found Arizona's charter sector underperforming relative to similar students in public district schools.

The CREDO study partnered with twenty-seven state departments of education and uses both student and school level data. It captures student-level demographics and achievement test scores in reading and math—and due to the structure of No Child Left Behind's testing regime—has most consistent data for grades 3–8. In Arizona for grades 3–8 and grade 10, for each two-year combination, CREDO focuses on student growth in their test scores. For Arizona growth data was available from 2006 to 2007 through 2010 to 2011.

The primary challenge in evaluating educational outcomes is finding an appropriate comparison group. You can't compare how a student does in a charter school with how she would have performed if she stayed at her neighborhood district public school.

CREDO's means of overcoming this challenge is to create a Virtual Control Record (VCR) that creates a "virtual twin" of each charter school student by identifying students with identical traits and very similar prior test scores in nearby traditional public schools. Traits included grade level, gender, race/ethnicity, free or reduced lunch eligibility, English Language Learner status, Special Education Status, and prior test score on state achievement tests.

CREDO's results can be seen in figure 10.1 for both 2009 and 2013. Arizona appears in the lower left quadrant for both reading and math. The lower left quadrant represents those states that in CREDO's 2009 study and 2013 study had charter results inferior to traditional public schools when comparing charter student performance with a virtual identical twin (Raymond, 2013).

In reading, Arizona's performance relate to the earlier study deteriorated somewhat, while in math the results were about the same in 2009 and 2013. Collectively though Arizona stands out as one of the worst performing charter school states in the country when compared to equivalent students in traditional public schools.

The CREDO data does have limitations. Because the first test scores are in third grade, any charter school impact prior to third grade would not be captured. In addition, CREDO does not differentiate by grade level or the educational mission of the school: rigorous, general, arts, alternative, etc.

CREDO has also done studies that focused on metropolitan areas and with charters that do online instruction. For Arizona the metro areas covered were Phoenix, Mesa, and Tucson. That 2015 study found students in Phoenix and Mesa who attended charter schools did significantly poorer in reading and math than equivalent students in traditional public schools.

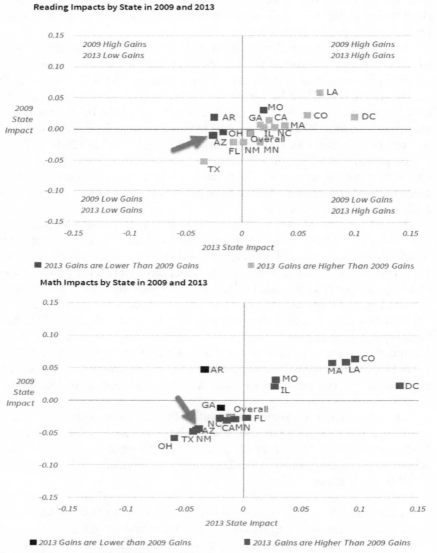

Figure 10.1. Academic Performances by State

CREDO Analysis of Charter School Academic Performance by State

In Tucson, the charter students did better in math and had no difference in reading. For Mesa and Phoenix, white students suffered the most by attending charter schools. For Tucson, black students gained the most and white students gained modestly.

CREDO also evaluated online charter instruction in 2015. They found nationwide online charters were doing a *deplorable job*. In Arizona, attending an online charter meant losing more than 80 days of learning compared to a district public school for an equivalent student, and for math the loss was 180 days—an entire year (James L. Woodworth, 2015).

These results alone suggest the state should be carefully scrutinizing and possibly terminating online charter operators.

SCAMMING THE ACADEMIC RATING SYSTEM

The Big Switch The charter board's own data on academic performance reveals that most online schools are not meeting academic performance standards.

This result is in spite of the fact that most online schools are considered alternative schools.

A Tipping Point In 2013, prior to the new rankings, there were 120 charter schools that converted to *Alternative School* status. This was in a group of 371 schools that went through a financial and academic rating in 2012. A full 32 percent of charters opted to *lower their academic standards for grading by the charter board by switching to alternative status in 2013*.

This move was a blatant effort to manipulate the academic rating system by lowering the academic bar to "alternative" status. How do you call yourself an academy and change your academic label to alternative?

Statistics on Academic Performances

The Goldwater Institute was concerned by the 2013 CREDO test results and contracted with the Brookings Institution to do a more careful evaluation of charter performance aimed at overcoming the limitations with the CREDO methodology. The Arizona Department of Education (AZDOE) provided student test score, school enrollment, demographic, and program participation data for academic years 2005–2006 through 2011–2012. AZDOE did not fully cooperate with researchers, so some student-level data was incomplete forcing researchers to use methods of estimation to fill the gaps.

The Brookings study focused on middle schools, so they could have multiple years of test data from the state's AIMS test, so as to identify students with similar demographics and test scores prior to middle school. Students could then be tracked across their middle school years.

The Brookings results also show marginally worse results overall for students in charter schools compared to traditional public schools with nonurban charters doing particularly poorly. The researchers also found stronger negative impacts in math for above-average students and negative impacts in reading and math for non-ELL students and non-SPED students. ELL students gained the most from being in charters.

Charters classified as rigorous modestly improved math performance, while general, art specialized, at-risk, and online ones retarded math performance. In reading, at-risk and online charter schools had the worst performance.

As with the CREDO study, the online charter school performance was atrocious. Researchers suggested possible missing variables related to students attending them, but that may be charitable. The state charter board needs to carefully scrutinize online charter operators.

Overall, they find "charter schools at every grade level have been modestly less effective than traditional public schools in raising student achievement." We are giving up publicly held property and overpaying for "modestly less effective" schools. Even with a consumer-centered focus, that equation does not make sense.

The CREDO study despite any limitations with its data shows that Arizona's charter sector is underperforming relative to other states—though some of those states restrict the student populations to inner cities. Though clearly some charter schools are succeeding, both CREDO and the Brookings study show lackluster performance overall among charters contradicting the notion that choice invariably improves outcomes.

Why does choice fall short? Neither of these studies publish school-specific results. Arizona's state rating systems also has inherent biases toward schools with more favorable socioeconomic demographics relative to student performance based on passing rates.

As noted earlier, 100 charters are now classified as "Alternative," *which excludes the category for lowest growth students as well as drop out and graduation rates.* All of which is to suggest state classifications of A to F may not accurately reflect how that school performs compared to a traditional public school.

Distorted Demographics

Free markets rely on complete information to function without distortions. Consequently, with incomplete information, we shouldn't be surprised that "choice" leads in many instances to suboptimal outcomes for students when they move to charters.

We know from psychology that once people make a choice, they tend to mentally justify that decision. Opting out of and moving out of public schools is a significant decision. We should expect to see choice-supported bias in, for instance, parental satisfaction surveys of charter school parents.

However, besides limited academic information, parents are not provided with transparency on the financial aspects of charter schools. Parents are provided no financial disclosures on how much top administrators make, the extent of related party transactions, whether the school is in the black or red, and how teacher salaries compare with traditional district schools. With that information, parents would be better informed when making their decisions, and the schools would be more accountable. *They would also be able to assess whether the school will survive financially.*

Factors in Success

No one is doubting the academic results schools like BASIS and Great Hearts are attaining. However, their insistence that their schools are not populated by children that are in the top quartile of the bell curve ignores the facts.

There is a vast chasm in the data regarding children who enter BASIS charter schools and their graduating class size. BASIS needs to acknowledge it and embrace what they are doing. The Navy Seals do not apologize for candidates that have to ring the bell and leave the program. They don't pretend they have "average sailors and marines" in their program or that everyone will succeed. It's okay to provide this type of "choice" under the existing charter laws, that is, it is authorized.

BASIS' finances and governance are what the data analysis undertaken takes exception to, not their stellar academic performance. Leasing teachers instead of continuing the company's initial practice of providing them with membership in the Arizona State Retirement System (terminated in 2010)

Table 10.1. IRS 990 Data from BASIS

Revenue Less Expenses	Net Assets Beginning of Year	Net Assets End of Year
$(2,868,549)	$(762,662)	$(2,105,887)
Revenue Less Expenses	Net Assets Beginning of Year	Net Assets End of Year
$(4,439,846)	$(2,105,887)	$(6,545,733)
Revenue Less Expenses	Net Assets Beginning of Year	Net Assets End of Year
$(4,217,998)	$(6,545,733)	$(15,292,723)
	Other Changes	
	$(4,528,992)	

IRS 990 Filings for BASIS FY 12, 13, and 14

Table 10.2.   BASIS Financial Data from Audits for Four Years

BASIS Financial Data from Audit Filings for FY 2013–FY 2016				
Total Revenue	*Total Expenses*	*Revenue Less Expenses*	*Net Assets Beg. of Year*	*Net Assets End of Year*
$43,952,493 FY 2013	$43,337,245 Loss on Disposal of Assets −$2,821,029	$615,248 Deficit on Net after Loss −$2,205,781 2013–2014	$688,632	−$1,517,149
Total Revenue	*Total Expenses*	*Revenue Less Expenses*	*Net Assets Beg. of Year*	*Net Assets End of Year*
$61,818,112 FY 2014	$66,108,317	−$4,290,205 2014–2015	−$1,517,149	−$5,807,354
Total Revenue	*Total Expenses*	*Revenue Less Expenses*	*Net Asset Beg. of Year*	*Net Assets End of Year*
$84,472,972 FY 2015	$87,547,289	−$3,074,317 Write off of Loan Issuance Costs −$4,528,992 2015–2016	−$5,708,917	−$13,312,226
Total Revenue	*Total Expenses*	*Revenue Less Expenses*	*Net Asset Beg. of Year*	*Net Assets End of Year*
$103,344,392 FY 2016	$103,099,711	$244,681 Write off of Loan Issuance Costs −$9,921,879	−$13,312,226	−$22,989,424

does not reward their performance based pay packages. The economic theory that competition will benefit teachers' compensation and benefits is a myth. Charters need to stop pretending that they reward teachers' stellar performances with performance pay. The data does not bear that theory out.

Tables 10.1 and 10.2 illustrate that BASIS' stellar academic performances are also not a guarantee of financial success. Their deficits continue to grow as the company is funding its expansion with excessive debt.

The Bell Curve Exists

The regular Navy is a bit more accepting of the general population. We as a society don't underfund the Navy to pay for the Seals. Public schools and many charters accept and keep all comers.

If we do not understand that money and inputs matter to educational quality, then consider this. Why does a dish of ice cream cost so much at a premium branded[2] outlet? These outlets do not set up shop in neighborhoods where the average consumer can't afford their product.

A former critic of public schools, Jamie Volmer, an ice cream executive, opened his mind when he took the time to understand what public schools really accomplish with the inputs that show up at their doors. Each child is known and treated as an individual in the best public schools. No matter where they fall on the bell curve.

Politicians suggesting that the loss of the top percentile of the student population choosing to migrate to an elite program does not affect the scores of the other institutions in that neighborhood are not fooling anyone. The overemphasis on these outlier academic successes in charters suggests that they either don't understand mathematics, normal distribution curves, or factor analysis. The other explanation is they have never been in real contact with their fellow citizens. The bell curve is real; it is not fake news.

Premising funding on performance makes sense in professional sports. All of the children playing in leagues and on high school teams do not make it to the professional ranks. Our children are scattered throughout the bell curve academically and physically. Public schools are for all of our children. Using funding as a triage tool for deciding whose schools live or die is anathema to our values. The child who is having difficulty sitting still may grow up to be the fireman who saves your family. They become the type of citizen who runs into danger rather than away from it. We call these type of citizens' "heroes." Academic growth is important to all of our children. All of our citizens count.

"What the best and brightest parents want for their child, so must we want for all children. Anything else is unlovely and a threat to our Democracy." Separate but equal rulings came because the separate schools were proven to be underfunded and unequal. Do we really want to move in that direction? Special-needs children were confined to state hospitals at one time. We are better than that.

Imagine hospitals whose staff said, "Stop bringing us sick and injured people. We are tired of dealing with them." "Send only healthy people to us. Those sick people hurt our 'wellness' scores."

A premise in the original theories of "greater parental control" has not been delivered. The market theory assumes there is an average consumer of its goods and services making informed decisions regarding where to send their child. Consequently, the informational pre-requisites for choice as a means of applying market-based economics to schools falls short in Arizona. The result is a resegregation of our schools, by "choice." Choice rhetoric appeals to our baser instincts of looking out for ourselves first our community second.

This is the antithesis of what Lincoln called for after the Civil War, "every living heart and hearthstone all over this broad land, will yet swell the chorus of the Union, when again touched, as surely they will be, by the better angels of our nature."[3]

Human and Cultural Capital

In addition to social capital, other influences, most notably the child's mother's level of education, are factors in academic success. The concept of human capital is the easiest to understand. Human capital is an individuals' knowledge, skills, and abilities, which they develop primarily through their parents, education, and social interactions and then "capitalize" on in the workforce. In the realm of parenting, a college degree or the knowledge and skills that level of education stands for drives how parents interact with their children.

Robert Marzano's work on the role of vocabulary development in a child's ability to take in information. Scholars estimate that children of parents on welfare hear thirty million fewer words by the age of four than the children of professional parents (Marzano, 2004). These children need to be engaged in interactions *with children who did have parents reading and speaking rich vocabularies*. This doesn't happen when those children are in different schools.

The gap is not only about the quantity of words you hear but also the quality. Better educated parents also use a wider vocabulary, and they dole out affirmations more generously than less educated parents. Learning a plethora of words early in life is tied to better academic outcomes down the road. Parents' early conversations with their children have long-lasting implications.

Mothers' education level also matters later in childhood: College-educated mothers are "able to more appropriately tailor cognitively stimulating activities to their children's developmental level," and they are better equipped to help kids do homework and study for tests.

There is little chance for a child living in poverty of interacting with children who have benefitted from parents who want the best for their children if they don't meet those children in a common forum. Cultural capital also helps kids to navigate the education system successfully without getting into trouble. Educated mothers are more comfortable with schools, so they are more likely to advocate for their kids there. *A critical mass of this type of parent in a school is vital to the school's success*.

These are all parts of our highly performing schools whether they are charters, private, or district schools. When we segregate ourselves by cognitive ability and social class the human, cultural and social capital that come from parents and children of all skill levels interacting are marginalized.

We are here to help each other through this thing we call life whatever it might be. Relying on outlier data to promote the myth that charters are academically superior with general populations is misleading at best. The myths about choice and academic prowess need debunking.

NOTES

1. "Freedom" and "liberty" that are often used as synonyms are defined here as the author makes the distinction in several discussions. Liberty is granted to people by an external control, that is, the freedom was granted. Freedom is a state of being capable of making decisions without external control.

2. Jamie Volmer, once a critic of the Public Schools, is indicative of the type of reflecting thinking the author hopes results from this work. https://www.youtube.com/watch?v=O9TUrHMZMno.

3. Lincoln was using Shakespeare's phrase, "the better angels of our nature," within this quote.

Chapter 11

Real Choice: Debunking the Rhetoric

THE BETTER ANGELS OF CHOICE

Charter schools locating in areas with an "A plus"–rated public schools are often offering the same programs that the district offers at one or many of its school sites.

Is this new "competition" going to improve academic outcomes for all students? If we left the children in their original district placement, would they have performed the same way?

Parents already have the choice to send their children to a different district in Arizona. This open enrollment feature removed the "you are stuck with the school you live near" argument from the charter advocate's quiver. Recognizing parents choose schools for other reasons, like sports, a serious rewrite of athletic eligibility rules occurred. A solution to this selecting for sports is provided here.

The charter schools in New Hampshire that were noted earlier were featured in the book, American Schools, by Sam Chaltain. They were also recognized by the Association for Supervision and Curriculum Development (ASCD). The MC^2 program is a cross-curricula program unlike the offerings at the local highly rated district schools. Students learn in a high stakes environment that is project oriented and where the testing is done through presentations to professionals, parents, and peers. In short, MC^2 is completely different learning approach from the local high performing schools.

The school district it is located in also offers lettering programs for sports that are not in their offerings at the district's school. They don't claim credit for those highly performing athlete's performance. They do recognize their performance.

Community: It's in the Name

If you attend the charter Monadnock Community Connections, MC^2, you are able to play sports at your hometown high school. If you are a world-class gymnast in a school district that doesn't have a gymnastics team, you can still earn a letter in your sport. You count as an individual in your community.

WORD PLAYS

The words "choice" and "freedom" are used analogously with words like "deregulation" as it is used by "free-market" economists. Who doesn't want to deregulate? The implication is that the alternatives to this free market, the public districts, are over regulated and bureaucratic.

We are psychologically and slavishly following a flawed "battle plan" even though we can plainly see the financial and governance faults in that plan. We have entrenched ourselves in opposing lines between charter and voucher advocates and districts only mentalities. It has devolved into a trench war of financial attrition.

The charter and choice movement's lobbyists chose words that have stuck in the public's collective minds. Isolated successes are sold as indicators of the efficacy of the plan. An example of this type of language manipulation in action follows.

THE RHETORIC: "DISTRICT SCHOOLS ARE BUREAUCRATIC"

There is nothing "arbitrary or routine," key descriptors in definition for the word "bureaucratic," in the majority of the rules governing public schools. The word "bureaucracy" originated in Europe where it was used when describing government workers who worked for the monarchies of the time. Our public school leaders work for the local community through their elected boards, not monarchs. They are champions for children.

Who do most charter owners work for?

- Charters school leaders, CEOs, work for corporate boards that are often related parties. If the board is the owner, they work for themselves.
- Corporate boards of one, the CEO themselves, are allowed. An oligarchy. When the property is passed to a son or daughter, it becomes an ancestral monarchy.
- Corporate boards comprised of two, the married couple who owns the charter are another variation on the same theme.

• Another permutation is corporate boards of related parties that are dealing with other for-profit corporations made up of the same members.

Autocracies and oligarchies are bureaucracies without the interceding middle management. The best charters have community based corporate boards with diverse representative membership. That corporate board structure is a common factor in 23 percent of charters identified in the data.

OLIGARCHIES MONOPOLIZE THE CHARTER "FREE MARKET"

While Milton Friedman argued against "socialist enterprises," it is incumbent on anyone interested in this theory to contemplate what he said after the comma in that argument. We would be wise to recall he wrote this piece in the 1960s. A time period immediately following the McCarthyism of the 1950s. A time of hyperbole regarding "socialism."

> The situation is wholly different with a socialist enterprise like the public school system, or, for that matter, a private monopoly. The true customers of the public schools—parents and children—have come to exercise less and less influence over the schools as the schools have become more and more centralized and bureaucratic.
>
> *When school districts were numerous and small, parents could exercise considerable influence. A superintendent or principal who misjudged the "merit" of teachers—in the eyes of consumers—would not have remained in these positions for long.*
>
> —Milton Friedman in *Newsweek*, December 5, 1983

Who Really Has the Monopoly?

The financial dealings within a small highly related group at many charter's companies *are monopolistic* not "efficient" as is claimed by their defenders. Typically, these types of charters move into areas where results are guaranteed because of the demographics of the communities where they locate their schools. One only need look at the addresses listed in the data to prove this point.

What do we call it when a charter group controls hundreds of schools and tens of thousands of students in the country like the Gulen Schools (Daisy Inc. in Arizona) and the mega-charter firm K-12 Inc. (known as Practical Portable Education in Arizona)? A listing of some of the largest charter groups in Arizona yields the following Average Daily Membership counts

Table 11.1. Largest Charters by ADM

Charter Group	ADM at June 2015	Charter Group	ADM at June 2015
Great Hearts	8871	Basis Inc.	8000
Imagine Inc.	7663	Leona Group	7071
Legacy	6890	K-12 Inc. PPE	5403
Primavera	5771	Edkey Inc.	5090

(the count the charter was paid on). The charters listed are managed by a management group.

Crony capitalism is not what is idealized in the espoused theory of free market systems rhetoric. The prevailing view, held by charter advocates, of district customer relationships is embodied in the statement, "The true customers of the public schools parents and children have come to exercise less and less influence over the schools *as the schools have become more and more centralized and by extension bureaucratic.*" So, what have we switched to?

An oligarchy of charter school operators has developed in Arizona. These oligarchies uses related party transactions, controlled labor pools (through leasing of employees), high management fees to management companies that are owned by the same owner, and corporate oversight of their schools to control the management group's interests. They run schools for the adults.

Sound familiar? The original quote with the reality of charter management goes like this, "The true customers of the public schools parents and children have come to exercise less and less influence over the schools *as the schools have become more and more centralized and oligarchic.*"

These schools pick and choose who they will let through the doors. Recall this statistic. The Arizona Department of Education report entitled *10/1/2009 Federal Child Count by PEA (Public Education Agency) updated as of 2/1/2010* indicated that nearly *93 percent of all special-needs students in the state are enrolled in traditional public schools.* In spite of this fact, we are expected to believe charters are not assisting special-needs children and their parents to "look elsewhere for special services."

The rhetoric regarding bureaucracies is dated. Most public districts moved to *site based management* in the 1980s.

CORPORATE NONPROFITS WITH FOR-PROFIT SUBSIDIARIES

At the same time, 1994 on, large charters started developing replete with for-profit management companies that controlled all of their charters' operations.

For every management action they took over, they took a cut of the gross for that service. Leasing employees is a lucrative 10 percent of the payroll paid to the "employment" for-profit subsidiary of the company.

Accelerating leases with built in increases are paid to "real estate management" subsidiaries with the same ownership and board membership as the school. A separate for-profit branch that has the same owners and corporate board. See figure 11.1 that illustrates the modus operandi of many large charter groups in the country.

The corporate boards for these entities? Unelected related parties.

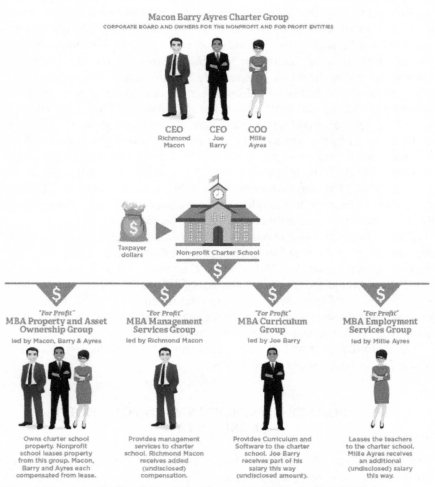

Figure 11.1.   Organizational Chart of a Nonprofit with For-Profit Subsidiaries

The "true customers" have lost influence at any level of management *except* by exiting from the charter. Parents and students are dealing with corporations instead of districts. The extent of this new management phenomena is illustrated in figure 11.1 a graphic representation of the management levels and subsidiary companies associated with many charter organizations. A detailed look at this type of organizational structure is provided in a later chapter. The chart is purposefully reused in that chapter.

Ignoring Voter Intent

When the public supports their schools by agreeing to overrides, warrant articles, and new taxes, they are expecting that the schools that are operating in their names are being fair to their teachers.

The public looks at teachers in the same way it regards police personnel and fire department personnel. How are charters treating their teachers? Are they meeting this public expectation?

First, we look at whether the myths regarding district teachers are true.

THE MYTH OF INEFFECTIVE TEACHERS IS JUST THAT, A MYTH

The inability of leadership in public district schools to dismiss a teacher is an urban legend. The author's own experience with highly unionized teachers and support staff in New England was uninhibited when decisions to dismiss were reached.

Unions have no vested interest in preventing the dismissal of ineffective teachers. It is never in a professional organization's best interest to allow mediocrity or incompetence to exist in its ranks. Are there issues? Of Course. They pale in comparison to the labor issues in deregulated charter schools.

Charter owners with employees that are related to them have a vested interest in those teachers. It is called nepotism. Experience in charters taught this writer that a unionized teacher is a lot easier for a manager to dismiss than a child of a corporate board member or the owner.

What unionized teachers do expect is that the dismissal is based on solid proof and due diligence by management. They expect and deserve to be treated as professionals.

Great teachers learn on the job. When states put forward evaluation requirements, they often leave out the primary cause of teacher failure, ineffective supervision. Dynamic and active supervision partnered with performance-based evaluation is the proper way to address the needs of teachers and the need for results based evaluations. When supervision is left out of the equation evaluation is meaningless. How do you evaluate a teacher you are not providing supervision and guidance to? Great charters and district schools provide expert supervision and evaluation to their staff.

If a district or a charter has ineffective teachers, it is a management issue. It is not a unionized teacher issue. Our educational professionals need to be treated as professionals. The data on charter turnover and compensation packages indicates they aren't being treated that way. That poor treatment is a "choice" that management at charter and private schools have free reign on. There aren't unions to blame for charter and private school management failures.

Corporate management at charters is supposed to enable management's ability to fire ineffective teachers.

Some of the rhetoric used in defense of charter management cites charter school's nimbleness in firing ineffective staff. Experience in the marketplace demonstrated that this "firing" of ineffective teachers often was motivated by an interest in reducing the payroll costs, not teacher inefficiency. A common sense question regarding this issue is asked here.

Who Is Harder to Fire?

- A unionized teacher or a blood relative of the CEO?
- A unionized teacher or a relative of a Corporate Board member?
- A certified principal nominated by a superintendent or an uncertified principal who is related to the CEO or a corporate board member?
- A CEO who is the president of the corporate board or a superintendent who is the agent of an elected board?

Providing teachers with experienced educational leadership professionals with successful teaching experience under their belts is a first step. We need people who know what they are doing through their own experience teaching children. Michael Polanyi called this type of knowing, personal knowledge. Learning to teach effectively is part of the artistry of the profession. Teaching is a vocation. A vocation that requires the practitioner to commit to life-long learning. Learning as a way of being.

In turn, the mentor supervisor needs experience and their own personal knowledge of the art of teaching to provide the developing teacher with carefully crafted feedback on their performance.

Think about this. If you were a new doctor in an internship,[1] would you want to be overseen by a business CEO or an experienced doctor? Plumbers learn under master plumbers. Police and fire personnel learn the nuances of their profession from sergeants and captains who actually worked in their field. We know the value of this approach intuitively.

Great salaries for teachers were another predicted result of privatizing education. Supply and demand would create a demand for highly compensated excellent teachers. Really?

NOTE

1. Internships were a part of the introduction to the profession that teachers received in the early part of the twentieth century. Internships are part of the best practices at schools of education across the country. A little known fact is that the medical profession copied the idea of an internship from the educational profession. See: The Flexner Report for details. There was a time when the medical profession was treated the same way as we are currently treating the teaching profession. That is, anyone could be a doctor.

Chapter 12

Teachers in the Charter and Private Systems

One of the theories of "competition" in the free markets was that schools in the charter and public sphere would be competing for excellent teachers. The standing logic was that competition would positively affect teachers' compensation packages as schools competed for the best teachers. That is compensation would increase based on supply and demand.

Teachers making over $100 K was one of the predictions made about compensation in a competitive education market by Milton Friedman in the 1970s. This was an extraordinary amount of money at that time.

The marketplace, it was postulated, would remove the need for unions, and money would be distributed based on a teacher's performance. In cases where there was a large influx of private money into the charter system that premise held up. The trouble with infusing charters with grants and donations is the sustainability of the effort once that funding goes away. There is also the fact that similar infusions often do not go into the "competing" district.

IGNORING HISTORICAL EVIDENCE

There was no real reason to believe this theory's predictions as there were many decades of union free schools prior to unionization. The "market" did not spontaneously provide improved salaries then for teachers or any other labor groups. Steel mills and coal mines didn't raise salaries because of "market forces."

There are exceptions. The CEOs and companies that do compete this way amounted to roughly a quarter of the marketplace. Remarkably close to the 23 percent of charter that are operating that way in Arizona. We call them enlightened owners. Their grounding in fairness can be from their own personal religious convictions. They demonstrate their faith by their ethical behavior in a business environment.

Malden Mills owner Aaron Feuerstein is a shining example of a family-owned business where a religious principal guided his decision making. For guidance, Mr. Feuerstein turned to the Torah, the book of Jewish law. "You are not permitted to oppress the working man, because he's poor and he's needy, amongst your brethren and amongst the non-Jew in your community," was a famous Feuerstein quote. It was his answer to those who questioned his business decisions.

After a devastating fire at Malden Mills, Feuerstein spent $300 million of the insurance money and then borrowed $100 million more to build a new plant that was both environmentally friendly and worker friendly. In December of 2015, twenty years after the fire, the company went bankrupt.

Why cite this exemplar from the business world?

Probing the data shows several of the charter schools that are in that 23 percent that are trying to behave in a morally and ethical way toward their employee and their community. Like Malden Mills, several of these are struggling to survive financially. These are the charters the state and charter board should be helping with guidance and extra funding.

Thinking the market is going to take care of this issue by itself is naïve. Academic success is no guarantee of financial security for charter owners or their employees. Especially when the "competition" swamps the marketplace with shiny new "choices" subsidized by government loans. A cozy deal that even Friedman spoke against.[1] He called this type of lobbying for political favor, "business suicide."

Maps showing where charters have located indicate that the propensity of charters have located in affluent communities. This is not a surprise. *It makes excellent business sense.* Academic data declines in those schools when the demographics in the area changes. Many of the charter closings noted were in areas where this occurred, that is, they left the area when the community composition changed.

Changing Markets

Freidman's theory was that the free market would provide competition for exemplary teachers. That pay would be based on the demand for a teacher's exemplary student academic performance like higher-compensated private school teachers. This comparison was made in the 1960s when private schools often *did* pay more than public schools.

The theory's premise is not the case as of 2013. Private schools average pay nationally was $36,000 compared to public school salary averages of $50,000 as of June 2013. The reason cited for teachers selecting to teach at private schools is the working conditions, not salary. Private school teachers are also often in their first three years of teaching. Private schools also have high turnover rates.

Sectarian schools traditionally underpay their staff. The academically successful Catholic school system that is often pointed to as an example of a faith-based system deserving of educational opportunity scholarships systematically underpaid teachers and employed nuns, priests, and brothers for even less in order to keep labor costs low. The school day in the late 1950s and 1960s included daily mass and one hour of religious instruction per day. It still does in many of these schools. Every facet of the day is infused with Catholic doctrine. The market and financial model for these schools changed when the level of vocations in the church sank in the 1960s.

As an incentive to entice teachers to work for charter schools, the legislature provided access to the Arizona State Retirement System to charters who desired to provide this benefit to their teachers. How did the unregulated charter industry react to the legislature's invitation?

RETIREMENT HEIST

What has the result of voluntary participation in the Arizona State Retirement System been? Participation in the Arizona Retirement can be found in several places in the data. The data was probed in steps to obtain an answer to this question.

Step 1   Finding and listing all of the participants in the Arizona State Retirement System from the AZRS website.
Step 2   Gathering audit information regarding contributions to the various "retirement" plans provided by charters in Arizona. This information was checked against the AZRS listing of participants.
Step 3   Perform an analysis of benefits to payroll. This yielded a percentage of benefits as it related to the overall amount spent on salaries.

There are several statuses regarding retirement plans for charter teachers:

Status 1:   Charter participates in AZRS: *155 charters are in AZRS.*
Status 2:   Charter provides an alternative to AZRS: *84 charters* have an alternative retirement plan. These plans are matches to 403b plans that range from 4–6 percent of the employee's contribution up to a fixed percentage of the employee's salary.
Status 3:   Charter provides no retirement plan for its employees. *180 charters provide no retirement plan for their employees.*

Table 12.1. Charter School Retirement System Participation

AZRS	Retirement Alternative	No Retirement Plan
155	84	180

Table 12.2. Percentages Regarding Retirement Packages

AZRS	Alternative Plan Offered	No Retirement Plan
36.99	20.05	42.96

There were 419 plans (or lack of plans) noted in the data. There is some redundancy in the statistics as two charters offer both (AZRS) and another savings plan. A total of 422 answers on the retirement benefit question. Three charters of the 420 in business offer both the AZRS and a matching 403b. They are an admirable exception to the rule.

Fully 180 or 42.65 percent of charter schools *offer no retirement package* as part of their benefits packages.

The 20.14 percent that provided an alternative plan contributed a total of $2,295,390 to the plans. The employees at those charters contributed a like amount. The funds went into limited IRAs, savings plans, and other strategies.

There were multiple cases of the investments being made into companies held by related parties. One example was found where the money invested was lost. There are examples like this in the national data also. Probing the Arizona data showed that the investment companies that were owned by corporate board members went out of business. There were also six charters in the data that had not paid their payroll taxes (federal and state) in a timely manner.

AN EXAMPLE OF THE ISSUE

Primavera, a large online charter of 5,172 students, contributed $60,000 on total salaries of $10,032,456 in fiscal 2014. *This is a 0.5981 percent contribution rate.*

The company's financial success is not driving the way it acts regarding benefits. The company netted $776,400 in 2014–2015. Net assets (liabilities) at the end of the year were $45,452,111. The company is flush with cash and investment income from its numerous investments ($36.1 million in investments as of June 2014).

The owners are pocketing and investing their money rather than providing salary and benefit enticements for their teachers. The company also owed millions back to the Arizona Department of Education at the end of 2014 for overpayments of Arizona Equalization Payments. A total of $11.6 million. They are allowed, as all charters are, to pay this money back over time through reductions to the same fund during the next fiscal year. With overpayments showing up in each year, it appears to be an endless cycle of interest free money to the charter.

As a comparison to the 0.6 rate donated by Primavera, the required rate for Arizona State Retirement System donations is 11.1 percent for employers and employees. The company would have paid $1.1 million instead of $60 K if it had been in the retirement system. The company paid its own "for-profit" subsidiary $12 million for software licenses in fiscal year 2014.

Another large group, Legacy Charter Schools, with a student ADM of 6,870 students paid in $77,000 of retirement matching funds at one of its sites, Maricopa, Arizona. This was on salaries of $7,849,664 *a contribution rate of 0.98 percent.*[2]

The cited champion of great charter schools, Arizona Equine and Agriculture, provides AZRS, does not lease its teachers, and does not collect leases. It makes money the old fashion way, it earns it. Their leader is true to the promise of charter schools. The bulk of the 23 percent cited as exemplary charters are also participants in the retirement system.

Low to Zero Participation in Alternatives Noted

There were five cases in the study of zero dollars being put into matching plans. Salaries at those sites were so low that teachers and staff *could not afford to contribute.* Every charter in the study has data in the retirement section of their audit unless they do not participate in any plan at all. The case in 180 charters.

Saving Money by Denying Benefits

Required payments to AZRS for the 37.2 percent of charters participating in AZRS were: $18,421,248. When charters participated in in AZRS, they contributed 803 percent more to their employee's retirement (or pension fund) than was contributed to alternative retirement savings programs at other charters. This constitutes a stunning and disturbing difference with implications for the entire retirement system's future viability.

The alternative retirement savings programs, as a whole, were limited to 4 percent (high of 6 percent at Imagine Schools) of salary. The AZRS rate in the years being studied was 11.2 percent plus (contributions by employee and employer were over 22 percent of salary). This is on top of what the employees and employers pay into Social Security and Medicare. Most charters only offer a paid single person medical plan. Fees noted for family plans averaged $1,000 per month; $12,000 on an average salary of $35,300.

DROPPING STATE RETIREMENT PARTICIPATION TO INCREASE PROFITS

A troubling finding in the data occurred when a charter (company) went from being a participant in the retirement system and then dropped the retirement program to save money. This was the case for several major charters. Notes in the data for these cases read, "No Longer Participating or Contributing to AZRS."

Trends Noted in Companies Dropping AZRS

There were at least two companies that dropped AZRS for their employees *after the owners*, who were participants in AZRS, were fully vested in the retirement system at an inflated salary (i.e., they, the owners, will collect the maximum benefit in a system that their company no longer participates in or contributes to). In two cases, this involved a husband and wife ownership team maxing out their benefit in AZRS prior to dropping the program for their employees.

The legislature, to their credit, is looking into enacting a Nonparticipating Liability bill—Senate Bill 1178. The bill's sponsor, an outspoken charter and voucher promoter, cited the University of Arizona system's move to a self-funded plan as the impetus for the bill. Charter misuse and abuse of the system should have been a part of her argument. It wasn't even mentioned in her videoed presentation to the legislature. The sponsor of the bill is a staunch charter school supporter with "selective" concerns about the retirement system's viability.

Dangers to the System's Financial Picture

There are several charters that participate in AZRS in one charter and not in others in the same group. The charters (participating and nonparticipating) are owned by the same people. A disturbing trend in the data showed the charter owners at those charter school groups *were paid from the charter that was in the Arizona State Retirement System. As a result the owner could participate in AZRS*. This unfair labor practice is a form of gaming the retirement system for personal gain.

Consequences of Gaming the Retirement System

As noted several charters have dropped out of the AZRS system when the benefit to key managers (owners) was maximized. The owners in those cases had attained at least thirty years of contributions into the system as they were in public schools prior to starting charters. This type of gaming the system leaves the other members in the system picking up the costs associated with the charters that left.

SOLVENCY ISSUE

Consider the rate that teachers *pay* into the retirement system along with their employer. A combined 22.3 percent of their salary goes into the system. By way of comparison, annuity companies often use the number 10 percent as a proposed saving's rate for their clients. One (Prudential) even implies that by increasing to 11 percent the picture for your retirement bliss changes dramatically. The Arizona retirement rate of contribution is more than double what the businesses that are in the retirement business suggest.

In the long run, there are financial implications to the entire retirement system's viability from this fiscal manipulation at charters. This is a self-created problem similar to the draining of funds that was perpetrated on the retirement systems studied in *Retirement Heist* (Schultz 2011). In most of the companies explored in *Retirement Heist*, the profits from shorting the employees' retirement funds went to compensate upper management with golden-parachute retirement benefits. Profits from the heist also were added to the company's bottom line. The data on charters retirement practices paints a similar picture. Golden parachutes in the state retirement system are being created for owners on the employees' backs.

This gaming of the system in all of the forms listed here weakens the financial stability of the retirement system.

Legislators that are in a charters with the AZRS have the ability to collect on two and sometimes three of Arizona's state retirement plans if they also draw a salary from their charter operations. This is referred to in the vernacular as "double dipping." In fairness to the legislature, the salaries they are paid as members of the legislature are not in keeping with the job's responsibilities ($24,000 per year with a per diem of $35).

Neither are teachers' salaries in keeping with their responsibilities. Some common empathy needs to guide legislative decision making. Comments like those attributed to a member of the legislature, "they (teachers) should get a second job" are insulting and unnecessary. Most teachers do have a second and sometimes a third job. This doesn't mean they should not be compensated fairly for their primary job. What happened to that prediction about market driven compensation?

Districts and Charters Are Paying for This Heist

When the system needs more money to continue providing benefits, it is taken by increasing charges to the participating schools and the employees. In 2014–2015, teachers were putting in 11.2 percent of their gross while districts put in 11.1 percent more as a match. De facto a 22.3 percent savings account. This uptick in contribution rates was in order to keep the system solvent. The current rate is burdensome.

Financial Windfalls

Legacy Charter in Maricopa, a part of a group that has an ADM of 6,870, has a matching 401K that matches employee donations up to 6 percent. Contributions totaled $70,000 for the year ending on June 30, 2014. The salary accounts for that same year were $7,849.664. The contributions noted are less than 1 percent of the payroll. If the charter participated in the AZRS, they would have spent $879,162 matching the employee's contributions (an equal amount).

The company saved $809 K by not participating in AZRS—a normal employment benefit in a school district. This charter's statistics are an example. The practice is a norm.

The Money Saved Does Not Go to the Classroom

The fact that participation in the AZRS is so low is reflected in the amount that charters contribute to retirement benefits. This difference shows up in the amount of money making it into the Classroom Spending category on the Annual Financial Review. This money categorized under teacher benefits normally is counted in the Classroom Spending area.

To clarify this point, the money that would have been spent in the Teachers' Salary and Benefits section of the 1000 Accounts under *Classroom Spending* instead went toward *Administrative Costs*.

This shift in spending is exasperated when the company is also leasing the teachers from management companies (for-profit related parties), which charge upward of 10 percent of payroll for this "service." This amount is uncannily close to the 11.1 percent they would have to contribute if the teachers were in the AZRS. *The amount taken isn't coincidental.*

Conveniently, leased teachers cannot participate in the state retirement system. This makes it easy for management to explain why they don't offer the benefit. The decision of management to make money on leasing teachers makes it impossible for teachers to receive an Arizona state retirement benefit. Managers do things right, leaders do the right thing. Some leadership on the part of charter management is sorely needed in this area.

BASIS made this type of management decision four years into its existence (2010). This school group is rightfully proud of their academic results. Didn't their highly qualified staff have something to do with those results? BASIS' public defenders often cite their "firing" rate as proof that they only take and keep excellent teachers. They should be able to point to excellent salaries and benefits for those prime teachers who survive.

The "choice and freedom" rhetoric is that teachers in the public schools are only worried about their salaries and pensions. Charter companies that use their savings on those pensions are enriching their own retirement options on their employees' backs.

A GREAT ARIZONA LARGE CHARTER IN THE 23 PERCENT

There is a large charter group that does it all without any of the shenanigans and self-dealing. Linda Proctor Dowling's Arizona Agricultural and Equine charters provide a unique charter choice. This charter offers a true alternative to district offerings. Under Ms. Proctor Dowling's leadership, the organization fairly compensates their staff, provides AZ Retirement benefits, and does not overcompensate management. Their board is diverse and represents their public. All this while AAEC schools are providing a program with academic and financial results, we can be proud to call a public charter school.

There is no evidence that this stellar charter selectively picks their students. The espoused theories of action at this charter match their theory is use. Northland Charter in Flagstaff is a small charter operator with similar ethical behavior toward its employees. They prove the fact that small and medium charters can do the right thing and still make money.

Who chooses, who loses in the companies that aren't operating like the Arizona Agricultural and Equine centers in the mix? Do the companies make up for the lack of benefits by paying the teachers more some other way?

It isn't made up on the salary side of the equation.

NOTES

1. See (Friedman, 1999) *Policy Forum on Business Suicide*.
2. AARP was started by a teacher who was appalled when she found out that a local teacher was "retired" and living in a chicken coop. What will happen to teachers in a "public" system without a retirement plan?

Chapter 13

Teacher Compensation in Charters

Data on teacher compensation in charters in Arizona is difficult to obtain. Salary scales are available at only a few of the charters studied. The only place to locate any "official" information is on the Annual Financial Review[1] sent to AZDOE. On Page 7 of this document, one finds the following entry points regarding the organization's expenditures for teachers.

Item G on Page 7 of the school's Annual Financial Review (AFR) is the entry point for information regarding how many teachers the charter has in each category. An example of the listing is provided here.

In the example case (a BASIS Site [one school]), Item G lists:

1. Number of Full-Time Equivalent Certified Teachers   1
2. Number of Full-Time Equivalent Non Certified Teachers   42
3. Number of Full-Time Equivalent Contracted Teachers   0

This example appears to be incorrectly answered as BASIS uses certified teachers who are contracted. It isn't. The fact of their teachers' employment as contracted labor is reflected in the report by listing them as noncertified/contracted teachers. BASIS is no longer a participant in the Arizona State Retirement System. BASIS schools lease their teachers from one of the management company's related party for-profit businesses. BASIS was in the retirement system prior to fiscal year 2010–2011.

HANDLING THE DATA AS IT EXISTS

When a charter was a known user of contracted teachers, these teachers were counted as certified (or at least highly qualified). Taking the sum of all of the teachers at every charter and the declared amount spent at the site allowed for an average teacher compensation to be determined.

Known Limitations to This Method

There are few teacher salary schedules at charters. However, some charters list starting pay on their websites. Also there are factors that make for uneven pay distributions within a particular charter, experience and longevity do not seem to be factors, neither does merit or student outcomes. The statistics on salaries in the annual AFR are not checked for accuracy. This limits the accuracy of the data source. This is a self-inflicted (by the charter holders) limitation as many of the AFR reports read were not filled in accurately. *This fact limits the statistical veracity of the data.* The statistics that follow acknowledge that limitation. Using an averaging method, the following statistics emerged:

Charters are significant players in the teacher employment market. They are competing with private schools and districts for teaching talent. The salaries in the data do not appear to support the premise that competition for those jobs is reflected in teacher compensation at charters or, as noted earlier, in private schools.

Math and science teachers have been in short supply since the 1970s. Teachers in these areas seem to understand that investing $40 to $100 K and more into an education for a job that pays $32 K is not a good return on investment. The idea of running things like a business apparently does not translate into competitive salaries for the employees at charters and private schools.

Table 13.1.   Average Teacher Pay at Charters

Uncertified or Contracted Teachers	Certified Teachers
3,349.5	5,819
Total ALL Charter Teachers 9,168.5	
Percent of Uncertified or Contracted Teachers 36.53	Percent of Certified Teachers 63.47

Table 13.2.   Comparison of Wages Districts to Charters

Charters Compared to Average District Wages for Teachers Total Paid to Teachers P7 Data AZDOE $323,037,981	Average Pay $35,233

Average Pay for a Charter Teacher

In the year 2013–2014, Districts in Arizona had an average starting salary of $31,874 and an average salary of $49,855.[2] Charter teachers are low paid in a state where teacher pay is low to begin with. The panacea of choice and competition to impact "free market" wages is not working. What has really happened is a clawing back of hard won benefits and salary gains.

ABERRATIONS NOTED IN EXPERIENCE

It was not uncommon in the charters the author worked in to have a vast difference relating to the salary offered to a candidate for an open teaching positions. One charter was hiring new teachers at the same pay (or greater) than the existing staff. A proposition that was inappropriately compared to the workers in the vineyard parable from the New Testament.

This disparity was the market creating a demand for higher starting salaries and then a decision by ownership to allow discrepancies in pay for the veterans. Performance rankings on the company created evaluation for the existing staff were checked prior to making this statement. The teacher's performance rating did not make a difference. Market forces did not change the outcome, that is, the new hires were being paid at the same rate as veterans, not because the veterans were underperforming but because new teachers were hard to come by at the old starting salary.

Cronyism and Nepotism

An egregious example, also from experience, of the problems inherent in this free for all method of determining a starting teacher's pay is provided here. This example involved an inexperienced male teacher being hired at $50,000. This "starting salary" was in a system that usually offered $32,000 to new teachers.

The case cited, as might be expected, was a related party hire. The explanation was *he* needed the pay to "take care of *his* family." This was the excuse that was given to the principal and the charter's superintendent by the CEO for the starting pay assigned to this male teacher.

There are no rules against this practice. In the case noted, the CEO bypassed their normal four-page long hiring procedure[3] for hiring by excluding the superintendent from the discussion. The hiring "policy" called for the superintendent to sign off on salaries for new hires. After calling the lapse to the CEOs attention, he, the superintendent refused to sign off on the hire.

Why didn't anyone file a complaint with Equal Employment Opportunity Commission?

The staff knew that getting "released" from their employment agreement was a real possibility. The ability to fire teachers is one of the points that advocates of charters like to bring up with pride. It is referred to as releasing underperforming teachers. In the cases, witnessed merit did not enter into the decision making regarding dismissal.

The CEO who approved the hire in question was also the highest appeal level for complaints. His first act as CEO was to make changes to the existing policy that established this final appeal level at the CEO level.

MARKET-DRIVEN SALARIES ARE NOT THE CASE

In a *market-driven business* when another firm desires to hire one of your key employees away, there is often managerial leeway to counter-offer the employee in order to keep them. This was not the observed case in the charter marketplace. The data illustrated in this chapter indicates that teachers (and other employees) are not benefiting from the "market-driven" theories regarding salaries. Similar disparities were also seen in principal's salaries at the same organization.

Charters are supposed to be market-driven employment environments. In a market place in which the primary goal was quality results for students, a proof of that goal being realized would be a market-driven valuing of key employees (highly effective teachers).

The data collected and analyzed for this book does not support the premise that a desire for educational quality is driving the resulting salary statistics for charter schools. Charter average salaries of $35 K are $14 K less than the average for Arizona teachers in the public system.[4]

Reacting to the market value of employees with improved compensation is nonexistent. One of Edkey Inc.'s best schools was the fine arts school known as Arizona Conservatory for Arts and Academics. A highly performing unique school both academically and financially.

During a two-year period, five excellent teachers (rated as such by the company's own evaluation tool) were hired away from the school by surrounding districts who offered them salaries that were $10 to $15 K higher than the salaries they were offered at ACAA. This created a talent drain for a highly performing school that could have been solved by higher pay for teachers and less spending on debt. No such counter offers were authorized or made.

A common claim of the "Open Marketplace and Choice Industry" is this: "Unions make it impossible to fire poor teachers, and reward the best teachers." There is *nothing* preventing charters from rewarding their best teachers. There are often reasons unrelated to unions that bad teachers and administrators are kept in place. Those reasons include the fact that some employees are related to the owner or a board member. A practice known as nepotism.

Some of the rhetoric seen (printed) and heard (in official pronouncements) is used in defense of charter management when citing data on charter school's firing of staff. Those writers should really reflect on the overall charter record in this area before citing their data on dismissals as proofs of their efficiency and teachers' accountability for student performance.

How are charters treating their teachers? The data tells the story.

AN EXEMPLAR OF FAIR AND EQUITABLE TREATMENT: MASADA CHARTER SCHOOL

In several cases in the data where the majority of the employees were related, the teachers' salaries *were higher than the norm*. This example is given to illustrate that point. The school is one of the schools in the 23 percent doing the right thing. *Hiring relatives isn't always a bad thing if management is ethical in their execution of the practice. This example is an exception, not the rule.*

The Masada[5] Charter School has eleven related parties on a staff of twenty-eight. Their average salary of $46 K represents what a charter average should look like *if the argument for eliminating unions were valid.* The argument goes like this, "competition for teachers will increase teachers' wages." *Masada is a well-run company that uses the advantages of charter laws to provide its public service, education, in an ethical and moral manner.*

Masada Charter is an exemplar of the promise of charter schools. Average pay at this school was $46 K, which is close to the public school average pay in Arizona.

Praise for Masada Charter School: The salaries to related people were declared, and this company was meticulous in its related party reporting to IRS and on its audit. *Masada set the standard for transparent reporting in the data set.* This school is used as a positive example here as they did the *detailed reporting on the form 990 that should be on every nonprofit form 990.* They have also moved money into a reserve fund for future equipment replacements rather than paying themselves more.

The company is vibrant, making money, being fair with its employees, and making money for its owner. Those earnings are justified by the bottom lines on its financials. The academic performances at Masada[6] are very good with an "A" being received in 2014. The sustainability of the company is excellent. There was no evidence outside of the name of the school that the school was promoting one religion over another. Other examples of this type of ethical charter management practices are listed here.

23 Percent of Arizona's Charters Are Exemplars

- There were several struggling charters where related parties were *taking less* than the average for pay. This appears to be an effort to help ownership keep costs down at schools with a low ADM.
- There were several examples of charters that *are* paying a premium for excellent teachers.
- The Rose Schools, a network of several for-profit schools, has a high average pay for teachers at the majority of its sites and offers Arizona State Retirement System Benefits to its employees. The Rose Schools are listed as alternative schools with an aggregate score of Alternative-C. They are meeting the needs of their student body. Their alternative status is earned. Their Alternative-C reflects their population.
- There was another for profit where the owners injected their own money into the school. A form of "reverse distribution" known as "Paid in Equity." This move protected the teachers from job loss and the students from cuts to their education. The school identified itself as a Montessori School. Marie Montessori would be proud of this type of charter.
- Many charters do require certification for their principals. All should.

  ○ Charters participate in leadership academies for principals. The Arizona Charter Association provides this training along with several other providers.
  ○ The Charter Association has excellent resources for training administrative staff and teachers. They also provide outstanding annual gatherings where successful methods are demonstrated and shared.

- Charters that invested in staff development were noted. This included paying for college courses and helping staff maintain certifications. These charters are true learning organizations.
- Several charters noted provide classroom funds for teacher designated purposes. This empowers the teachers. Great charter schools encourage and support their staffs. They don't "brag" about their staff attrition rates.
- The charters that participate in AZRS are true competitors in the marketplace. Participation needs to be 100 percent. American leadership academies lead the way in this area. Their management and financial practices are meticulous and sound.

- There are charters in the data that do not own the property they operate in. A deliberate choice to save money and concentrate on their primary mission.
- Charters that are doing it right can and do cost less to run. The charters that the author started in New Hampshire illustrate this along with the 23 percent of charters doing it right in Arizona. These types of charters serve as a proof of concept. They deserve our support. They are true public schools of choice that serve their communities.

NOTES

1. These files are publicly available on the Arizona Department of Education's website. All references to pages are in regard to the Annual Financial Reviews from 2014–2015. Three years of AFRs were reviewed in the original study.

2. Source: http://www.teacherportal.com/salary/Arizona-teacher-salary. Other sources list the average at $45,000 for Arizona. The same source (www.teacherprotal.com) ranked Arizona as twenty-eighth in the nation regarding teacher compensation.

3. No one seemed to think that long drawn out procedures for hiring practices were "bureaucratic." The procedures witnessed were several pages longer than any experienced in the district world. Reason: CEOs wanted control over their employees' compensation and free rein to pay related parties more money.

4. See also: Gross 2010.

5. The term "Masada" is a reference to the historic battle of the Israelites with the Roman Army from 37 B.C. to 31 B.C. It is a proud name.

6. Masada was an ancient battle site where the Jewish defenders committed mass suicide rather than surrender to the Roman army that laid siege to the site.

Chapter 14

Administrative Costs versus Classroom Spending

SHIFTING THE CONVERSATION

A small jump in the percentage that districts are spending on administration resulted in a call for the Arizona Auditor General to develop a special report on how districts were spending their equalized payments from the state. The report was entitled, "The Arizona School District Spending (Classroom Dollars) Fiscal Year 2015" (Davenport 2016). *The report (and similar national reports "generated from facts") appear to be political theater.* The input, district school data, ignores the same issues (amplified) in the charter school segment of the marketplace the reports are evaluating.

The Arizona Auditor General's report was commissioned in a State where the state's own statistics (Source: 2014–2015 AZDOE AFRs and the Superintendent's Reports) show charter school spending on management and administration to be 20.53 percent of operational costs to Public School District spending of 10.73 percent. (A figure for charters that is inaccurate [too low], as was demonstrated in the data.) Ten years of that data are in the original study.

CHARTERS HAVE ALWAYS BEEN MORE COSTLY TO ADMINISTER THAN DISTRICTS IN ARIZONA

Senate President, Steve Yarborough has assigned Deb Lesko (AZ Senate), a known promoter of tax credits for private placements, to further investigate how much money is being sent into the classroom *at districts*. They are barking up the wrong tree. Other legislators and charter advocacy groups have joined the fray hounding districts about administrative costs.

As Joe Friday would say, "Just the facts ma'am."

In fact from 2013–2014 to 2014–2015, both districts and charters edged up in the percentage they spend each year on administration. In 2013–2014, districts were at 10.33 percent, and in fiscal 2014–2015 districts were at *10.71 percent (a .42 percent change)* while charter school's edged upward (*20.49 percent to 20.53 percent [a .04 percent change]*). *The figure used for the report is incorrect. The true figure using the information that charters send to the U.S. Department of Education is 22.3 percent (Source: Page 10 data for all charters of the Annual Financial Review FY 2014).*

When the dollar differences are looked at district costs went up (from *$774.05 to $819.66*), while charters moved down from (*$1,419.91 to $1,402.06* [a decline]). The dollar change is significant (this change is looked at in the main report) and could be one reason for the call for the report from the auditor general's office. However, the dollars per ADM spent on charter administration *are still too high. They also do not represent the true administrative costs, which are higher.*

This overcharging for administration at charters is evident without considering the other ways (previously discussed), the owners of charters with for-profit subsidiaries profiteer from their businesses. Even the 22.3 percent figure ignores the other ways management rewards itself financially.

ADMINISTRATIVE ACCOUNTING AT CHARTERS IS FUNDAMENTALLY FLAWED

The documents used for collecting data on administrative costs and general financial practices in charters are *inconsistent and flawed.* The current system is unable to capture the true cost of ownership (management costs) of charter schools. The tools used to monitor charter finances are not up to the issue of related party transactions. These types of transactions are deeply embedded in the finances and governance at our charter and private schools. These are transactions with for-profit subsidiaries that often go to management's bottom line through distribution payments to ownership from those subsidiaries.

Contrast this with districts' financial and governance practices. District administrators and boards do not own the assets or collect rent on the properties the school operates. They do not hold the contracts for maintenance and other necessities. They are restricted from conducting business with board members, their own families, or related parties.

These "rules" for districts have evolved because such dealings were a problem in the past. Reports that view these type of rules as endangering autonomy and variety at charters miss the point. The rules concerning finances are a check on human nature. That is what financial regulations are designed to do. Free markets are not exempt from the same human frailties around money as public entities.

The traducing[1] and fault finding laid on district boards' and administrators' feet continues. There is currently a proposal to cap administrative salaries at two times the rate that the highest teacher is paid. This is another attempt to leave the local school board out of their decision-making ability on salaries that those boards contract for.

COMPARING APPLES TO WATERMELONS

The proposal on the salary cap includes charters. The major problem with that is their (charter ownership's) salary is not what they earn. *It is one piece of some of the administrative costs at charters.* District superintendents are not owners. Superintendents earn a negotiated salary from their boards. It's the board's prerogative, by law, to do this. The legislature does not belong in the negotiations between a local district and their administration. Capping administration salaries in charters doesn't solve the issue either.

Owners in charters and private schools can *and do* get a cut of.

- Management fees from for-profit related subsidiaries
- Distributions (Dividends) from for-profit related subsidiaries
- Leases and rents paid to for-profit related subsidiaries
- Leases on contracts for leased employees from for-profit related subsidiaries
- Percentages on related party contracts

The sale of charter property also produces a capital gain on the sale *for the owner(s)*.

All of these transactions are conveniently hidden in the "for-profit" reports that are not part of the auditing process. The people looking into this administrative salary "problem" know about this practice.

The excuse given that these entities are not part of the "charter school" is like claiming Mopar is not a part of Chrysler. Worse yet it is similar to having an "off shore" entity where the public cannot see what is going on. When a private business acts this way, they are rightfully accused of money laundering. There are numerous cases nationally where this type of activity has become so widespread and egregious that charter owners have been charged with a crime.

The Orange County Register reported in an audit prepared by the Fiscal Crisis & Management Assistance Team that the founder of Oxford Preparatory Academy created a system of payments between for-profit companies staffed by families and friends (the definition of a related party) that diverted public school funds to her and her associates' bank accounts.

Particularly disturbing is when this type of money laundering is used to finance activities like the recent coup attempt in Turkey. A senior state department official believes the director of the Gulen-linked charities and educational institutions in the United States (with over 136 charters nation-wide) look "a lot like the ways in which organized crime sets itself up . . . to hide money for money laundering." The Federal Bureau of Investigation is investigating claims that the teachers, who are brought into the United States on work visas, *are coerced into supporting the Gulen Movement*. Six of these "charter schools" are located in Arizona. Our tax dollars at work.

The Gulen network is one of the largest users of work visas in the country. Importing teachers in "critically short areas." Instead of encouraging invest-ments in American teachers by paying them a premium for these areas, this player in the charter market responds by bringing in cheaper foreign workers.

Financial and academic red flags abound.

NOTE

1. Traduce: To speak badly of or tell lies about (someone) so as to damage their reputation.

Chapter 15

Academic Red Flags

Red flags are present in the warnings signs in the data. The governing agencies for charters are systematically ignoring the red flags in the limited charter financial and academic data that is publicly available. The country's recent brushes with financial collapse were caused by inflated mortgage-backed bonds, junk bonds, and the selling of worthless bonds as "AAA." It occurred because the people in charge of regulating the market, and the public, ignored the red flags in the data.

We were offered choices and freedom from bureaucratic banking regulations for fast and loose mortgages. Those mortgages were financed by high-risk junk bonds masked by false bond risk ratings of "AAA." The same charade is happening again. Academically and financially.

Legislators whose answer to the current malaise and improprieties is denial need to open their eyes, minds, ears, and souls. Citizens need to demand accountability and assess what their commitment to the local community means as it applies to a citizen in a democratic republic.

Are we allowing ourselves to "choose" our way to another financial disaster?

We need to pay attention to data that is readily available, the academic data on charters. In order to do so, we need to understand what we are looking at.

ACADEMIC SCORE "LAUNDERING"

In 2013, prior to the new academic rankings, there were *120 schools that converted to Alternative School status*. This was in a group of 371 schools that went through a financial and academic rating in 2012. That is, 32 percent opted to lower their standards for grading by the charter board by switching to alternative status in 2013.

Hidden in the data on charter school academic success is the fact that when the academic standards were enforced in 2012, the category listings of over 32 percent of the state's charters were changed to lower tier rating category.

Isn't lowering the academic bar one of the complaints about districts cited by critics of those districts? There was no evidence that districts made these type of category changes during the time period reviewed.

The total number of grades assigned by the Arizona State Board for Charters in 2014 was 458.

The percentage of alternative schools in the chart mix was 26.2 percent. Only 113 of the 120 identified as alternative schools were rated; small schools were not rated. Alternative schools were more likely to have no score (a blank) recorded in the graduation rate area of the academic ratings. *This lack of scoring on graduation rates was especially true for online charters.*

Several charters with physical sites only went up to grade 11. This move allows them to sidestep the graduation cohort counts. Graduation counts affect the scores in table 15.1. That is, *if* you have twelfth grade.

Are we really allowing this to count for "charter academic performance"? Rating schools this way, on alternative scores is akin to rating junk bonds as AAA.

We don't live in Lake Wobegon. If charters *were taking all types of students,* shouldn't the propensity of the scores in a well performing charter or district be in the C range? In reality, we get a different kind of distribution when we look at the scores teachers pass out, in districts and charters. The propensity of those scores bunch up in the A to B ranges.[1] Grade inflation is real. It occurs at charters, private schools, and districts.

Children fall all over the normal distribution curve. We need to embrace that fact as we "test" for teacher accountability via test scores.

What do inflated academic scores have to do with finances?

A fair question to ask of someone who made the comparisons between what is going on in charter financing and junk bonds would be this.

Why compare the bond markets involved in the mortgage crash to what is going on with charter school finances?

During the last financial crisis, the public learned that rating agencies had rated junk bonds as AAA that were really CCC. The same type of financial

Table 15.1. Academic Rating Scores in 2014

A	B	C	D	F
32.75%	21.18%	15.07%	4.80%	1.53%
Alt A	**Alt B**	**Alt C**	**Alt D**	**F**
1.97%	8.08%	11.79%	2.84%	0.00%

Grades for Charter Schools in Arizona for Year Ending 2014

Table 15.2. The Bell Curve

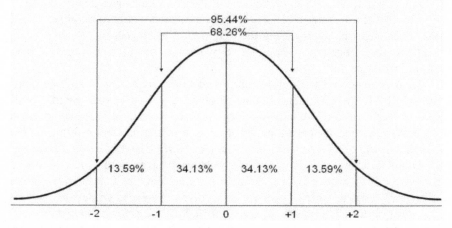

risk assessment is going on in the charter school financing world. Financial ratings are not the only thing being manipulated. Academic ratings are also being compromised by changing a charter's academic rating category. Making yourself an alternative school is similar to grading using "junk grade" academic valuations on your test scores.

After the last financial collapse, the media pointed out that there *were* whistle blowers who either lost their jobs or were marginalized by the firms they worked for. Those whistle blowers were vindicated after the collapses occurred at those same firms. Hindsight, which is always a perfect 20–20, revealed we really knew something bad was going on. We went along for the ride.

Who was put in charge of cleaning up the financial mess?

CEOs from firms that were involved in creating it. They even passed out bonuses to the perpetrators at the firms involved. Bonuses are often used in the charter world. Bonuses were noted in the audit data at charters that were losing money, a disturbing but unsurprising discovery.

Responsible ethical charter owners do not allow themselves to get into financial difficulty. They need to be held up as exemplars. Whistle blowers who were in the charter business and saw abuses firsthand need to be heeded. *Critics of the charter and private school industry also need to recognize what is right about providing a real choice as they critique those finances*. There will be enough blame to go around when financial failures in charters hit a critical mass.

When queried regarding financial inconsistencies noted in an Arizona Republic report on financial dealings at charter, the charter advocacy group's leader responded to the reporter by saying, "Ultimately, though, the state is looking broadly at whether a school is accomplishing what it was founded to do. Are they educating kids? We're looking at that first."

With over one-third opting for alternative status, we should add "or at least accomplishing the alternative to a traditional education?" to that answer.

The answer was an attempt to shift the conversation from finances to academics. The academics after 2012 were tainted by the move to reclassify 34 percent of the charters in Arizona to Alternative School Status.

The next chapter focuses on the critical financial red flags in the data, financing irregularities.

NOTE

1. The author gathered report cards after each semester for twenty years of his practice. The results were posted in the teachers' work area. Discussions at the follow on teachers' meeting were initiated by writing several "quotes" from staff regarding their stated remarks regarding pupil performance. The data on how those same pupils were scored by their teachers was revealed next. Grades changed to a more even distribution in the following semester. However, without constant vigilance they shifted back to the original inflated grade pattern within two grading periods.

Chapter 16

Unsustainable Debt and Financing Irregularities

The Financial Industry Regulatory Authority (FINRA) announced on May 30, 2016, that it had filed a complaint against Phoenix-based firm, Lawson Financial Corporation, Inc. (LFC), and Robert Lawson, the firm's President and Chief Executive Officer. The complaint charged the firm and the CEO with securities fraud in connection with the sale of millions of dollars of municipal revenue bonds to customers.[1] Lawson Financial is a fixture at charter school conferences. The firm has supported many charter schools as they negotiate financing deals for building bonds and refinancing debt.

The market in charter debt relies on the fact that charters will refinance their debt on a regular basis. This was how many people allowed themselves to become "underwater" on their mortgages during the last mortgage crisis. The scheme then was you would remortgage prior to the balloon payment on your loan coming due. A situation that many of the charters analyzed showed in their financials (balloon payments due in year 6 of the loan). Districts, by way of comparison, pay off their debt. They do this without refinancing several years into the loan.

In addition to the primary charge, the complaint against Lawson Financial also charged the owners of the finance company with self-dealing. The complaint alleges that the firm abused their positions as co-trustees of a charitable remainder trust and improperly using the trust funds to indirectly prop up the struggling offerings in the charter finance arm of the firm.

This type of covering up of the losses in charter bonds and at the charters themselves is manifest in the financial data. In this case, the charges stemmed from the transfers of millions of dollars from a charitable remainder trust account, the complaint also charges Robert Lawson with misuse of customer funds.

The municipal revenue bonds at issue in the complaint include: (1) a $10.5 million bond offering in October 2014 for bonds relating to an Arizona charter school (author's note: This was Hillcrest Academy) was underwritten by LFC and sold to LFC customers, as well as subsequent sales of these bonds to LFC customers in the secondary market; (2) secondary market bond sales to LFC customers in 2015 of earlier-issued municipal revenue bonds relating to the corporate predecessor of the same Arizona charter school; and (3) secondary market sales to LFC customers between January 2013 and July 2015 of earlier-issued municipal revenue bonds concerning two different assisted living facilities in Alabama.

The complaint alleges that Robert Lawson and LFC carried out their fraudulent scheme by transferring millions of dollars from a deceased customer's charitable trust account to parties associated with the conduit borrowers to hide the financial condition of the bond borrowers and the risks posed to the municipal revenue bonds. In particular, the complaint alleges that LFC and Robert Lawson hid from LFC customers who purchased the bonds the material fact that Robert Lawson—in his role as co-trustee of the charitable trust account, and with the knowledge of his wife Pamela Lawson—was improperly transferring millions of dollars of funds from the charitable remainder trust account to various parties associated with the bond borrowers when the borrowers were not able to pay their operating expenses and, for certain of the bonds, were not able to make the required interest payments on the bonds.

—FINRA, Financial Industry Regulatory Authority

COLLUSION

If FINRA looked at the corporate boards as a part of their investigation in Arizona, they would find Pamela Lawson, various contractors (who build and profit from those charter school loans), and multiple cases of owners of one group of charter schools on the corporate boards of other charters. The term for this type of inbreeding at the corporate board level is collusion. Several large charters have dealings with "development companies" who own and lease the land and buildings to the school.

There are no rules in place to disallow this type of "compromised" board composition. Under the charter laws, there is nothing illegal about this kind of arrangement. Charter laws are like a religion that doesn't have a set of Ten Commandments guiding their ethics. Anything goes.

There are also cases where the land owner selling property to a charter was in collusion with the charter owners. Overpriced land deals were witnessed by the author on several occasions. Including $250,000 per acre "deals" for undeveloped (no water, electric or sewer) desert property. The charter group had been "locked" into this deal by signing a lease that included a clause regarding purchasing the land within a certain time frame. A poison pill.

CASE STUDY: HILLCREST ACADEMY FAILURE
OCTOBER 2016

The Case Study here details some of the misrepresentation of bond risk involved in the FINRA case. The case involved the defunct Hillcrest Academy in Mesa. Hillcrest was a struggling charter school that went out of business at the start of the 2016 school year.

The year prior to their demise, 2015–2016, Hillcrest reported a positive *net* of $105,136 to the Arizona Department of Education on their Annual Financial Review. *This figure was "misleading" the AZDOE at best.* The more likely proposition is that the report to the Department of Education was financial deception.

Cross-checking of what is being reported to the Arizona Department of Education and what the same company reports to the Arizona Charter Board is not occurring. *That type of simple collaboration between those agencies does not require new laws or bureaucratic meddling. It requires cooperation and comparisons of data. There is no excuse for this lack of oversight.*

The reality of Hillcrest's financial position was a net loss of (–$4,084,353). Hillcrest was in debt to a Florida based financial company (bond holder) among others when they went bankrupt in October of 2016. The IDA was the source of lending for the bonds in the FINRA report.

The deception used by the bond company involved misappropriation of funds from another one of their accounts to "prop up" the failing charter group's portfolio on paper. The financials posted to AZ Charter Board for several years showed the type of Net Assets (Deficits) that the forensic accounting report supporting this work lays out. In this case the (–$4,084,353) amount of Net (Deficit) at Hillcrest at the end of fiscal year 2014–2015. *A blind person could see there was a problem. This school should have been shut down by the governing agency.*

This type of illegal activity is one trick in the accounting practices that the full study details. By way of comparison, districts are required to end the year in the black. When they don't, there are consequences. Charter advocates like to cite the fact that the Phoenix Arizona based Roosevelt District had a net loss in 2015. The fact is that 153 charters suffered net losses in 2014–2015. Those charters were not subject to the same rigorous financial corrections districts like Roosevelt is obliged to take when they have a deficit in a fiscal year.

If the district has a deficit, it has to cut staff and other expenses to balance their books. The district's fiscal situation is sometimes the result of the random appearance of a charter in the same area. In Arizona, deficits in districts are often created by the movement of students from the districts' ADM to a new charter. The proliferation of new "choices" is a planning nightmare for the business office staff trying to calculate their ADM for the next school year. Districts can also be taken over by the state. The fact that districts have less net losses than charters is testimony to the sound financial practices at those districts. District business managers are trained professionals.

Charters are using financing schemes to erect brand new schools next to or near existing district schools. A shiny new school is often the reason parents "choose" the new school in the neighborhood. This type of government sanctioned funding source, IDA loans, RAZA loans, and guaranteed state-backed lending allows the charter to set up shop with a new facility. The loans are guaranteed by the expected payments from the Arizona Equalization Funding, which is based on ADM.

Districts can't use some of the financial tricks available to charter groups. Large charters can afford to wait out small charters and districts in the same area by absorbing their operating losses throughout their organization. This shifting of debt between entities happens in many charters. Building a well-appointed new school makes the charter attractive to parents especially when the district schools are deteriorating as a result of underfunding of the repair and maintenance fund at the state level.

CONSOLIDATING TO CONCEAL

A *Consolidated Audit* is a single audit for multiple charters. This accounting tool can be used to manipulate the financial data of a group of charters under one management company. This type of shifting *is not allowed between districts. Districts can't consolidate with other districts to hide problems in one of the district's finances.*

An example of Consolidating: Charter Group "Super Schools" Inc. (fictional entity) has four charters. They filed a Consolidated Audit for all four schools that has a positive balance (net) showing for all schools. The individual charters show a different story on the individually filed AFRs filed with the state. Consolidation is also used on IRS Form 990 filings for nonprofits.

By consolidating the audits, the fact that two out of the four schools in the example are operating at a loss is "hidden" in the overall data. This allows the charter group to receive a positive Consolidated Financial Performance Rating. Presto, that consolidated report then shows the group *passes* the financial measures set by the charter board.

A superintendent of multiple public school districts *cannot* cover one district's financial losses by consolidating all of the districts in their area onto one audit. This is only one of multiple accounting sleights of hand employed and allowed in charter financial reports.

Table 16.1.   **Consolidating Audits to Conceal Losses**

Charter	NET 2014 Fiscal Year	NET Assets EOY
A	$1,200,000	2,000,000
B	–$750,000	–$1,200,000
C	–$500,000	–$500,000
D	$250,000	$300,000
Totals	**$200,000**	**$600,000**

Consolidating also allows a charter to operate in multiple states and report all schools under the same audit. Funds can also be moved from state to state in multistate and multinational charters to cover up losses.

This shifting of funds is often done by "forgiving" debt. The debt is not really forgiven. It is delayed. This gets it off the books for that year. By doing this the charter can report a net result for the year that just nudges it into positive numbers. There were fifteen charters in the middle of the data that just made it into the black. Probing their data revealed the accounting manipulations that allowed them to stay in the black. In other words the number that are *really* suffering net losses is higher than 153.

PRIVATE SCHOOLS ARE NOT IMMUNE TO FAILURE

Private schools in the New England states have been struggling financially for decades. Closures for some of the biggest names in private academies were common in the Connecticut River Valley. This is in a place where private academies once flourished.

We have data on voucher (these are called "opportunity scholarships" in Arizona) funded private schools from the first state that approved vouchers, Wisconsin. *A total of 41 percent of all private schools that participated in Milwaukee's private school voucher program between 1991 and 2015 failed.*

The author of the study that published this information was a voucher and private school advocate. He noted, *"I do not mean failed as in they did not deliver academically, I mean failed as in they no longer exist."*

In his report University of Wisconsin-Oshkosh Professor, Michael Ford wrote, "These 102 schools either closed after having their voucher revenue cut off by the Department of Public Instruction, *or simply shut their doors. The failure rate for entrepreneurial start-up schools is even worse: 67.8 percent.*" Ford is a former vice president of School Choice Wisconsin. His honest assessment is refreshing.

In a summary of his study, Ford concluded, "The larger, perhaps more troubling legacy of the first 25 years of the Milwaukee voucher experience is the problem of externalities. When a school closes, students and parents must find new schools, student records may be lost, student achievement will likely suffer, and *the public investment in failed institutions is lost.*"

As vouchers continue to be expanded, many of the schools now calling themselves, charters will most likely move to private school status. This will effectively remove them from public scrutiny. *As the statistics on private schools show, this does not mean they will thrive.*

Is This What Disruptive Innovation Means?

Dr. Ford posits the issue of disruption in market-based school reform, "In other words school closures are disruptive, and inevitable in market-based school reforms that encourage entrepreneurship. Anyone in Milwaukee over the past two decades can remember specific cases of school failures, so the fact that failure occurred is likely not surprising, but Dr. Ford was admittedly stunned by the high failure rates."

Dr. Ford continues, "It speaks to something someone said to me back when I was on the front lines of school voucher policy. *We have underestimated just how hard it is to build a quality choice school.*"

In discussions with members of the charter school movement, this information about failure rates was cavalierly answered with a response one would expect from Pee Wee Herman, "We meant for that to happen. That's the marketplace working."

In Arizona, the failure rate statistics analyzed also tracked charters closing during the school year. The figures are stunning.

Charter schools that closed during the school year from 1995 to October 31, 2016: sixty-seven cases. For this figure a closure between October and March of the school year was counted as a closure during the school year in the study.

Retirement Fund Effects of Charter Financial Instability

A little discussed effect of the last financial collapse was its effect on pension plans and the retirement savings of the general public. Particularly the hit taken by several major teacher retirement plans. As a part of the meta-analysis, the author looked into the funds that are invested in charter school financing instruments. The question asked of the data assessed, "Whose money is at risk when charters fail?"

In order to pursue this line of thought, an inquiry into K-12 Inc.'s institutional ownership was undertaken. The two examples cited in table 16.2 of institutional investors in K–12 will be of interest to teachers in the public systems in California. *Their state teacher retirement plans are vested in the "competition."*

Table 16.2.   State Retirement Systems Vested in Charters

California State Teachers Retirement System	December 31, 2016	69,681	(1,700)	(2.38)	1,283
Teachers Advisors, LLC	December 31, 2016	62,728	(11,025)	(14.95)	1,155

Who is making those investment decisions? The answer state retirement fund managers.[2] Who is recommending these purchases? Wall Street investment firms.

HIDDEN FIGURES

Earlier in this report a reference was made to a rating firm, Moody's, giving high scores for charter financing and bonds. The critique posted about this score was that Moody's was counting *repayments of loans that the charters were refinancing as positive factors in their analysis.* The issue of course is the new refinancing of that debt *at ever-increasing amounts.*

An example of a recent case in Arizona (Hillcrest Academy) was posited in this chapter. There are 138 charters currently in financial difficulty according to the Arizona Charter Board's own rating system. Over one-third of all charters ended their year in the red in 2014–2015. Another ninety are red flagged in the cash flow component of their financial performance ratings.

These are red flags in the Arizona data. The picture gets particularly frightening when California's experience with charter financing is probed.

The Center for Popular Democracy report dated April 2015 found mismanagement of funds, fraud, and abuse of $80 billion, or $160,000 per child. The amount was spread across all California charter schools. The same report noted that California could lose another $100 million in 2015 to charter school fraud. Is this what is meant by fiscally conservative practices?

One of the recommendations of the Grand Canyon Institute Report, this book draws some of its statistics from is the need for more auditors and the Department of Education and at the Arizona State Board for Charter Schools. The staff at the Arizona State Board for Charter Schools is an honest, hardworking team. They do not have the resources they need to monitor the financial issues or to investigate known problems. A similar finding was posited in the California study.

The Center for Popular Democracy report found that charter schools in California undergo *little monitoring of finances, and the districts that oversee charter schools do not have the resources to provide sufficient oversight. This understaffing appears to be a deliberate tactic designed to make the problems difficult to discover.*

Like Arizona charter schools, California's were created to bridge the achievement gap by granting increased freedom to administrators, teachers, and parents to innovate without being subject to most California education laws.

The commentator for the cited article has impressive charter credentials. His assessment:

> As a former entrepreneur and venture investor, I am all for freedom, innovation, competition and choice. But the charter school financial model is at risk of failing.

—R. Blanchard in the *Mercury News*[3]

When faced with a catastrophic system failure on Apollo 13, Gene Kranz, the mission leader, famously stated, "Failure is not an option." Our children's educational future demands the same kind of thinking.

Identification of the red flags in the data is the first step in preventing financial failure.

NOTES

1. The case study Hillcrest Academy that is presented in the Grand Canyon Report: "Following the Money" was the charter school in question in this case.

2. Read more at: http://www.nasdaq.com/symbol/lrn/institutional-holdings?page =4#ixzz4ZXb4ZabJ.

3. See: http://www.mercurynews.com/2015/04/09/charter-financing-study-finds-too-little-accountability-in-california/.

Chapter 17

Failure Is Not an Option

ANALYSIS OF THE METADATA ON CHARTER VIABILITY SINCE 1994

A meta-analysis is a comprehensive look at the issue under investigation using all sources of data. With the exceptions noted previously and here, the data set includes all of the charters in Arizona since the establishment of charter schools in 1994 (first openings 1995). This type of forensic meta-analysis approach uses the full data set rather than a random sample. There were some exclusions.

The data set used excludes district charters from the early period that would have skewed the data on charter failures higher than reported here. This caveat makes the data set comprehensive for charters controlled by the Arizona Charter School Board, not those set up by local districts. The data set referred to as metadata is over 12,500 rows deep and over 150 columns wide. There are subsidiary data sets compiling the data in the main Excel files. That subsidiary set provides collated factual statistics. The raw data is presented here.

STATISTICS ON CHARTER SCHOOLS OPENED/CLOSED AS OF OCTOBER 2016

Charter Schools open and closed from 1995 to June 30, 2016, are as follows:

- The total number of charter *schools* (*schools as opposed to charter holders*) still in existence as of October 2016: 567

- The total number of charter schools closed (*out of business*) as of October 2014: 424

  ○ The data does not include district or university authorized charters. Districts ability to start charters was halted several years ago. The "free market" of charter schools is no longer open to districts. This is a disturbing anti-competition clause reminiscent of a monopolistic power grab.

- Total number of charter schools opened since 1995 (end date June 2015):991
- Percentage of charter schools still in business at October 31, 2016: 57.21 percent
- Percentage of charter schools closed (out of business) September 1995 through the end date of October 31, 2016: 42.79 percent
- Charter schools that closed *during the school year* 1995 to October 31, 2016: 67

  ○ A closure between October and March of the school year was counted as a closure during the school year in this study.

- The most recent copy of charter closures (2016 Audit) shows that an additional fifteen charters closed between 6/30/2015 and 9/30/2016. During the same time period twelve new charters were started the majority of these were existing charter groups expanding. The net loss was three charters during this time period. Source: Annual Arizona State Board for Charter Schools Report for Fiscal Year 2016. Net closure rate as of June 30, 2016, is now 43 percent.

Charters that reopened under another name or owner are accounted for in this data.

Educational Impact: Closures of charter schools and private schools cause academic and other disruptions to parents and students alike. Districts cannot absorb large influxes of displaced students when their buildings have been closed due to "competition."

CONSEQUENCES OF CHARTER SCHOOL LEVEL FAILURES DURING A SCHOOL YEAR

The displacement of students who must then seek open space in either another charter or a district school creates issues for the receiving school(s). The larger the size of the closing charter school, the greater the impact to other charters and districts. Charter school closures after the 100th day, which are not uncommon, resulted in a loss of funding to the receiving school as funding is based on the 100-day count.[1]

What this 100-day count funding translates to is that the district or charter school accepting the displaced student *may not receive further funding as the first charter has already collected the maximum for the year.* They accept the students without compensation. *Some charters do, a credit to their ethics.* Unfortunately, this largesse is offset by charters that "cut" students during the weeks prior to testing and post 100 days. This "cutting" is another cause of student displacement in mid-year. Districts must accept any and all displaced children.

Firsthand verification of the statement regarding "cut day" is provided here. The author ran a charter school in a Maricopa, Arizona, that had several charters in it. Prior to testing a substantive uptick in the students registering at the charter school, the author managed was noted. Several teachers who left the charter school where the students came from spoke about the "cut day" phenomenon to the author. It is a real practice. This practice discriminates against special-needs children and needs to be stopped.

Following the Money: What happens to the ADM collected for those students?

The money lost in a closure, which is paid in advance, is usually unrecoverable by the state. This is a problem in all of the states that have charter laws similar to Arizona.

Note on Districts Closing a School: Unless a catastrophic event occurs (fire, flood, etc.), districts never close schools during a school year to avoid disrupting the child's education. The receiving school that takes the student after 100 days is doing so without compensation.

The next set of facts is derived from the data researched regarding charter level closures. In this subset, the charter holder lost or gave up their charter. Cases where another charter picked up the charter that closed were not counted in the data.

- Total of Charter Organizations since 1994: 641
- Charters still in Business in the Arizona Charter Market: 422
- Charters that have closed or left the Arizona Marketplace: 219
- Percentage of Charter Organizations still in business as of October 2016: 65.83 percent
- Percentage of Charter Organization that have given up their charter or left the Arizona Marketplace: 34.17 percent

IGNORING FINANCIAL WARNING SIGNS

As noted charters are allowed to submit consolidated financials. Several charters submit this type of audit. For example, Edkey Inc. consists of multiple charters but files a consolidated audit for all of its independent charters. The consolidated numbers are the statistics used to generate the financial statistics kept by the charter board.

There is an effect from this consolidation on the numbers of charter groups being reported on here: The resulting shortage of 16 charters counting in the data below is because of this factor, that is, the difference between 422 and 409. This segment clarifies the methodology used to generate the numbers reported. Charter Groups are being reported on in these numbers, not individual charter schools.

- Total of Charter Audits Studied: 409
- Charters and Consolidated Charter Groups that MET the Arizona State Board for Charter School's Financial Performance Recommendation: 270
- Charters and Consolidated Charter Groups that DID NOT MEET the Arizona State Board for Charter School's Financial Performance Recommendation: 139
- Percentage that MET the Standard: 66.01 percent
- Percentage that DID NOT MEET the Standard: 33.99 percent.

Meaning of the Statistics

Fully one-third of the Charters that are still in business in Arizona are struggling financially. They *do not meet* the AZCB Financial Performance Expectations. Another ninety beyond this count *did not pass the Cash Flow Standard*.[2] As has been noted, this is not the only way to assess whether a charter is struggling financially.

There are schools that passed the financial performance recommendations that *will not survive financially due to effects that are not measured in the AZCB Financial Performance Recommendations*. The full version of the report, Red Flags, calls attention to those factors.

As noted, other methods for looking at the financials suggest the problem is greater than the charter board's data suggests. *This statement does not mean nor is it meant to imply that the Arizona State Board for Charter Schools is dishonestly reporting the data. The board is stuck with the data that is presented to them in the audits.*

EXAMPLE OF THE ISSUE

Manifestations of this issue were experienced firsthand by the author. The low Dun and Bradstreet rating for bonding that one of the charters the author worked for received when they applied for a bond rating. The charter group received a bond rating of (CCC)[3] in 2013–2014.

The data the audits provided did not point out this problem in a clear way. Due diligence by Dun and Bradstreet and their agents identified the gaps. Author's note: At the time the Edkey charter group was working on this financing with the same financial firm implicated in the Hillcrest example earlier.

Student Growth Statistics Are Not Keeping up with the Debt

The number of students listed in the count that follows was taken from the data set on Annual Daily Membership (i.e., the information the schools reported on their Annual Financial Report).

ADM (Average Daily Membership) for All Charters by Year

- 2013–2014 ADM 148,044
- 2014–2015 ADM 156,335
- Change: Up 8,291

Charters as a whole grew at a 5.6 percent rate from 2013–2014 to 2014–2015. These are new students into the charter system. They include children that were not in the prior year's student count (i.e., kindergarteners). The uptick does not include students that moved from one charter to another as those students were already in the prior year counts.

Note: Figure used is total from data set, *not* the Superintendent's Report. The Superintendent's Report shows 150,120 ADM in 2013–2014 as it included charters from districts and university sites.

Realities of Ponzi Schemes

Charters, like Ponzi Schemes, rely on new students moving into the system. This growth (5.6 percent in 2014–2015) is masking some of the issues identified in this report. Masking but not hiding. The financing schemes in play depend on ever-increasing ADM counts that are beyond what the experienced growth has delivered. This is further exasperated when debt is growing faster than the ADM rate. An analysis of this long-range issue will be the subject of a future scholarly report on the topic. In their 2016 Audit Report, the Arizona Charter Board reported fifteen closures and twelve openings of new charters, mostly with existing large charter groups.

The over-extension of charter debt is being financed by deals that are "anticipating" (projecting) continued market share (student counts). *When the numbers do not materialize,[4] cash flow issues develop first. Cash flow issues have continued to escalate.*

Year-to-year growth in Average Daily Membership is noted in the data set. There are many charters that are losing students and, therefore, the ADM numbers that drive their revenue stream. Charter students moving from one charter to the other do not help the overall numbers for charters. That student movement (charter to charter) is similar to rearranging the deck chairs on the Titanic. *Charter students moving to private placements negatively impact the viability of other charters. Several well-known charter advocates in the legislature opposed the expansion of private school scholarships.*

Much of the growth being reported in the data in the past comes from new charters opening up at a greater rate than the number that are going out of business in the same year. That was not the case in the data on 2015. New buildings means new debt without the resources to pay for that debt. The marketplace is glutted in areas where higher performing students live. There were multiple charters within one mile of the failed Hillcrest School in the case study *including four "A rated" districts.* Building projects funded by state-backed debt allow this to occur. It is a house of cards.

Cash Flow Issues at For-Profit Charters

The data included here looks at the Cash Flow element of the AZCB Financial Performance Standards. Twenty-two of the thirty-two "for-profit" charters received a *"does not meet" rating in the Cash Flow* element of the AZ Charter Board rating.

Meaning of the Data: 71 percent of all charters in business in Arizona were struggling with cash flow issues. Cash flow is a canary in the coalmine of charter (or any business') finances.

In addition to Cash Flow, there were cases where the Debt to Income Ratios reported on the audit *did not match the Arizona Charter Board's financial report.* A subset report regarding "for-profit" viability was also conducted.

Question asked of the data: Do "For-profit" Charter Schools exhibit greater financial viability in the data?

Data Subset Reporting: "For Profits"

- For-profit charter schools still open in Arizona: 51
- For-profit charter schools that have closed in Arizona: 51
- A 50 percent success rate matched by a 50 percent failure rate

Charter Schools versus Charter Organizations

Individual charters can have multiple schools under that charter while some charter holders only have one school under each charter. As noted, there are many permutations. The total number of charter schools that were for-profit in 2013–2014 was 102.

- Twenty-one "for-profit" charters groups have gone out of business in Arizona since 1995.
- This loss is out of a total group of fifty-two "for-profit" charter groups. Several of these companies still operate some charters in Arizona.
  - Likewise, some charter holders had multiple charters with a single school. Some "for profits" also went nonprofit in this time period. They are noted in the data set.
- The "for-profit" failure rate at the charter organization level is: 38.46 percent

AZCB Financial Performance Ratings for Thirty-One "For Profits"

- For profits (existing) that met the AZCB Financial Performance Recommendations: 24
- For profits (existing) that *did not meet* the AZCB Financial Performance Recommendations: 7
- Percentage that met the Financial Performance Standard: 77.42 percent
- Percentage of for profits that *did not meet* the Financial Performance Standard: 22.58 percent
- These statistics are counterbalanced by the 71 percent figure on Cash Flow at for profits.
  - Seventy-one percent did *not meet* the Cash Flow element. *An issue.*

CASH FLOW ISSUES AT FOR PROFITS

The data here looks at the Cash Flow element of the AZCB Financial Performance Standards. Twenty-two of the thirty-one "for-profit" charters had a "*does not meet*" rating in the Cash Flow element of the Arizona Charter Board rating.

Meaning: *71 percent of "for profits" are struggling with cash flow issues.*

ADM (Average Daily Membership): For Profits in Arizona

- For-profit charters grew from 13,281 students in 2013–2014 to 14,299 in Fiscal Year 2014–2015.
  - The figures here indicate a growth rate of 2.27 percent.
  - A numerical change of 318.

Notes: Data Exclusion Reasoning: The reason that charter schools and groups that were organized by school districts (charters authorized by districts) were not included was to present data that was gleaned down to those charters that were authorized by either the Arizona State Board for charter schools or a university authorizer.

The School Districts with charters, municipalities, and universities are not included in the financial data used in this report. *Their sites are listed in the data set.* The resulting statistics for failure rates would move up significantly for the entire grouping (nonprofits and for profits together) if these other authorizers were included.

The statistics with regard to for profits presented on this page and the previous section are reflective of a market segment "for-profit charters." School districts were never involved in this segment of the market.

The Arizona Charter Association rightly cites the fact that charters are growing in Arizona. Each year charters have a greater number of students.

- *The growth in student ADM is not keeping up with the debt loads those charters have taken on.*

Note about the State of Arizona's Superintendent's Report: The State of Arizona has a system that reports schools at the county level. That is the schools are organized based on which county the school is located. This listing by county makes sense for districts.

The organizational listing by county *does not make sense for charters that can be located throughout the state.* The data set used for the meta-analysis collated this data by charter organizations. This method allowed the researcher to locate all of the schools financial entities and tie that information to the physical locations and the identification of common governance bodies.

What does this statement mean?

All of the Legacy Schools are located together in the dataset. Legacy schools are located by county in the Superintendent's Report. Every charter was tied to its owner and board to accomplish this. This was done using board and ownership listings in the Arizona Charter Board's informational system. The Arizona Charter Board also does a good job of organizing its data by charter group.

The resulting organization of the data makes it easier to "follow the money."

NOTES

1. The 100-day count is the student count (Average Daily Membership rate) at the 100th day of school. The figure is used to calculate ADM payments that are distributed throughout the year in Arizona by payments from AZDOE.

2. The charter board measures Cash Flow, Liquidity, Net Income, and Fixed Charge Coverage Ratio for its financial performance expectations.

3. AAA is the highest rating for a Dun and Bradstreet Bond Rating. Junk bonds have low scores on a Dun and Bradstreet rating scale. This is well into the junk bond rating that begins in the B section of the ratings.

4. The latest audit report from the Arizona State Board for Charter Schools shows fifteen new closures and twelve new charters opening. Growth did not match the closure rate for 2015–2016.

Chapter 18

Following the Money

A billion here, a billion there, and pretty soon you're talking about real money.

—E. Dirksen

BILLIONS ARE AT STAKE

The National Center for Education Statistics reported that total expenditures for public elementary and secondary schools in the United States amounted to $620 billion in fiscal year 2012–2013.[1] This is equivalent to $12,296 per public school student enrolled in the fall (in constant 2014–2015 dollars, based on the Consumer Price Index).

These expenditures include $11,011 per student in current expenditures for the operation of schools; $931 for capital outlay (i.e., expenditures for property and for buildings and alterations completed by school district staff or contractors); and $355 for interest on school debt.[2]

The National Center for Education Statistics figures make the public education system (a system that was once immune, from the "free market's" gyrations) a target for financial manipulation. The substantive amount of property being moved from public to private hands make these educational real estate and asset acquisitions possible.

Good Faith

The standard for these transactions is that they need to be done in "good faith." This makes this type of real estate dealings both legal and profitable. Senator Dirksen's witticism regarding a billion here and a billion there is attracting sharks to this pool of "real money" involved in charter school real estate and schooling in general. The first thing gobbled up is "good faith."

In 2014–2015, the Arizona Superintendent's Report reported charter schools average expenditures per ADM was $8,158. The lion's share of that money comes from the State of Arizona's Equalization funding. This number is an average. Charters have other ingenious ways of creating revenue streams for the owners and their backers that tap this source of revenue.

The ways charters can increase revenues are as follows:

- Federal title programs
- Grants
- Donations
- Before and after school programs
- Preschools
- Fee-based activities for sports and extracurricular programs
- Facilities fees
- Some charters "recommend" a donation amount for every child enrolled.
  ∘ Many have created *separate funding agencies* that seek donations. All known cases of this are listed and tracked in the original dataset. Donations run into the tens of millions.

This transfer of public assets, paid for with tax dollars, to private ownership and corporate board governance has the same unseemly underbelly that was seen during the mortgage meltdown and financial failures of 2007 and the savings and loan debacles. The hedge fund collapses and junk bond scams created several other market crashes in the past including pension failures.

The financing schemes used to finance charter schools are contributing to a financial bubble that is bursting. The problem is over-extension and over-leveraging financed by the new quasi-government lending funded by junk bonds. The problem shows up in the financial data. It manifests in net returns and net assets *that are in the red despite other sources of revenue.*

WE'VE BEEN THERE AND HAD IT DONE TO US BEFORE

Deregulation always leads to opportunistic financial schemes. The raiding of pension and retirement funds immortalized in the book *Retirement Heist* saw the loss of millions of workers pension[3] savings. "The roots of this crisis took hold two decades ago, when corporate pension plans, by and large, were well funded, thanks in part to rules enacted in the 1970s." New accounting rules in the 1990s paved the way for the pension heist then. They called it "deregulating."

The rules for charter school finances and governance allow the heist going on in the educational marketplace to remain hidden until it is too late. The failure rate at charters and in some cases private schools is symptomatic of the problem. The 43 percent failure rate can be compared to the mortgage default rates. In the crisis year of 2007, California had a 9.1 percent annual mortgage default rate.

The public generally responds to these inside job heists with dismay, disgust, and disbelief. Especially when they are personally impacted. The fact that most companies no longer provide pension plans impacts all workers.

The public's awareness of the market failure caused by deregulating occurs when they are hit by the bill for the financial manipulations carried out in their names. This awareness phase is followed by disbelief when the "culprits" are named and exonerated.

We are told, "They didn't break any laws." They didn't.

How Did This Happen We Ask?

"Why Didn't Anyone go to Jail?" It happens because, as the perpetrators often correctly say, "they didn't break any laws."

They didn't! When the author informed the Arizona Charter Association about the research and its findings, they replied, "Well, everything you have discovered is legal under the charter laws."

It is! That's the problem. The cavalier response reflects the industries' attitude and their inability *or motivation to correct the problem themselves.*

The *laws were changed before and during the robbery to allow the heists to occur in a deregulated (ergo legal) environment. The same modus operandi that was used for the other financial heists referred to in this work. Perpetrated nationally by the same players.*

INSIDER TRADING

An inside job in the financial world occurs when the laws are changed to transform a financial "taboo" (using public funds for private gain) into a legal "deregulated" change designed to make the heist "legal."

Legal, but unethical and immoral when you are talking about a public good.

Earlier, the issue of corporate ownership of the daycare centers in the United States was mentioned. We aren't asking the right questions. Is there really a need for a price tag of $250 per week ($13 K per year, per child)? This is a marketplace that underpays its employees and hires minimum wage help to run its "child-based" educational centers.

Who is profiting from these prices and the tax credits for child care? Is it coincidental that the price charged is always just ahead of the tax credit? Private school tuition will probably go up now that there are vouchers to help "the disadvantaged." This is similar to the price gauging at private and public colleges attributable to the availability of fast and loose federally sponsored college loans. Eventually that model collapses on itself.

There are always opportunities when great sums of money change hands. This is especially true, when that money comes from public coffers. This is where fiscal conservatives are correct. Sometimes government is the problem!

Financial and real estate lawyers, hedge fund managers, and Wall Street investment firms are always looking for large sums of money changing hands. That's their job. *They are great CEOs by that standard.*

Is it really happenstance that there are so many lawyers and investment brokers in the Charter School business in Arizona and in other states? The laws passed make sense when one recognizes they are designed to authorize the heist being perpetrated on the public. The charter laws in Arizona were written by lawyers. To be fair, most laws are written by legal experts. They know how to keep things legal when they deregulate to their advantage.

This truism was noted by Kurt Vonnegut in *God Bless You, Mr. Rosewater*. The story is a fictional tale of a millionaire trying to use his fortune to help his fellow citizens. He is opposed by an attorney who is trying to capture a large piece of the money for himself.

In every big transaction, there is a magic moment during which a man has surrendered a treasure, and during which the man who is due to receive it has not yet done so. An alert lawyer will make that moment his own, possessing the treasure for a magic microsecond, taking a little of it, passing it on.

If the man who is to receive the treasure is unused to wealth, has an inferiority complex and shapeless feelings of guilt, as most people do, the lawyer can often take as much as half the bundle, and still receive the recipient's blubbering thanks.

—Kurt Vonnegut, *God Bless You, Mr. Rosewater*

The magic moment, in the case of public schools, is the transfer of taxpayer dollars raised to fund public education to the quasi-public schools (charters and private).

An opportunity has been created that allows opportunists to use money designated for a public good to enrich middlemen, promoters, investors, and themselves. This opportunity allows for massive legal skimming from the money we have designated to educate future citizens. Money that is not going into the local economy. Taxpayer funds, earmarked for education, that are not going into the classroom.

We have been giving our blubbering thanks to the perpetrators of this scheme. "Oh, thank you for allowing me to choose where I send my child to school." The accolades for providing vouchers to special-needs students continue to pour in. Ergo, we will expand the program to everyone. "Thank you for my entitlement."

We keep electing people to office who are benefitting financially from the "free market" in education. Some of these "representatives" are on charter corporate boards, some own their own charters, and still others benefit from the secondary market. An example alluded to earlier is the Arizona State Senate President. A recent *New York Times* post that was verified using IRS Form 990 filings noted:

- From 2010 to 2014 the largest voucher granting group. The Arizona Christian School Tuition Organization ACSTO received $72.9 million in donations.

  ∘ The donations were ultimately financed by the state through tax credits.

- The director, Senator Yarborough, collected $125,000 in 2014 for his services. He claimed forty hours a week as the time spent on running the organization.

  ∘ He is also a practicing attorney and a full-time state senator.

- HY Processing handles the details of the organization. The Y stands for Yarborough. Of course, there is a fee for this service.
- The organization pays rent of $52,000 to the landlord, Steve Yarborough.
- The company bought a $16,000 car for the director in June of 2012.

The original research for the Grand Canyon Institute report went even deeper. A great deal of the charters researched had separate nonprofit fund raising wings. There are fifty such organizations in Arizona. The facts beg these questions.

- Where is the outcry against *large centrally controlled* charter organizations? Groups that typically take more for administration and "management" than any district? (Grand Canyon Institute Study)
- Where are the concerns that Catholic Schools had to deal with regarding separation of church and state since their very inception?

  ∘ Is it really okay that there are charter groups controlled and run by faith-based groups?
    – Imagine the outcry that would ensue if a publicly funded school was run by Catholic Bishops and Nuns or a Rabbi, yet many charters are

run by Bishops and church clergy (ministers, imams, and deacons) from other faiths with public funds moving from one aspect of the operation to another.

○ Your Arizona tax credit for contributing to a "Christian School Tuition Organization" like Mr. Yarborough's *specifically excludes Catholic schools.*

– For a tax credit, Catholics have to use another version of the "rules." Really?

• It gets worse. A 2014–2015 update on ACSTO by the Arizona Republic asked, "How is it that the Senate president of the Arizona State Senate, can simultaneously be the executive director of a $17,064,168 organization, The Arizona Christian School Tuition Organization Inc., while having control over all of the bills that come up for voting in the Senate including those that benefit his organization?"

– This while collecting a salary and other compensation of $145,705 per annum in 2014–2015 (a raise of $20 K from the prior year)[4] for directing the ACSTO. Figure does not include related party rents and other charged services. They were following the same scheme that charter organizations use regarding leases and rented space. Surprise, related parties are on the payroll of the organization. (Source: IRS 990 FY 2013)

○ Researching the organization in question one finds a list of the "participating schools" (2013–2014). That list as noted earlier is devoid of any Catholic Schools or Mormon Schools.[5] Again, do they not fit the organization's definition of Christian Schools? Would having a Muslim or Hindu Tax Credit group be okay with the legislature? As of April 2017, there are over fifty "Christian" schools supported by this organization. A Greek Orthodox Church school is in the mix. Roman Catholics need not apply.

• The Catholic Education Arizona is another IRS 501(c) (3) nonprofit charitable organization and has never accepted gifts designated for individual students. Per state law, a school tuition organization cannot award, restrict, or reserve scholarships solely on the basis of donor recommendation. A taxpayer may not claim a tax credit if the taxpayer agrees to swap donations with another taxpayer to benefit either taxpayer's own dependent.

○ The rules for donating to a Catholic Educational Program speak volumes to the previous complaint regarding what is a Christian School. It required separate rules to "allow" the donations to go to Catholic

Schools. The restrictions make it impossible for one to donate for their own child's (or grandchildren's) tuition.

– This is a taxpayer-funded way to provide the scholarships that Catholics used to provide in their donations to the church of their choice.
– The leadership at this charity received compensation of $131,115 in fiscal year 2013–2014. This was on revenue of $16,269,022.[6]

"Freedom to choose" for religious purposes *has always been an option* in this country. Catholics chose to create Catholic schools. Jewish parents chose temple schools based at their synagogues. There are Hindu schools and Muslim schools in this country.

In the past, these faiths funded this choice with sacrifice and tuitions that were subsidized by their church, synagogue, or mosque, not by diverting funds meant to support the public schools to their religion. Credit is due to the director and the philosophy driving the Jewish Tuition Organization.

• *The Jewish Tuition Organization*[7] *is another 501 C specifically to provide scholarship or grants to attend Jewish primary and secondary schools.*

• *The executive director at the Jewish Tuition Organization has a salary of $70,000 as of fiscal year 2013–2014. This is on revenue of $2,922,316.*

The fact that there are religiously based nonprofits working to garner the tuition tax credit is a further proof that we are moving toward "schooling alone." This time instead of declaring that "separate is not equal," we are moving toward a government subsidy to separate by religion.

This is not an issue if you are funding it with the religion's own funding mechanism. It is a big problem for the separation of church and state if you are taking Caesar's revenue to do it.

The total for all three organizations was $36,255,506 in 2014–2015. Are we to believe these schools are not designed to promote a specific religion? Do churches that insist on and collect tithes of 10 percent from the faithful need the public to donate to their schools also? If you are collecting tax money to operate, should your organization be deemed tax exempt?

Since the tax credits for tuition program were introduced in 2011, Arizona has spent $99.7 million funding ESAs. Funding a massive expansion would require raising taxes *or* dramatic cuts to K–12 public schools and other parts of the state's budget.

Aren't these organizations' charter schools and their supporting "tuition credit" organizations hierarchical bureaucracies? Aren't religious organizations by their very design hierarchies? Isn't this the rhetorical organizational type that the folks demanding "choice" were leaving the district schools they were complaining about for? There are already charters in place that are being run by specific denominations, the comingling of funds is already taking place. Enough already.

Violating Public Trust

The public's trust is being played through slick advertising campaigns. Spending on advertising at charters is sometimes a million dollar plus expense item with most multisite organizations spending money on billboards, television, theatres, and on the Internet. The advertising pays.

- Comments heard while interviewing for this report are as follows:
  - ○ "The claims must be true, I saw it on T.V.!"
  - ○ "Charters perform better than districts." Wrong.
  - ○ "The charter school my child goes to must be Arizona's Best Charter School. It says so on their webpage."

Our investments in our children are being used to enrich investors at the expense of our children's education. The heist includes for-profit charter schools that pay out "distributions" to shareholders that exceed what the company netted for that year. For-profit distributions are a multimillion dollar drain on educational funding. The distributions are often hidden from view when nonprofit charter schools have for-profit subsidiary companies with the same ownership and board involved in. The subsidiary for profits can be:

- Management "for profits" that assess a fee for management costs. (Ranges seen 9 percent to 15 percent of the school's gross.)
- Employee leasing subsidiaries that lease at 10 percent of payroll costs.

  - ○ Leased Employees are ineligible for the Arizona State Retirement System saving the company 11.1 percent of payroll.

- Leasing Facilities subsidiaries that lease or rent the school sites at ever-increasing multiyear fixed leases.
- Holding property and assets in "for-profit" property management group subsidiaries.

  - ○ Guaranteeing their (the property management group's) loan payments by encumbering their payments from the state through intercepts.
  - ○ These subsidiaries are often paying less out on the loans then they are charging the schools for leases and rents.

- Selling their school's curriculum and software to the school through fees.
- Hiding upper management salaries in the "for-profit" subsidiaries.
- Paying Distributions from companies that are not subject to the AZCB Audits.
- Paying bonuses in years where the school lost money.

We are putting profits for entrepreneurs ahead of our children's educational opportunities.

NOTES

1. National Figures for 2012–2013 were probed for the data displayed here.

2. Source: National Center for Education Statistics.

3. The fact is that charters are taking money that normally would have gone into the Arizona State Retirement System for teacher retirements and using it to bolster their bottom lines. See: Participation in the Arizona State Retirement System for Charter Schools. This is also a retirement heist as most voters believe that teachers in all systems are receiving this benefit.

4. These types of raises are particularly annoying when one considers that there never seems to be any money to give teachers a raise. When it does happen, they are limited to 2 percent. Bonuses for critical skill areas are talked about. The amount bandied about is $1,000—twenty times less than the raise seen by the Senate President in one year without the extras being counted.

5. See: http://acsto.org/about/our-partner-schools.

6. The figures seem to indicate that the salaries generated are based on the gross amount taken in for the year. For details, see: http://www.guidestar.org/FinDocuments/2014/860/937/2014-860937587-0b8e0571-9.pdf.

7. See: http://www.jtophoenix.org/take-the-credit/. Also see: *Form 990 FY 2013 JTO:* http://www.guidestar.org/FinDocuments/2014/860/970/2014-860970081-0b26cdec-9.pdf.

Chapter 19

Choosing Profits over Children

"Choice" and "freedom" are really the best words to describe the choices and freedom that *businesses* gained from the charter laws as they exist. Businesses were given choices and freedom of operation. Choosing profits over children is a consequence of that freedom of choice.

"'The only social responsibility' of the 'public' charter or private school business is to use its resources and engage in activities designed to increase its profits."—Paraphrasing Milton Friedman.

For-profit charters and private schools are controlled by "shareholders" or "partners." As a ruse, many nonprofit charters are actually controlled by separate subsidiary for-profit companies controlled by the same owner(s) and corporate board.

An example of how this works in the real world follows: We will call this "fictional" charter "Macon, Barry and Ayres Charter Academy." The owners of the venture are three attorneys.

Business choices:

- The partners *choose* to run Macon, Barry and Ayres Academies as nonprofits. The schools get all of the tax benefits that emulate from this designation. The designation also makes them eligible for special funding that only nonprofits have access to.
- The partners *choose* a for-profit subsidiary that leases the teachers to the charters "Macon, Barry and Ayres Employment Services." The same ownership and corporate board runs this shell company.

  ○ This move allows them to deny participation in the Arizona State Retirement System to their leased teachers. Teachers get to choose to participate in an alternative plan.

- This choice generates an immediate savings of 11.1 percent to the partners. They substitute a "voluntary" retirement 403b. They contribute 0.98 percent to the fund. For some reason their underpaid teachers choose not to participate in the plan.

- The subsidiary that owns the "real estate" the school occupies is another related party company "Macon, Barry and Ayres Realty" with the same ownership and corporate board. The owners choose to do business with their own subsidiary.
- The partners choose to run a subsidiary "for-profit" management company named "Macon, Barry and Ayres Management" that collects a fee based on the number of students at "Macon, Barry and Ayres Academies." They choose a standard fee of 10 percent of the gross receipts for this choice.
- The partners choose to use the ADM for the school as the guarantor of the debt held by the "Macon, Barry and Ayres Real Estate Company." By guaranteeing the debt with the ADM they save a percentage on the interest rate charged on the debt.
- The Macon, Barry and Ayres Academies "choose" to pay leases to the "Macon, Barry and Ayres Real Estate Group."

  - The lease is set up to increase year to year. Five percent to ten percent is the norm. It is clearly stated in the school's audit under "Commitments."
  - The lease generates more money than the holding company owes on the debt the "for-profit" holding company is guaranteeing to the lender with the school's ADM money. This is profit for "Macon, Barry and Ayres Realty." The owners choose to collect distributions on this for-profit subsidiary's income.
  - The owners choose to have the school pay the real estate taxes for the bond holding company "Macon, Barry and Ayres Holdings." There is no choice here for the school they are the tenant with a locked down commitment to the lease.
  - The bondholders on the property choose to get their money directly from the Arizona DOE as an intercepted payment. Investors first, children second.
  - Macon, Barry and Ayres Academies is sent what is left over to run the school.

- The school "chooses" to pay a fee to the "Macon, Barry and Ayres Employment Company" along with the cost of salaries, taxes and benefits. This is usually in the 10 percent range. On a $10 million payroll the fee is $1 million a year.

  - Distributions from the "for profits" go to the owners of the for-profit shares. Macon, Barry and Ayres are listed as owners of those shares.

In the scenario described, the fees collected from the nonprofit schools are visible on the "Macon, Barry and Ayres Academies" audit collected by the Arizona State Board for Charter Schools. What is not visible is the profit from those fees. Those fees are hidden in the for profit's accounting system.

In "for profits" with a single charter entity reporting, the distributions are visible for that side (the actual nonprofit charter school). The results of those distributions are in the audits. Profits can go either to distributions or into shareholder/partner equity.

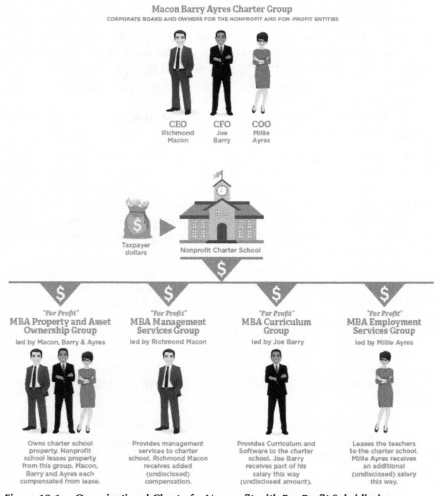

Figure 19.1.   Organizational Chart of a Nonprofit with For-Profit Subsidiaries

In cases where the owners and the board take more in distributions than the company netted for the year, a net deficit is created. The public can't see all of the "other" Macon, Barry and Ayres company audits. Why?

They are different types of businesses. Those companies' audits and the salaries, distributions, and profits paid out from them are invisible to the public. Many of the charters operating like the example are in the red on their net for the year.

They are also in a net deficit on their balance sheets in the charter side of the business. The cause: *Too much money is going to the subsidiaries in fees.*

This distribution tap on company's equity leads to fiscal problems when the company suddenly needs to make capital purchases or major repairs on its buildings. Some companies pay out distributions that are either a high percentage of their net or exceed that net. Sound shareholder held businesses in the free market *do not behave this way.*

In the "unregulated" free markets known as charter schools, the practice infects a high percentage of the "for profits" analyzed. The corporate boards of these schools are typically, two married members (also the stockholders). There are cases where the "oversight" provided by the corporate board is one member. That one member being the CEO owner. All permissible structures in the corporate management world of charter schools.

The chart in Figure 19.1, which was used earlier, is provided here as an illustration. The reuse of this chart here is purposeful as it relates to the topic of distribution that follows.

THE GOOD, THE BAD, AND THE UGLY IN DISTRIBUTION DATA

The bad and the ugly of "for-profit" distributions are illustrated in table 19.1. The chart is followed by a break out of how much of the money that was supposed to be being used to educate children went to distributions for the corporate owner(s). Good is green, bad is yellow, and orange indicates ugly practices. The names of the companies are in the original report.

Distributions are shown as negative numbers as the amount is being paid out of the revenues from the fiscal year. Table 19.1 shows eight of the for-profit charters. There were for-profit charters that also had for-profit subsidiaries listed on their audit. Benjamin Franklin schools was one of those companies. Benjamin Franklin Charter School has not paid out a distribution during the course of their history. The profits have been going into owner equity. A sound business practice. The company also does not take federal grant money. Their theory regarding taking federal funds matches their practice. The various columns show:

Table 19.1. Excess Distributions

Distributions taken by eight for-profit charters in Arizona in 2014–2015

Charter Holder Corporate Name Column A	Revenue Column B	Expenses Column C	Distribution (Paid Out Dividends) Column D	Percent of Revenue for the Year Column E	Percent of Expenses for the Year Column F	Percent of the NET for the Year Column G
Pinnacle Education—Tempe, Inc.	$3,896,153	$2,393,190	–$1,744,085	44.76	72.88	116.04
GAR, LLC	$2,641,942	$1,455,860	–$1,034,734	39.17	71.07	87.24
Accelerated Learning Center	$1,542,026	$1,124,862	–$382,400	24.80	34.00	91.67
Pinnacle Education—WMCB, Inc.	$383,617	$348,745	–$58,871	15.35	16.88	168.82
Pinnacle Education—Kino, Inc.	$434,077	$373,813	–$53,393	12.30	14.28	88.60
SELF DEVELOPMENT ACADEMY	$3,012,379	$2,468,026	–$447,000	14.84	18.11	82.12
American Basic Schools, LLC	$5,687,457	$5,621,225	–$421,654	7.41	7.50	636.63
Consolidated Report for Rose Academies	$8,105,340	$8,194,503	–$256,941	3.17	3.14	288.17

Note: Payouts (distributions) are always negative on financial sheets.

Column A: Corporation
Column B: Revenue for the Year
Column C: Expenses for the Year
Column D: Shows the distributions paid out at eight for-profit charters
Column E: Shows the percentage of the charters' revenue the distribution
             represents (i.e., Example one paid themselves 44.76 percent of
             their revenue as distributions)
Column F: Shows the percent of expenses represented by the distribution
             payout
Column G: Shows the percentage of the NET for the year represented by
             the payout

Table 19.2 illustrates that not all for-profits are engaging in questionable distributions to shareholders. Accelerated Learning Center from table 19.1 is shown below for comparison, but both Alan Cochran Enterprises and Bright Beginnings School, Inc. illustrate acceptable stakeholder distributions. Ben Franklin Charter School shows what you should see when the school runs a loss, no distribution to shareholders.

Answer heard back from one of the company's spokesperson, "What's so bad and ugly here? Aren't for profits supposed to make money? Aren't they businesses?"

Yes, they are businesses. But, If you are receiving $5,158[1] per ADM and the shareholders are taking 41.65 percent as a distribution, then that means out of $5,158 you took $2,148.50 for yourself.

This means you did not spend the money on educating children. Your first imperative.

Table 19.2.   Fair Distributions

Charter Holder	Net Revenue	Distributed	Retained Earnings	Distributed as a Percent of Revenue	Distributed as a Percent of Expenses	Distributed as a Percent of Net
Accelerated Learning Center	$417,164	–$382,400	$288,592	24.80	34.00	91.67
Alan Cochran Enterprises	$332,668	–$194,485	$537,073	7.53	8.64	58.30
Ben Franklin Charter School	($88,304)	$0	$4,451,920	0	0	0
Bright Beginnings Inc.		–$31,000	$654,668	1.09	1.13	28.90

When you paid out over 100 percent of your net, then you choose to not save for things you will eventually need to replace. Bad and ugly business practices even in a free market, Mr. Business CEO. Who is choosing, who is losing.

Legitimate Question: So, are you saying then the fact that the company made a profit is bad? Yes, when that profit is coming from creative reporting on your financials, it is a problem.

Creative Reporting

The company in the example, Pinnacle Tempe, had total revenue of $3,896,153 in the year ending on June 30, 2015. Their expenses were $2,393,190. The result is a net income of $1,610,462. *That is until the owners took $1,744,085 for a distribution. This payout to ownership (the shareholders) drove the net for the year to (−$133,623).*

In this example, the charter school, Pinnacle Tempe Inc., spent 44.76 percent of its revenue on distributions. Those distributions represented 72.88 percent of its expenditures. A review of the data for all of their for-profit charters shows that the company did this at several of their charters. They took several million in distributions overall that fiscal year.

When the companies that are nonprofits pay management fees, leasing fees, and lease their employees from "for-profit" companies with the same owners and board, the dividends paid out and salaries taken at those entities become invisible to the public. It is apparent, when an analysis is performed on the administrative costs, that the total costs reported on the Superintendent's Report for Administration *often do not contain this information.*

Several "for-profits" reject this type of management style. They choose ethical methods of running their "for-profits." Their names: The Rose Schools, Montessori School House of Tucson, and Allen Cochran Enterprises. You can run a "for-profit charter" without gouging the public funds you are entrusted with.

This Type of Financial Manipulation Is Occurring on a Regular Basis

Deregulation is a buzzword for changing laws designed to protect the public and the public's property interests. We have seen these types of heists before. Time fogs our collective memories regarding the travesties perpetrated on the savings and loans in the 1980s; the ENRON Scandal, junk bonds in the late 1980s and 1990s; retirement funds in the early 1990s; and the last "crash" caused by the mortgage and bond markets supporting those mortgages. We were allowed freedom and choice on those deals. Who won? Who lost?

Are we that gullible?

NOTE

1. The Charter here is Pinnacle Tempe. The ADM for 2014–2015 was $5,158 at this school. (*Education* 2015)

Chapter 20

Selective Memory

The current generation of parents sending their children into corporate run charters has little or no "generational memory" about past abuses of public trust. Their memory of what a real public school system looks like is quickly fading. The last financial collapse in 2007 is now ten years old. Prior financial scandals are twenty to forty years in the past.

Financial memory is not the only memory missing. There are whole generations that have no memory of what playing for the "home" team really means. The hometown used to mean the team at their town's or neighborhood's high school. Being true to your charter school is difficult when 43 percent of them have gone broke. Where do the alumni reunions meet? Where are the academic records of your attendance? Answer: They are supposed to be in a central storage area at the charter board. Good luck finding them.

They, the current generation of parents, have been lied to about the successes of public education and local control. A system that was once, and in many cases still is, the envy of the world. There are many indications that China and other countries are still trying to emulate our schools. They admire our schools' output of American entrepreneurs and critical thinking citizens. Our public schools, in short, produce Americans. Caveat to the China reference here, *China millionaires are major holders of charter school bond debt.*

How have we let trusted democratically run institutions to become passé?

Do we really think this enterprise known as education should be left to the marketplace's whims? Do we really think the people who have chosen economic models that benefit shareholders and owners over children represent a good choice for our republic?

HISTORIC CONTEXT: REMEMBERING ANOTHER LOST INSTITUTION

There was a time when all mortgages came from local banks and the savings and loans in your community. These local entities didn't sell your mortgage to a mortgage brokerage after you took it out. They required the buyer to have a down payment of 10–20 percent of the value of the property. The decisions for lending were local. You knew the bankers from your community. They lived in and were from the community the bank was located in.

The savings and loans in this country and many individuals' savings were wiped out by the financial scandals in the 1980s. In simple terms, the savings and loan heist was the undoing of everything that the character George Bailey epitomized as he struggled with Mr. Potter in the classic 1946 film *It's a Wonderful Life*.

Mr. Potter finally figured out a way to win, it is called "deregulation." In *It's a Wonderful Life,* the Baileys run a building and loan business[1], their nemesis is Mr. Potter, a millionaire businessman, the villain in the story.

The new target for the "Potters" of the world is the public money used to fund our communities' schools. Schools and education have become the new financial playground[2] of the free marketers on their way to bankrupting and destroying the public school systems in their towns.

The demise of the savings and loans, locally controlled and owned small businesses, was a precursor of the mortgage meltdown that was implicated in the last financial crisis. Everything that the greatest generation learned from the Great Depression was thrown out the window by deregulating the bond markets that played fast and free with mortgage securities.

The result was the meltdown of our economy in 2007 and 2008.

The same thing is happening to the financial regulations that were designed to protect public educational funds from being looted. They have been deregulated. Once again at a cost to the communities the public schools exist within.

The financial machinations in the privatization of public schools nationally have caused a 41 percent failure rate due to financial issues coupled with another 24 percent for mismanagement. *Fully 65 percent of the failures are financial or mismanagement failures. Charters are not working financially. Only 18 percent are closed for academic reasons.*

The same "free market" concepts that apostles of charter schools and vouchers are now promoting were touted as solutions to our financial markets in the past. When will we learn?

Deregulating school finance rules and the "opening" of the educational "markets" to choice are rallying cries of the charter school and private school voucher movements nationally. After twenty years, it is time to really investigate what the financial results of this deregulation process have been. It is time to look at how the rhetoric has played itself out in the real world.

In short, a reality check is long overdue before it is too late.

NOTES

1. Mr. Potter is the millionaire investor in the story. He buys up all of the local businesses and banks during a "bank panic" in the story. This leaves the building and loan as the only place the local people can get approved for their mortgages.

2. One of the absentee charter owners for whom I worked referred to managing a charter as, "Playing in the sandbox of charter schools," a phrase I heard several times over the years.

Chapter 21

Running Schools for the Adults

It is not a coincidence that some of the nation's largest chains of charter schools are owned by or in debt to the same junk bond, hedge fund, and Wall Street firms that precipitated the latest collapse of the financial markets.

Is it really a surprise that they are invested in this market opportunity? Books extolling the money to be made in charters have been around since the early 1970s. The days of claiming charters as "disruptive innovations" as some claim are now twenty-two years old. It is time for an assessment of the damage that "disruption" has caused.

A major disruptor in the marketplace is K-12 Inc.

The former junk bond dealer Milken brothers set their sights on the $600 billion public education free "market"(value at that time). They did this by forming new companies including Knowledge Universe and Knowledge Learning, parent company of the KinderCare childcare chain. With his $10 million stake in K-12 Inc., Milken aided by one of his vice presidents[1] and another junk dealer, Ron Packard, who specialized in mergers and acquisitions for Goldman Sachs back in the 1980s. Goldman Sacks is invested in several Arizona charters.

The team prepared to exploit the "guaranteed" funding used to operate the public education sector. "Various educational ventures have made Milken one[2] of the richest men in America. Mr. Milken raked in[3] over $16 million in compensation and options from 2008 to 2012 as CEO of K-12 Inc."

In their previous careers, the Milken Brothers specialized in Junk bonds. The quotes contained here are from Mother Jones,[4] the August 18, 2011, issue.

"Junk bonds—the high-risk issues of corporate debt that were Drexel Burnham's specialty—eventually led to the collapse of a number of large S&L partnerships in the United States in the late 1980s and early 1990s.

Those collapses (often of firms with close ties to Drexel Burnham and the Milkens) fueled the larger savings and loan crisis, which eventually cost taxpayers some $500 billion."

"To a very great extent, the market [in junk bonds] owed its existence to a single individual, Michael Milken, who acted, literally, as the auctioneer," economists George Akerlof (a Nobel laureate) and Paul Romer explained in a 1993 paper, "Looting: The Economic Underworld of Bankruptcy for Profit." Akerlof and Romer argue that Drexel Burnham's junk bond business was likely based on "manipulating the market."

"Michael Milken was *the* high-paid Wall Street executive in the 1980s, and his brother (who's still his business partner to this day) was right there with him. As Kurt Eichenwald reported in the *New York Times* the week after the Milkens were indicted: "[Michael] Milken's compensation, which topped $550 million in 1987 alone, exceeded $1 billion in a four-year period. Surely no one in American history has earned anywhere near as much in a year as Mr. Milken." Eichenwald later noted that even after accounting for inflation, J.P. Morgan's "income never matched Mr. Milken's." A Drexel Burnham lawyer later testified that Lowell had told him that "the Milkens want to become the richest family in America," according to Stewart."

The junk bond kings are back. Peddling charter schools and the financing of those schools on our public school taxpayer funds. The bulk of all of the money in those salaries and compensations to Milken enterprises from 2008 to 2012 came from U.S. taxpayers. An example of running schools for the adults.

RUNNING SCHOOLS FOR THE ADULTS

One of the critiques of our public schools used by the privatization lobby goes like this: "The public schools are being run for the adults not the children." The implication of this statement is that the teachers and administrators at those schools only care about their salaries and benefits. The enemy we are led to believe is the "unions" and district administrators.

The antithesis of that argument is exposed by findings that reveal who is really benefiting from "choice" and privatization.

Analysis of the financial and governance data reveals that the carpetbaggers and scalawags are the ones running schools for adults. This "real" purpose for charter schools manifests itself in the data. The data exposes who is running schools for the adults.

* Running schools for the adults shows up as dividends that are equal to 47 percent of your revenues at your "for-profit" charter organization.

Money that went to ownership not to educate children. On top of this revenue source, dividends from subsidiary for profits are hidden from public view, except, of course, from the adults running the for-profit subsidiary companies.

- Running schools for the adults happens when 63 percent of your "free market" business transactions *are with related adult parties in subsidiary companies you own.* You are running schools for adults and friends of those adults.
- Running schools for the adults shows up when you lease your school from a related party that "owns" the school building and land for more than the payments on the property. You, the private owner(s), and your corporate board own the subsidiary company holding this property holding entity and the leasing company.
  - These leases often have built in increases of 5 percent to 10 percent a year. That amount goes into the pockets of the adults as "revenue" for the related "property company" that owns the buildings not to the children in the classroom.
- Running schools for the adults shows up in employee counts that include five or more relatives of the owner and board members.
  - It shows up in compensation packages for those relatives that exceed what you are paying other employees in the same employment category.
- When the sale's price of a school facility is inflated 150 percent or more (compared to the value declared on your audit), you are running schools for the adults.
  - This payout to adults (related parties) impacts your ability to pay for the things you need to educate the children you are being paid to educate. The property, as most charter property is, has become *over-leveraged.*
- Running schools for adults occurs when your travel expenses for adults exceed $50,000. Money spent traveling to other states and countries (China is a favorite) to promote "business." One company, Portable Practical Education (K-12 Inc.), had travel expenses of over $1 million dollars in 2013–2014. The bulk of the money being spent on moving corporate officers about the country.
- Running schools for adults happens when you pay yourself substantially more than a comparable CEO in the districts (where the CEO is called the superintendent).
  - This statement is made and illustrated using data comparing districts and charter salaries for the same numbers of children under the CEOs care.

- Running schools for the adults is giving out tax credits and vouchers, so well-heeled adults can "choose" to send their children to private schools at public expense. Who chooses, who loses?
- Running schools for the adults is profiteering from your payroll by "leasing" teachers to the schools.

  ○ This strategic move allows you to deny the teachers access to the state retirement program because they are "leased employees." It also allows you to pocket the amount that you would have spent matching the retirement contribution of the teachers (11.2 percent in Arizona).

- Running schools for the adults is hiding your free market use of taxpayer funds into multiple "for-profit" entities.
- Running schools for adults is reflected in excessive administrative costs.

  ○ This includes extravagant management fees and purchased administrative services.

For-profit charters by their designation as such are running schools for adults. National trends on for profits from The National Education Policy Center found that the number of commercial "education management organizations" rose from 95 to 97 in 2011–2012, the most recent year studied. *But while the number of operators did not increase by much, student enrollment in public schools run by for-profits spiked, from 411,000 to 463,000 in just the most recent year.*

Those numbers reflect a major departure from the mid-1990s, when hardly any students—only about 1,000—were served by public schools run by for-profit providers, the report notes. The largest for-profit operators, as measured by the number of schools they are managing, are Imagine Schools[5] with 89; Academica, 76; National Heritage Academies, 68; K-12 Inc., 57; and Edison Learning, 53, according to the authors' 2011–2012 estimates.

California is putting forward legislation, Assembly Bill 406, to stop some of the "running schools for adults." In a recent article. it was reported that K-12 Inc., the state's largest for-profit education management organization, received $310 million in state funding over the past dozen years. In 2016, it reported revenue of $872 million, including $89 million paid to its Wall Street investors.

Management benefits at the expense of teachers in the system. K–12 pays millions to top executives while its average teacher salary is $36,000. This is thanks to heavy recruitment among young, inexperienced teachers, and rapid turnover. K-12 Inc. operates sixteen schools in California with about 13,000 students. The average graduation rate of its charter schools in California is 40 percent compared to the statewide rate, which is 83 percent.

Like many for-profit and nonprofit online charter companies, K-12 also overstates student performance and attendance data. Students who logged onto their computers for one minute per day were reportedly counted as full-time students, giving the corporation full average daily attendance funding from the state. In Arizona, the total of these overpayments was in the millions of dollars. Here the company has an interest free loan as they "repay" the overpayments through reductions in the next year's payments.

In California, they went after the overpayments aggressively. In 2016, after the state sued the company for manipulating attendance records and overstating student success, the company settled for $168.5 million. These for-profit companies also have significant influence over other charter school boards and, in many instances, place corporate officers on their school boards. A pattern that is evident in the board listings in Arizona also.

According to a National Education Policy Center report, K–12 opens charter schools and then requires the schools to contract with them for most or all their services, including financial management, curriculum, technology and the hiring and firing of staff.

Online charter schools have also grown exponentially across South Carolina and the nation. South Carolina has started asking the right questions about their effectiveness.

According to a report in the *Post & Courier*, "Today, the state has five virtual charter schools that together enroll roughly 10,000 students, *up dramatically from about 2,100 students nine years ago when the state's first cyber schools opened.* A 2007 bipartisan bill fueled their growth by authorizing the state's virtual schools program, and since then, taxpayers have footed the bill to the tune of more than $350 million."

"Despite this hefty investment, online charter schools in South Carolina have produced dismal results on almost all academic metrics, according to state and district data. On average, less than half of their students graduate on time. At one cyber-school, nearly a third of students dropped out last school year. Data from the South Carolina Public Charter School District, which oversees these schools, shows just one in two virtual students enroll for a full year."

Who is really running schools for adults? A hard look at the data on management and administrative overhead reveals the answer. High administrative costs are being chosen by the management firms controlling charters. A wise choice, if you are one of the lucky managers.

NOTES

1. See Bloomberg Article Link: http://www.bloomberg.com/research/stocks/people/person.asp?personId=901591&privcapId=4973712.

2. See *Forbes*: Richest men in America.

3. See link for verification of data: over $16 million.

4. See *Mother Jones* Article: http://www.motherjones.com/politics/2011/08/lowell-milken-institute-ucla/.

5. Imagine is not in the listings used in data for the Arizona report as their charter sites here are nonprofit. The management company, Imagine Inc. is a for-profit company.

Chapter 22

Choosing High Administrative Costs

MANAGEMENT SALARY DISPARITIES

By any measure, management costs are higher at charters than at districts. The data was probed and analyzed to provide a comparison between district administrative costs and charter administrative costs.

THE GOOD, THE BAD, AND THE UGLY IN THE DATA

The Good: Charter Management Teams that pay themselves comparable salaries to districts of the same size. Examples:

- A charter of 619 students paying their CEO $109 K.

  ○ A comparably sized public district of 819 students paid $91 K to its superintendent. *This is an example of the good, but the salary is still $18 K higher in the charter*.

The Bad: Charter Management Groups that "look" at the salaries of districts that have thousands of students and sets their compensation to match it (the district with thousands of students).

- A CEO and a "parliamentarian" who paid themselves $225 K and $276 K respectively for a school with 296 students. In addition, they had other administrators actually running the school.

  ○ A comparably district of 290 students paid $75 K to its superintendent/ principal.

The Ugly: Salaries at large corporate charters with a minimal footprint in Arizona

The charter cited offers no benefits and low wages for teachers running the school in Arizona.

- The corporate salary of the president was $759.7 K. This was in a multistate organization. The chief financial officer earned $562.7 K.
- Prior reporting in this work illustrated the large compensation packages at international online schools like K-12 Inc. Deep dives into the data reveal several owner in the millions of dollars. They are paid out of the "for-profit" subsidiaries. They are also shareholders in those subsidiaries, which means they can collect distributions.
- As noted some of the distributions were in the millions of dollars. Usually to a single or two married owners.

Sources for Superintendent and Other Salaries: Published Superintendent's Salaries and IRS Form 990 for the Nonprofits.

HIDDEN FIGURES

The salaries do not tell the full story. There are several multistate, multinational companies that run their management groups as "for profits." This type of corporate status (for-profit) shields the group from publishing the salaries being paid out of those entities.

Related party transactions compound the management salary excesses. This use of widespread under-reporting includes management teams that are paying themselves large salaries and then cashing in on related party transactions on:

- Leased employees from related for-profit companies
- Property leases with related for-profit companies (i.e., the same owners)
- Rents with related for-profit companies (i.e., the same owners)
- Service contracts with related parties
- Property and assets sales to for-profit related parties
- Bonuses paid to management
- Personal loans made to the firm at high interest rates (interest only loans were often the case with interest rates from 6 percent to 30 percent noted).
- Distributions to shareholders (typically the owners). When the company is split into separate entities for management, leases, schools, land, etc., each subsidiary company is a separate for-profit entity. The only report seen

by the Arizona Charter Board is the report dealing with the charter school entity(ies). That is the nonprofit entity.
* *Repeat distributions in the "for-profit" subsidiary companies are not in the audits as those "related companies" are not audited. Salary and distribution payments in those companies are not visible to the public.*

Compounding this deception is the recording of administrative costs on the Annual Financial Reviews provided to the Arizona Department of Education.

ADMINISTRATIVE PURCHASED SERVICES A TELL IN THE FINANCIAL REPORTS

The *Administrative Salaries and Benefits* total for all charters in Arizona was $115,126,310 in fiscal year 2013–2014. That same year charters reported $96,770,380 in expenditures for *Administrative Purchased Services. These figures indicate that Administrative Purchased Services are equal to 84.06 percent of what was claimed as salaries and benefits.*

The majority of those services were with related parties, that is, companies managed by the same CEO and corporate board in subsidiaries set up as *"for profits."*

In a school district, this type of lopsided administrative charging for administration purchased services would never be tolerated.

The issue: The owner can be paying themselves under the salary portion of the administrative expenses. They can *also be paid* from the amounts going to Administrative Purchased Services. When administrative data to the AFR was compromised, it was usually done by not counting account 2,500. This account represents Central Administrative charges.

The data on Administrative Costs generated by AZDOE are not accurate. There is contradictory information about administrative costs. *There is evidence that this is a deliberate misrepresentation.*

Table 22.1.   Disparate Data Reporting on AFRs

Administration from Page 7 (Used for Superintendent's Report)
$303,238
27.32%
Actual Administration P2 Totals
$477,340
43.00%
Administration from Page 10 AZDOE Report to the Federal DOE
$410,629
36.99%

Proof in the data: *The self-calculating feature of the AZDOE form has been suppressed (deleted). This causes different totals for administration costs to register on the page the Arizona Superintendent's Report draws its data from. What should be the same totals are often reported differently on Page 7 (which is used for the Superintendent's Report) and Page 10 that goes to the federal government.* The simple directions on the Annual Financial Review are listed here:

Instructions for Administration
Includes current Expenses Coded to Functions
2300, 2400, 2500, and 2900
Does not include Program Codes
700, 800, and 900

Administrative costs *should be the sum of all Administrative Costs submitted on Page 2 of the AZDOE Report. There should not be any variation.* This is an unambiguous set of directions.

Table 22.1 illustrates the issue.

There are three pages in the AFR where data is collated. Page 2 provides the expenditure detail. The data here is "supposed to" automatically fill in the Page 7 data that is used in the Annual Superintendent's Report. The source of the state's public data on charters and districts. Page 10 should also draw from Page 2. Page 10 data is reported to the federal government. Table 22.1 shows the problem being described here. Disparities were present in over 20 percent of the cases.

Management fees and overages are only one profit center. Like the real estate market in the early 2000s, the real money transfers happen when the owners flip the charter property.

Chapter 23

Inside Job: Real Estate Acquisitions

The result of running charter schools for adults has been a transfer of publicly paid for and financed (through government sponsored and backed loans) properties to private ownership. A takeover of local assets and property that is sponsored, in part, by the federal government's sponsorship of charters and its current advocacy for vouchers.

The primary players in the municipal bond and lending markets for charters are Wall Street Hedge Fund Managers, junk bond investors, private philanthropists (with a vested interest in the charter marketplace), real estate venture capitalists who buy the properties and "lease" to an "unrelated" charter school group, and, most commonly, the charter's owners who own for-profit real estate subsidiaries.

Once commonly held public school properties are becoming charter owners privately held schools. *Properties that are owned by the private owners, not the public.* The goal, real estate acquisition and ownership for the adults involved in this private takeover of formerly public properties.

These free market properties can then be "flipped" at opportune times enriching owners and investors while simultaneously creating debt for the new charter holder that becomes unsustainable. This is yet another way of saying, "We are running our schools like businesses." This scenario describes the way the same players ran the mortgage industry into the ground in 2007.

Lest one think that this flipping of property is of benefit to Arizona businesses and, therefore, good for Arizona's businesses consider this.

Residency in Arizona is not a prerequisite of owning an Arizona charter.

- There are no "rules" that prohibit out of state (or country) ownership of charters in Arizona. Several Arizona charters borrow IDA money and spend that money in other states. This is justified as investing in the local economy by citing the company's Arizona headquarters.

- Residency in Arizona (or most other states) is not a prerequisite for corporate board membership. Foreign nationals are on many charter corporate boards. Other foreign nationals own the charter outright. The Gulen Schools, AKA Daisy Inc. is owned by an exiled Turkish Imam who lives in Pennsylvania. There is also evidence that China is a major holder of the charter school bonding debt.
- There are examples of individuals that are collecting salaries for "educating" students in Arizona charters that have never set foot here or been in contact with students in Arizona. The same is true in other states.

PRELUDE TO UNDERSTANDING THE ISSUE

The basic issues uncovered in finances and governance of charter schools serve as a prelude to a deeper understanding of what is happening. The next chapter will delve into the language written into charter laws that permitted the application of situational ethics to charter finances and governance. The National definition for charter schools was given in an earlier chapter.

A FOCUS ON ARIZONA WITH REFERENCES TO OTHER STATES

Why Focus on Arizona?

Arizona is cited by charter advocacy groups, most notably Edreform, as an exemplar of charter school "reform" in this country. Charter and voucher advocates note that charters here receive a "blanket waiver" from most rules and regulations used to govern traditional public schools. Charters in Arizona are also exempt from district contracted work rules (bidding processes).

The recent passing of legislation to expand tuition vouchers in Arizona is in the national spotlight. The call has gone out to advocacy groups to follow Arizona's lead. It is a road to perdition.

On the financing fronts, Arizona just established a $100 million fund to guarantee charter debt with government-backed securities. A slippery slope. On the positive side, the first two companies to garner these loans are exemplary charters in the 23 percent. However, the pattern for this largesse in the past is to start with this type of charter and then expand to the 77 percent.

While Arizona is the focus of this study, many of the issues discussed here exist in other states. There are currently (2017) forty-two states and the

District of Columbia that authorize charter schools within their borders. Arizona is home to at least thirteen charter groups that have their headquarters in other states. Arizona's charter and private school "tuition reimbursements" are manifestations of the financial and governance issues that have been written into law.

As of June 2015, there are 2.9 million of America's School Children in over 6,700 charter schools. The year 1991 was the first year charter schools were granted on the national stage. Arizona granted their first charter in 1994. The laws that started that process are the subject of the next chapter.

WHO ARE THESE CHARTER PROMOTERS?

The Associated Press examined political contributions over a ten-year period by the people who have been major contributors to advance school-choice measures such as public charter schools and programs to use taxpayer funding to pay for private school tuition.

Some key findings of the AP study:

- Forty-eight individuals or married couples donated at least $100,000 from the years 2000 to 2016 to support statewide ballot measures advocating for the creation or expansion of charter schools or taxpayer-funded scholarships that can be used for K–12 private school tuition.
- Those contributors account for more than three-fifths of funding to support the ballot measures since 2000.
- The support from those contributors totaled nearly $64 million,[1] nearly equal to the amount all *opponents of the measures reported spending.*
- Despite the proponents' spending, *voters rejected seven of nine statewide school-choice ballot measures.*
- The contributors also are major donors to officeholders, candidates, and political causes. They donated a total of nearly $225 million from 2007 through last year. The biggest portion of their contributions went to candidates, party, and general ideological political action committees. Some of the candidates they supported are known for their support of school-choice measures.
- Their spending was roughly even over that period on school-choice causes, other education measures that were not specifically advocating for school choice, and causes that are not linked directly to education.
- *The wealthy school-choice advocates also put millions into nonprofit groups that advocate for, study, and fund school-choice measures.*
- The school-choice advocates generally support public charter schools, which are run under different rules than traditional schools and often fall

outside the oversight of local school districts. Their views diverge on the role of vouchers, which use taxpayer money to pay tuition at private schools.

- During the same time period, the teachers' unions spent 2.5 times as much working against these proposals. The unions represent 4.5 million employees. They are a vested interest.

As noted, charter and voucher advocates' first move is to write laws that "legitimize" the financial and governance "rules" for charter schools and tuition credits for private schools.

The laws that allow the financial and governance practices described in this report are the topic of the next chapter.

NOTE

1. See also http://www.edweek.org/ew/articles/2017/05/13/key-findings-on-poli tical-spending-by_ap.html?cmp=eml-enl-eu-news1.

Chapter 24

Charter Law in Arizona

AZ 15–181: CHARTER SCHOOLS; PURPOSE; SCOPE

A. Charter schools may be established pursuant to this article to provide a learning environment that will improve pupil achievement. Charter schools provide additional academic choices for parents and pupils. Charter schools may consist of new schools or all or any portion of an existing school. Charter schools are public schools that serve as alternatives[1] to traditional public schools and charter schools are not subject to the requirements of article XI, section 1, Constitution of Arizona, or chapter 16 of this title.

    a. *Author's note 1 on AZ 15–181*: The article noted (article XI, section 1, Constitution of Arizona, or chapter 16 of this title) relates to public funding for construction and repairs at existing public schools. This restriction also applied to public school district properties that the district declared as a "charter school."

    b. *Author's note 2 on AZ 15–181*: Charters use funds generated from their equalized payments from the state to make payments for real estate, property, bonds, loans, leases, rents, transportation, and repairs. That money comes from, and is guaranteed by, revenue generated from state taxes.

    c. *Author's note 3 on AZ 15–181*: The legislature is currently (April 2017) expanding the role of government-backed securities in financing charter properties. Arizona has awarded the first two loan guarantees to privately owned charter schools in a program that has raised questions about its legality. The Academy of Math and Sciences is getting $24.8 million in what Gov. Doug Ducey is calling "credit enhancements." That will allow them to borrow money at lower rates to expand existing campuses in west Phoenix and South Tucson. The schools already can borrow money at lower rates from the IDA. The Arizona Agribusiness and Equine Center is receiving a loan of $17 million to expand an existing campus west of Phoenix and to build a new campus in Mesa. Author's Note: *Both of these charters are exemplary charters in the data.*

i.   The awards are the first since lawmakers agreed last year to set aside $100 million to help privately run charter schools borrow money at lower interest rates. That's because the state is effectively guaranteeing that lenders will not miss payments.

ii. The justification is that these schools—all with an A rating by the Arizona Department of Education—will now have a chance to expand with below-market borrowing costs. Put simply, if the state agrees to make payments if the borrower defaults, the lenders are more likely to demand lower interest rates.

iii. Chase Bank to its credit already provides charters with a low interest borrowing source. They have high standards for loaning this money. As they should.

iv. The Arizona Constitution says it is illegal for the state to "ever give or loan its credit in the aid of any individual, association or corporation." Taxpayers are being put on the hook for these payments to privately held companies.

d. *Author's note 4 on AZ 15–181*: The Goldwater Institute[2] did an investigative report in 2012 entitled, "Debt and Taxes: Arizona Taxpayers on Hook for $66 Billion Tab run up by State, Local Governments." While the report focused on "governmental debt" at the time, one cannot ignore that there are millions of dollars of charter debts currently out in IDA Loans. A portion of this debt was issued to failed charters. That is, some of these shuttered charters funded their seized properties through these types of bonds.

B. *Charter schools shall comply with all provisions of this article in order to receive state funding as prescribed in section 15–185.*

The purpose and scope defined in the laws seem innocuous. The devil is in the details, of which there are precious few.

The next section of the law legalizes the exemptions and immunities of charter schools. As will be stated multiple times, this is a system that legalizes the carpetbagging of the public schools in this country while protecting the perpetrators of this "educational innovation" from responsibility for their "actions taken in good faith."

GREAT FREEDOM WITHOUT RESPONSIBILITY

AZ 15–183. *Charter schools; application; requirements; immunity; exemptions; renewal of application; reprisal; fee; funds; annual reports.*

Author's note 1 on AZ 15–183: Sections S and T. These provisions are taken directly from the Charter School Legislation. They spell out the use of charter school property for credit purposes and state who owns the property accumulated by the charter school.

S. Charter schools may pledge, assign or encumber their assets to be used as collateral for loans or extensions of credit.

T. All property accumulated by a charter school shall remain the property of the charter school.

Author's note 2 on AZ 15–183: Prior to items S and T, items O and P of the same Charter Law *limited the liability* of the taxpayers (State) of the sponsors, the charter schools and their boards.

O. A sponsor, including members, officers and employees of the sponsor, is immune from personal liability for all acts done and actions taken in good faith within the scope of its authority.

P. Charter school sponsors and this state are not liable for the debts or financial obligations of a charter school or persons who operate charter schools.

The policymakers at the legislative level have applied a theory of action based on the application of free market economic theories to the public sector.

The public good known as Public Education has been financially compromised as a result of this deregulation.

CONSEQUENCES OF THE LAWS ENACTED

A legal real estate transfer from public to private owners was legitimized by the charter laws enacted in Arizona and other charter states.

Most of the voting public remains unaware of the provisions of the "public" charter schools laws that were put into place in Arizona in 1994 and other charter states with similar "freedom of choice."

What is meant by the term "unaware" here? The law is published isn't it?

The majority of people that were asked the question (over 100), "Who owns charter schools?" did not realize that the property of charter schools is owned by the charter owners. Most cannot begin to describe the financing used to build the new schools they see springing up.

The public also believes that "charter holders" are taking a financial risk by starting a charter school. Not true.

In addition, they assume that the charter holder will be held liable for the losses incurred by their charter in a free market. Also, not true.

In short, the public is assuming the same thing that they assumed regarding the funds in their pensions, retirement plans, mortgages, and the bond markets. That assumption being that the law protects them (the taxpayer), not the people they trusted their money with.

That Assumption Is Incorrect

The term "legislated" is an intentional use of language in this look at the flaws, philosophically, ethically, and financially of what passes for charter school law in this country. The laws were an intentional act by the policymakers of the state. A move that was guided in part by attorneys and interested parties who were promoters (lobbyists) for charter schools and vouchers.

The move to deregulate public education and the financial and governance protections (rules) that go with a publicly supported public good were the target of the policymakers in the Arizona legislature. The "dark money" support came from the charter and private school lobby. Groups that are supported and funded by corporate donations and "charitable foundations" whose owners will benefit financially from the privatization of public education.

Some of the arguments given for this transfer of real estate to private ownership versus public ownership include:

- The owners of charter schools do not receive funding specifically slated for property. They are excluded from the state's school building and maintenance rules and ineligible to receive funding from this source. This statement is true. Charters use their state equalization funding to pay for property along with the debt guaranteed by those payments.
- The most common answer given is that ownership makes the owners of the school responsible for the debt on the property, not the state.

  ○ This answer ignores the release from liability in Item P of AZ 15–183. "Charter school sponsors and this state are not liable for the debts or financial obligations of a charter school or persons who operate charter schools."

Charters routinely guarantee their financial obligations and debt by citing (as evidence they can pay) and then encumbering through intercepts[3] the state equalization payments coming to their charters. The state payments are based on the school's Average Daily Membership. *The audits, collected each year by the Arizona Charter Board, are filled with cases where the State Equalization Payments are the guarantor of payments to debt holders. That fact is stated in the audit.*

The arrangement used by financial institutions that hold the debt of each charter is spelt out in the audit section of each charter's dataset. Intercepts are tools used to send the state equalization money to the debt holder first. Debt payments trump payments to fund the actual education of students. This often results in late payments to vendors and issues with payrolls.

Ownership Is Not Equal to Fiscal Responsibility

Financial and governance *responsibility* has been dismissed by the language in the law. *"Sponsors and this state are not liable for the debts or financial obligations of a charter school or persons who operate charter schools."* Great freedom is granted without the great responsibility that normally attends great freedom. Leaders are people who are in the world with responsibility. The lack of fiscal responsibility for your situational ethics driven business decisions is not indicative of great leadership.

Property and assets, paid for with taxpayer funds, are lost (the properties go to the creditors) when charters fail. The charters with the least creditworthy scores often borrow from junk bond dealers at excessive interest rates. Charter school debts are also heavily financed by bonds held by the IDA (Industrial Development Authority Bonds). To understand the long-range financial problem requires some understanding of what an IDA loan is and how it is funded.

IDA Loans

The Industrial Development Authority is a political subdivision of the State of Arizona that serves to promote "industrial" development. The IDA does this by being the issuing agency for bonds for *private* economic activities. Charter school property purchases are authorized uses of IDA funds. Fees from these bond issues are paid to the IDA bondholders. The bonds are tax exempt, which makes them attractive to investors. The bonds are only available to Nonprofits.

IDAs were established under the Arizona Industrial Development Financing Act. They are covered under Arizona Revised Statutes Title 35, Chapter 5: "Industrial Development Financing." In Arizona, most of the state's counties and municipalities have an IDA lending agency. The IDA board members are appointed by the supervisors of the county they represent, or the council of the city or town they represent, to six terms. Because of the provisions of the law there is no liability for debt on any bond issued through IDAs to the counties or municipalities (ARS 35–742).

LIMITED LIABILITY IS IN QUESTION

As noted earlier Arizona just initiated a guaranteed loan program for charters. Initial funding is $100 M. The Goldwater Institute's[4] investigative report in 2012 entitled, "Debt and Taxes: Arizona Taxpayers on Hook for $66 Billion Tab run up by State, Local Governments" focused on "governmental debt" at the time. Since 2012, things have changed substantially. There are millions of dollars of charter debts currently out in IDA loans. A portion of this debt was issued to failed charters. Some of these shuttered charters funded their seized properties through these types of bonds.

The Goldwater Institute would do the public a service by revisiting their first study. An interesting figure would be the new amount their researchers deem the taxpayers are on the hook for.

The new funding source for charter construction and expansion passed in 2017. The opening funding provided is $100 million in state guaranteed loans. These loans *are unambiguously* guaranteed by the taxpayers.

Where in the law is the charter and legislative leadership's responsibility for financial and governance decisions that are being made in the service of charter or private schools? What happened to a system of checks and balances?

Districts are required to list all "unused" district properties. These properties can then be offered (or given) to charter groups at fire sale prices. *There is no reciprocal rule in place regarding the $400 million in property that failed charters have lost. Districts can't claim them. This is a double standard.*

When deregulation occurs and blanket freedom is given regarding the use of public money, situational ethics become the moral "standard" for corporate behavior.

What happens when a charter does not deliver?

NOTES

1. Alternative is used here to mean an alternative to the public schools. This is not to be confused with the term "alternative high school" or "alternative elementary school." These designations mean that the charter so listed (as an alternative school) has a lower academic standard to meet when it is ranked academically by the state. The rankings for this type of school are listed as ALT-Grade (Example: An ALT C ranking). When the academic standards were enforced in 2012, there was a move to

change the category listings of over 32 percent of the state's charters. In 2013, prior to the new rankings, there were *120 schools that converted to alternative school status.* This was in a group of 371 schools that went through a financial and academic rating in 2012. That is, 32 percent opted to lower their standards for grading by the charter board by switching to alternative status in 2013.

2. For a copy of the report see the addendum or: http://goldwaterinstitute.org/en/work/topics/free-enterprise/related-reforms-free/debt-and-taxes-arizona-taxpayers-on-hook-for-66-bi/.

3. An intercept is similar to a bank encumbering your salary. In this case, the lender is sent the money it is owed prior to the charter school receiving the funds to use for expenses related to educating the children. The money is intercepted at the Department of Education and sent to the lender. There is a contract regarding this transaction that is signed by the charter group at the closing of the loan. There are also additional fees and charges for this type of lending.

4. For a copy of the report see the addendum or: http://goldwaterinstitute.org/en/work/topics/free-enterprise/related-reforms-free/debt-and-taxes-arizona-taxpayers-on-hook-for-66-bi/.

Chapter 25

Stand and Deliver: Probe Vertically, See Horizontally

UNFULFILLED PROMISES

Educational opportunity has been promised to the public. Educational opportunism has been delivered in its place. Antinomianism, a disregard for ethics or morality, seems to be the modus operandi concerning taking public money meant for our children's education for personal and corporate financial gain in 77 percent of the cases studied. The statistics and facts in the audits verify that public education and teachers' economic viability are afterthoughts for these opportunists.

This opportunism is reflected in administrative costs running at *20.5 percent* of total charter costs (the average is actually higher 22.3 percent) versus 10.35 percent at districts. It is apparent in classroom instruction of *45.3 percent at charters* versus district classroom spending of *51.88 percent*[1] (Staff 2015). The lack of spending on retirement benefits is reflected in the low classroom spending numbers of charters. This type of spending (money put into pensions) counts toward classroom spending.

Begging the Question

With statistics from the state's own data collection pointing to classroom spending (too low) and over spending on administrative (too high at charters), why is the legislature ignoring the source of the problem? Unregulated, under-reported, and opaque spending at charter schools.

A deeper dig into the data reveals that the charters *that are spending more* on classroom supplies are buying those supplies from for-profit subsidiaries of the charter (related parties). Online schools buying their own software at inflated prices is another example.

164

The graduation rates and academic results at these online schools are usually C and below. They would be "D" and "F" *if the schools were rated as traditional schools* rather than as alternative schools. Fifty percent graduation rates are the norm at these alternate "schools." For some reason, some don't even report graduation rates.

SO WHAT ACADEMIC RESULTS ARE WE GETTING FOR THIS?

Portable Practical Education's online school is Arizona Virtual Academy. Their AZCB Academic Report is below. Nationally, that is, other online schools in the country, the statistics match what is seen here (Bottari 2013). A national disgrace.

Charter schools and the public money used to fund them have become the new mortgage and junk bond marketplace of the free marketers. They are a new investment tool in hedge fund managers' arsenal. This is happening on the national stage as well as the state and local levels.

This hostile takeover component of charter and private schools should be a concern to the public and to the core group of charter operators and private schools that are doing the right thing with the structure that is in place. These include the 23 percent of charters that have personal financial integrity and sound business practices that these charter owners combine to bring us exemplary charters. These real charters have a stake in getting the financial and governance model for all charters right.

PROBE VERTICALLY, SEE HORIZONTALLY

In his masterful work about the Spanish Flu Epidemic, The Great Influenza, *John M. Barry described the greatest challenge of scientific inquiry (Barry 2004). The challenge is asking the right question(s). It was the genius of one of the heroes in that story, Dr. William Henry Welch, and his ability to "probe vertically and see horizontally" that led to the end of the Spanish Flu Pandemic. This is the type of vertical probing that led to the discovery of the*

Table 25.1. Two Years of Academic Ratings for K–12 Charter Group

AZ Virtual Report	2014	2013
State Accountability	N R	C
Overall Rating Over Time	67.5	83.75
Graduation	*25*	*25*

influenza's causes. This discovery in turn guided the research leading to an eventual cure and strategies for preventing the disease's spread.

The invasive nature of financial and governance paradigms extolled upon and used in the free market approach to education need to be challenged. The models are responsible for a financial epidemic that threatens the financial and social fabric of our communities and our public schools financial health. The epidemic is going unchecked. As with past financial disasters, the public is unaware that they have contracted the disease of "Voodoo Economic theories."

The current model for charter financial management and governance allows for an invasive and unchecked assault on the funding the country dedicates to educating our future citizen. Its parasitic version latches onto the host source of funding and bleeds it dry. This in turn leaves the surviving healthy systems in a weakened financial state.

The disease has been disguised as an innovation. It is a parasitic invasion. Our financial immune systems were pre-weakened with bunk about our public schools and the teachers who work in those schools. The disease took hold and lay dormant. The spores that created the pandemic are out of the dormant stage after twenty years of incubation during a period of unchecked criticism of the public school system. The symptoms of financial malaise are now manifesting themselves.

Our legislatures are ignoring the symptoms. They continue to witch hunt the public school system rather than face the real problem. They frantically suggest more voodoo economic theories of action as a cure.

The complaints about publicly elected school boards, which included "concerns" regarding the democratic process used to elect those boards, could easily be made regarding city councils, elected state representatives, and Congress. Democracy is messy. It was designed to be that way.

Let's start calling this takeover what it really is. The financing schemes used in 77 percent of the cases are Ponzi schemes being played with public funds. A financial epidemic caused by malpractice is killing our public schools.

When one looks at how publicly funded, privately managed, and semiautonomous charters have played out in reality in the past twenty years, the facts point to the need for a paradigm shift in our thinking. A paradigm shift is what is called for when one looks seriously at the data and ignores the rhetoric of the entrenched "economic theorist's" theses used in defending the status quo.

Challenging the paradigm requires authentic leadership at the local and statehouse levels. Leadership that is willing to question the model and face the alienation that comes from authentic leadership (Heidegger 1962). Paradigm shifts are uncomfortable for the economic scientists and politicians challenging what has become a de facto mainstream economic theory. That is the nature of paradigm shifts. When leaders in the legislatures of the states with charters are participating in the market they are regulating they have become a part of the problem.

Without challenges to the new status quo scientific, fact based, scientifically sound revolutions do not occur (Kuhn 1996). We have been trusting the rhetoric of Friedman and Hayek's theories of economics as they relate to economics and education without verifying the outcomes of that rhetoric's implementation effects. We have trusted without verifying.

We have not acted like we have been sobered by our experiences.

NOTE

1. Source for both statistics: Arizona Superintendent's Report January 2015 for FY 2013–2014.

Chapter 26

Ideals versus Ideology

The data used to probe the essential questions asked by this inquiry came from all sides of the political spectrum, pro-charter, anti-charter (and private school funding using state funds [tax credits or vouchers]). The result is a comprehensive forensic accounting look at what has transpired as a consequence of deregulating public school financing and governance. The result is a sobering and honest presentation that is meant to challenge the financial and governance paradigm (based on a faulty economic theory of action) that has been established.

The ideas and ideologies developed to foment this sea change in how we view public education have been developed over a long period of time. A theory of economics that was developing in the 1950s has now fully bloomed.

School choice via privately owned publicly funded charters and a vouchering system, via tax incentives and direct state funding, for private school tuitions have become the norm. The financial results indicate the emperors of school-choice theories have no clothes. These results are being ignored or trivialized in pro-charter literature that pushes back on the research findings.

Kuhn's *Structure of Scientific Revolutions*, the source of the term "paradigm shift," predicts this type of push back. After twenty plus years, the charter paradigm is the new status quo.

The charter authorizers and the charter associations need to stop acting like lemmings leading their organizations off the cliff of financial demise. State charter boards and other authorizers need to get this right. Twenty-three percent of their constituents are already providing what the model idealizes. Support them. Encourage new charters to emulate their best practices as a condition of authorizing or re-authorizing the charter.

The paradigm that "free market economic theory works in public schools" has developed over a fifty-plus year stretch. The paradigm went into play in Arizona in 1994. Over twenty years have passed. We have historical data. It is time for reflection and thoughtful analysis of what that data shows us. The paradigm's "anomalies" (charters that do not improve academics as predicted) deserve to be studied and scrutinized.

The theories that were espoused regarding what would occur if we instituted charters and vouchers need to be probed vertically and horizontally.[1] There are 100 plus outliers in the data that make money and behave ethically. Ideological responses to critiques need to be replaced with hard data and course corrections based on the market facts.

The data gathered points to a conclusion that semi-autonomous decision making does not always lead to financially sound decisions. Private governance of a publicly financed public good is not working. If it was working, it would curtail abuses and protect the public's money. The umpires and governing agencies would have some control over the game.

The businesses that have used the paradigm presented in the charter school laws to provide themselves financial opportunities have resorted to practices that are opportunistic. Carpetbaggers and scalawags are thriving in an unregulated marketplace that is neither open nor free. Twenty years on the social experiment of charter schools in Arizona continues to grow without adequate monitoring and effective oversight. This lack of oversight is accompanied by a decided lack of transparency regarding how the public's money is being spent. Historically, ergo conservatively, control over how taxpayer funds are being used has been a major factor in school finances.

Private ownership of publicly paid for assets, a hallmark of the charter and private schools, is being pushed down the public's throat by politicians and promoters with vested interest in the resulting market opportunities. Too many politicians who are making the "rules" are benefitting from the rule-making in all of the states with charters. This is a clear and present danger and a conflict of interest.

In 2017, the efforts to access even more public funds and facilities through thinly veiled legislation to privatize the public schools of Arizona is being accelerated. Verification of the claims by those we trusted with our public funds needs to be intensified and expanded prior to any informed decision making on this topic. The "rules of this game" are rigged. Allies and publicists for the three sisters of spin are spinning the rules to their financial advantage[2] in a "market" that is supposed to be providing a public good (Moe 1996).

Enough already.

YOU DON'T KNOW WHAT YOU HAVE GOT TILL IT'S GONE

For many years, I've been worried as a citizen about things like the collapse of trust in public authorities. When I was growing up in the 1950s and 1960s, 75 percent of Americans said that they trusted their government to do the right thing. Last year, same survey, same question, it was 19 percent.

—Robert Putnam, AHEE interview 1995

When I was a child in Houston in the 1940s and 1950s, everyone I knew went to the neighborhood public school. Every child on my block and in my neighborhood went to the same elementary school, the same junior high school, and the same high school. We car-pooled together, we cheered for the same teams, we went to the same after school events and we traded stories about our teachers. I went to Montrose Elementary School until fifth grade, when my family moved to a new neighborhood and I enrolled in Sutton Elementary school. Then, along with everyone else who lived nearby, I went to Albert Sidney Johnston Junior High School and San Jacinto High School.

—Diane Ravitch, *The Death and Life of the*
Great American School System

My parents, part of the greatest generation, were products of the public education system in Jersey City, New Jersey. When it came time for them to send their five children and three foster children to school they paid for us to go to a private kindergarten then sent us to the local Catholic Schools in North Andover, MA. When we moved to Pennsylvania that Catholic education took place at St. Ann's in Emmaus and Central Catholic in Allentown, PA.

My parents never complained about the costs associated with their "choice" for their five sons and their foster children. It was a religious choice and as such they expected that they would have to sacrifice for that choice. They contributed, at their church to help pay other children's tuition. They continued to support the public school system knowing that it was that system that had provided them the opportunities they now exercised.

That same public minded sense of duty was reflected in my father's service at Peleliu and Okinawa as a Marine in the First Marine Division, The Old Breed. The public schools were a gateway to my mother's career as a nurse. A sense of community and connection to that community led that Italian immigrant to care for wounded soldiers coming home from overseas.

As an adult I elected to become a teacher in the public schools to return the opportunity that my parents had to new generations. Those children have not disappointed me. They have not disappointed their country. They were public district and charter children. The charters some of them were in emphasized community service and democratic values. They were and are Americans all.

—Curtis J. Cardine, author of this book

NOTES

1. The data set used is literally 12,500 lines vertically and over 100 columns horizontally. It has been probed in both of these dimensions and in time. (The time dimension is looking at historic and present follow on statistics [post 2014–2015] that are available).

2. See Moe (1996).

Chapter 27

Situational Ethics

The charter laws, by relying on "good faith," empower and enable the owners of charter schools (and private schools by lack of oversight) to use situational ethics when it comes to their application of the limited laws that are in place. The laws silence on ethical business practices is deafening.

Consider the law's wording: *"A sponsor, including members, officers and employees of the sponsor, is immune from personal liability for all acts done and actions taken in good faith within the scope of its authority." This is great freedom for actions taken by leadership and governing bodies at charter and private schools. It is granted without the great personal responsibility that should attend such freedom.*

There are no "clear cut" operational rules in place when you have given the type of "freedom" as described in the definition of charter schools. This freedom from responsibility is written into the Arizona Charter School Laws. *"They receive public funding similarly to traditional schools. However, they have more freedom over their budgets, staffing, curricula and other operations. In exchange for this freedom, they must deliver academic results and there must be enough community demand for them to remain open."*

DELIVER OR WHAT?

The theory of action in play is that the financial and governance freedom will be checked by the "responsibility" to deliver academic results. The theory also implies that if they don't deliver this result (academic results), then there will not be "community demand" for them to remain open. The exit theory verbalized by the charter industry is that parents who have a choice will leave poorly performing charters because of academics.

This thesis is not supported in the literature regarding why people exit from schools. The theory that academics will improve is implicit in the charter scope and purpose, "to provide a *learning environment that will improve pupil achievement." It is also a commonly used response when one makes inquiries about fiscal accountability in charters to charter promoters. "We are focusing on academic results first."*

A financial ethics void is created by the existing charter laws. When a void is created regarding what constitutes ethical practice, situational ethics are all that is left to "guide" the financial and governance practices that emerge. The belief system espoused by the charter school advocacy groups is akin to a religion without some version of the Ten Commandments providing a moral standard to the practitioners of that religion.

The result is the financial and governance abuses that are in play at 77 percent of charter schools studied. The fact is that 90 percent of charters have applied for and been exempted from the bidding and purchasing requirements that school districts and school boards are subject to is not a surprise. They have asked for (an intentional act) and have been granted that exemption.

LEADERSHIP IS UNACCOUNTABLE TO HIGHLY RELATED CORPORATE BOARDS

Situational ethics have allowed charters to have corporate boards with one or two members. The two usually being a husband and wife team. At times, the leadership and corporate board consists of two couples. At other times, it is *one person, the owner.* Oligarchies have been created. Any definition of the term, "oligarchy," leads to that conclusion.

Situational ethics allow wholly related corporate boards with monetary interests in the school and its infrastructure. This arrangement is covered under the term "other operations" in the definition. An exemption from liability is included in the law, "*A sponsor, including members, officers and employees of the sponsor, is immune from personal liability for all acts done and actions taken in good faith within the scope of its authority.*" De Facto, the organization is immunized from the financial disease that the organization itself is spreading.

Charters are allowed to use situational ethics to decide what is "right" for them regarding board size. This permission is implied *since the law is silent on corporate board size and composition.* The term, "in good faith within the scope of its authority" in item O, is stretched to its limits when one considers the situational ethics that are used to determine what "good faith" looks like in practice. In short, what constitutes "good faith" relies on the integrity of the humans carrying out the letter of the law.

The Financial Consequences of Situational Ethics

The consequences of twenty-three years under these laws and rules are the topic explored in this book. Lost publicly paid for property and assets are one aspect of this inquiry's findings. The losses are symptomatic of the underlying issues that created a national charter failure rate of 44 percent for "financial reasons" and another 21 percent caused by "mismanagement" (a total of 65 percent). These decisions occurred in a venue without the financial safeguards needed to ensure ethical practices are the norm, not the exception.

The results borne out in the data are what people have suspected would occur. The decision-making systems allowed by the vagaries of the law guarantee what normally would be termed malfeasance and fraud will occur. It has in 77 percent of the cases. We are told that once the money is paid to the charter it belongs to them, that is, it is no longer public. It is public money.

PUBLIC MONEY

An oft heard explanation of why this isn't public money being spent goes like this. The money now belongs to the charter provider. They can spend it like they wish. The following is the standard reply regarding this issue:

"We pay contractors to build the highways with state and federal funds and they use that money to buy and own their equipment." The equipment, yes, but they don't own the road or the land the road runs through.[1] That remains part of the public's property. They are also *responsible* for the proper construction of the roads and the debt they incurred in "good faith" when they paid for that equipment. How has that worked out?

The mismanagement of charters that leads to this kind of result is the result of many factors.

Table 27.1.   Property Value (and Property Losses) of All Charters in Arizona

Total of the privately held Assets of All Charter Schools in 2013–2014
$1,572,900,288
Property Value of All Charters Adjusted for Nonschool Properties and Depreciation:
   $1,189,017,107
Estimated Value of Property and Assets Lost through Charter Failures since 1994[2]:
   $400,000,000
Cumulative Sum of All Property and Asset from Individual Charters Audits FY 2013–2014

The data was probed looking at several years' worth of audits, IRS 990s, and AFRs.

The factors identified as causes of these losses include:

- Bankruptcies on over-leveraged properties
- Financial mismanagement
- Over extended credit
- Exploitive leases held by the same owners and boards that hold the properties (using different corporate entities for each aspect of the subsidiary operations)
- Profiteering through management fees and occupancy costs
- Overpaid executives and management
- And most seriously *by related party transactions at 77 percent of all the charters studied. (100 percent of Charter Board Authorized Charters financials for multiple years were reviewed for this study.)*

These and other financial and governance issues were explored and evaluated as factors in the *42.79 percent* failure rate of individual charter schools in Arizona since 1994. Closures in 2016 topped new charter openings. The percentage is now 43 percent and growing.

PUBLICLY FINANCED DEBT ON PRIVATE PROPERTY

A special report from the Arizona Chamber of Commerce in 2012 declared: "Charter schools though have proven to be good credit risks over time." The report cites a 2011 study showed that out of $1.2 billion in loans to charters analyzed, only 1 percent ended in foreclosure, with only 0.2 percent eventually written off. "A Decade of Results: Charter School Loan & Operating Performance" (Young, 2011). The report painted a rosy picture.

The report then talks about a specific case in Arizona. Despite this optimism, individual school failures can still affect risk perceptions. Things have changed since that 2011 report.

Moody's recently downgraded the credit rating of an Arizona Charter bond series after the announcement that the largest school in the charter bond pool was going to be shut down by the state. "Moody's downgrades I.D.A. of Maricopa County's (AZ) Education Revenue Bonds; $15 million of debt affected"; Moody's was correct in doing so.

The data on debt gathered for the Grand Canyon Institute Report is cited in the data for this report's look at Arizona's issues with over-leveraged property. The failure rates noted are a symptom of the financial problems seen in the data.

In 2014–2015, 153 charters in the state had a negative net result for the year. An increase of nine from the prior year. Figure does not include several schools who had adjusted their figures to attain a positive net (fifteen more).

The facts in the marketplace are changing. CCC ratings of major charters in the state are not indicative of low bond risk. The best Dun and Bradstreet rating listed in the audit data was BB (junk bond status).

Refinancing and Increasing Debt Loads

What was seen in the data was a continuous refinancing of debt on ever-increasing *bond and commercial loans*. In several cases, the cost of getting out of a previous debt (penalty fees) was in the millions. BASIS, a high performing charter school wrote off $9.9 million for loan issuance costs in 2015–2016. The prior year a write off $4.5 million was taken. The net assets (deficit) of the company were (−22,989,424) at the end of 2016. (Source: Audit data). This is what comes from refinancing ever-increasing debt loads.

Also noted were extensive related party dealings that were costing the school end of the operation to pay fees to related party management, property, leasing, and employment companies. Those subsidiaries are operating as "for profits." This profit taking excess coupled with known cases of fraud in the financing of charters in the state yields the negative results seen in the data on net (deficit)[3] for the year (over 150 charters reported negative net [deficits] for FY 2015) and net assets (liabilities) showed that 83 charter groups had a net (liability).

Financial Failure: A National Issue

The national figures for charter failures match and sometimes exceed this rate. When failures due to mismanagement, a form of financial failure caused by malfeasance and incompetence, are included in the national figures, the total rises to 65 percent (Consoletti 2011).

Revenue Sources for Charters

In Arizona, the formula used to determine the state's contribution to local education is based on a state property value equalization formula. Districts with a lower equalized property value receive equalization funds at a higher rate (thus the term equalization funding). Charters locating in Scottsdale receive their funding from the state through the formula even though the town does not receive state funding for its public schools.

Table 27.2. Revenue Data for Success School

AZ State Equalization	*$4,391,912*
AZ Classroom Site Funds	$276,009
AZ Instructional Improvement Funds	$26,698
Government Grants and Assistance	$690,354
Contributions	$47,866
Arizona Tax Credit Contributions	$8,779
Student Fees	$20,240
Rental	$21,393
Student Activities	$21,913
Extracurricular Activities	$31,205
Food Service	$21,731
Before and After School Care	$82,556
Miscellaneous	$38,062
Totals	$5,678,718

An Example of the Revenue side: Success School: The charter in the example is Success School (four sites). Success School did not meet the Arizona Charter Board's Financial Performance Expectations in fiscal 2013–2014 or 2015–2016. The FY 2013–2014 audit information for Success School is shown in the revenue statement. (This type of analysis was done for every charter school in Arizona.)

The schools had an ADM of 664 in 2013–2014. The school's academic performance was "A" (Highly Performing) with a 100 quality points scored for its graduation rate.

The school's expenses were *much greater* than its revenue. This resulted in a net loss for the fiscal year ending June 30, 2014. The school had a net loss of (−$943,930) *even with the extra sources of income listed on the financials*.

In the following year FY 2014–2015, the school saw a net loss of (−$138,789).

In 2015–2016, the charter showed another loss.

The FY 2013–2014 audit had an *expense item* shown of $1,043,334 (the amount was attributed to a "*loss on refunding of debt*"). This amount is the result of refinancing. It was not a singular case in the data. *It is the norm. Refinancing costs are paid when the company had a built in "refinancing fee" on the original loan. A common practice.*

Two board members are listed on the firms IRS Form 990 FY 2013 (those members are also the Chief Administrative Officer and Chief Operational Officer). The pair took salaries of $130 K and $124 K respectively. A similar size district in the data set paid its superintendent between $60 K and $108 K.

Administrative costs of $939,353 were listed on Page 10 of the Annual Financial Report to the Arizona Department of Education. The figures reported to AZDOE *do not reflect the loss reported to the AZCB. Those fig-ures report a net of $690 K for FY 2014–2015.*

The reports should agree. They don't.

The loss on refunding of debt accounting may be one of the reasons for the difference. It shouldn't be.

The figures in the revenue report show that bulk of the charter's funding comes from Arizona Equalization funding. However, *$1.3 M comes from other sources as noted. Even with the added revenue, the charter wound up in the red at the end of FY 2014 and FY 2015. Their cash position at the end of the year remained strong. This was in spite of the expense on refunding the debt* ($1,043,334).

The sustainability measures (AZCB Rating) for this example show that an "A"-rated school can have financially troublesome results.

This result is the antithesis of the theory posited by charter promoters (i.e., that academic success and financial viability of charters are highly cor-related with one another). The theory does not take into account the effects of high administrative costs, high debt loads, continuous refinancing, related party transaction, and the normal things that have an impact on a company's finances.

In short, the theory is not valid. The fact is the rhetoric is incorrect. It does not come down to the equation: "Academic success is equal and equivalent to financial success."

Fiscal discipline is not being imposed on the charter industry. Prior reports on financial issues recommended changes that included the monitoring of finances by the charter board. The next chart shows the sustainability mea-sures used for each charter. The Arizona Charter Board rated 138 of their charters as *not meeting* performance standards. Cash flow issues were noted in ninety additional charter organizations. Debt to income ratios, when pro-vided in the audit, often were not aligned to the fixed charge cover ratio in the charter board's rating system.

Every charter has a sustainability measure in the Arizona Charter Board's rating system. The information in the system is sometimes compromised by accounting tricks used to defeat the metric used for those measures. In the middle of the data set, there were twenty charters whose nets were close to $1. Probing the data turned up accounting manipulations that returned a positive number ($1 to $100). The original report details how this was accomplished.

Sustainability Measures

The Charter *Does Not Meet the Charter Board's Financial Performance Expectations.*

The company, Success School, owed $12,589,120 on bonds to IDA and to the RAZA[4] development fund at the end of 2014. This was up from $10,925,000 at the end of 2013.

Table 27.3. Sustainability Measures

(Negative numbers indicated by parentheses)				
Net Income	($138,789)	Does Not Meet	($56,622)	Does Not Meet
Fixed Charge Coverage Ratio	1.04	Does Not Meet	1.15	Meets
Cash Flow (3-Year Cumulative)	($629,720)	Does Not Meet	($424,901)	Does Not Meet
	FY 2015 ($205,653)		FY 2016 $57,715	
	FY 2014 ($276,963)		FY 2015 ($205,653)	
	FY 2013 ($147,104)		FY 2014 ($276,963)	

Table 27.4. Assets and Losses for Success School

Net (Loss) 13–14 AZCB Audit	EOY Assets 13–14 AZCB Audit
$ (−934,930)	$(−23,592)
Net (Loss) 14–15 AZCB Audit	EOY Assets 14–15 AZCB Audit
$ (−138,789)	$ (−162,381)
Net (Loss) 15–16 AZCB Audit	EOY Assets 15–16 AZCB Audit
$ (−56,632)	$ (−219,003)

FY 2013–2014 had an expense of $1,043,334 attributed to a "loss on refunding of debt." As noted, it appears the debt was refinanced at that time.

Refinancing is often a sign of borrowing from Peter to pay Paul. This type of borrowing (refinancing) often occurred when the former owner, "sold the charter to a related party for more than the Fair Market Value." The new owners were forced to take out more money (loans) to keep afloat.

Data from the 2015–2016 shows that the debt has increased to $14,045,803. The EOY net *assets continue to travel further into negative numbers despite the added debt borrowing. As noted, this was a randomly selected charter.*

Unfortunately, their story is the norm for many of the charters reviewed at the twenty-year mark for charter schools in Arizona.

NOTES

1. Promoters like to use the example of land rights given to the railroads as they developed the Transcontinental Railroad. They forget that this monopoly brought about the term "Robber Barons" in the 1880s.

2. An explanation of the method used for these calculation is presented later in this book. The figures are purposely conservative and at the lowest end of the true costs. See: 6 Over-Leveraged Property and Equipment.

3. The bracketing used on net (deficit) is meant to show that on a financial document a deficit shows up between brackets whereas a net gain is outside of brackets. The terms "assets" and "liabilities" are used on a balance sheet.

4. RAZA Mission: Raza Development Fund invests capital and creates financing solutions to increase opportunities for the Latino community and low-income families.

Chapter 28

Overspending of Revenues
AKA Net Losses

One of the selling points promoting charters was that Chief Executive Officers would bring financial accountability and savvy from the private sector to the charter world. Carpetbagging chief executives have not delivered on that promised "reform."

2013–2014:

- *There were eighty-six charters with over −$100K of net losses[1] (ten were over $1M).*
- *There were another fifty-eight charters with net losses between $1,000 and $100,000.*
- *Total: 144*
- *Another layer of the data consisted of sixteen that ended the year with $0 net. Several in this count used accounting tricks to get to this point.*

2014–2015:

- *There were ninety-seven charters with over −$100 K of net losses (nine were over $1M).*
- *There were another fifty-six between $1,000 and $100,000.*
- *Total: 153*
- *Another layer consisted of six that ended the year with $0 net. Several in this count used accounting tricks to get to this point.*

Several Charters with net losses over $1 M in 2014–2015 are reported here. Also listed is what *the organization claimed their net was to* AZDOE (on the

Table 28.1.   Six Highest Net Losses 2014–2015

Charter Name	Net as Reported to AZDOE	Net as Reported to AZCB	ABSOLUTE Difference
Hillcrest Academy, Inc.	$105,136	–$4,084,353	$4,189,489
BASIS System Wide Information	–$1,332,911	–$3,074,317	$1,741,406
Edkey Schools	–$658,531	–$1,265,948	$607,417
Imagine Prep Coolidge, Inc.	–$808,488	–$1,129,412	$320,924
Legacy Traditional School-Gilbert	–$543,745	–$1,117,552	$573,807
Bradley Academy of Excellence, Inc.	$211,521	–$1,011,727	$1,223,248

Six Charter Groups with over $1M loss in 2014–2015

Annual Financial Review [AFR]). The *absolute value* of the differences between the two reports is given to show the disparity or continuity of the reporting.

How bad is it? The chart below tells a part of the story regarding the differences in reporting for the same year, 2014–2015.

The first example on the list is Hillcrest Academy. A struggling charter school that went out of business at the start of the 2016 school year.

The year prior (2015–2016) Hillcrest reported a positive net to the Arizona Department of Education on their AFR. *This was "misleading" the AZDOE at best.* The reality was *a net loss of (–$4,084,343). As noted the AZCB audit showed that problem.*

Different Rules

School districts are required to end the year in the black. If the district has a deficit, they have to cut staff and other expenses to balance their books. Large charters can afford to wait out small charters in the same area by absorbing their costs and local losses throughout their organization. This shifting of debt between entities happens in many charters.

Compromised Competition

A superintendent of multiple public school districts cannot cover one district's financial losses by consolidating all of the districts onto one audit. As noted earlier, charters can hide their financial losses by consolidating their audits. *Funds can also be moved from state to state in multistate and the same holds for multinational charters.* Another method used is "forgiven debts." Interstate companies can "forgive" debt (usually temporarily) to "balance" the accounts of the debt ridden local charter."

Compromised Accounting for Distributions

Note on For Profits' Reporting on Distributions: As noted earlier, distributions are the amounts paid out to the owners of the corporation in a for-profit company.

In the data, there was a $6 M difference on the sum of all "for-profit" net differences. *This disparity was caused by some companies reporting pre-distribution Nets to the AZDOE. That is, they failed to take the distribution out of their Net. It should have been counted as an expense as the money is paid out, an expense on the year's revenue.*

The adjustments for this difference were calculated into the data on for profits. Proper accounting calls for reporting the Net *after the company pays out distributions*. Why is this so? Distributions[2] are an expense no matter how you look at it. That is why audits report the number paid out as a negative number. It is an expense.

"It is said that power corrupts, but actually it's truer that power attracts the corruptible. The sane are usually attracted by other things than power."
—David Brin

The deregulation of the laws and regulations regarding the use of public funds for education have had financial and governance consequences. These chapters have sought to inform the reader about the wording of the law. Once the reader has that background knowledge, the resulting consequences become easier to understand.

Circling Vultures

The Problem: We have put into place situations that attract the corruptible into a field that we, as a society, hope is filled with uncorrupted people. Power attracted them. The scent of easy money from tax-funded sources has that effect.

Uncorrupted people. People like the majority of teachers out there are not attracted to the education field by power:

The majority of teachers enter the education profession because they want to make a difference in the world and their communities. This is a noble and valiant purpose that you should always keep in the forefront of your mind. No matter the challenges you face in the classroom, your work truly does have positive ramifications for your students, their families, and the future. Give your best to each student and watch them grow. This is truly the greatest gift of all.
—Lewis 2017

School leadership used to come from the ranks of exceptional teachers. The ranks were people who went into teaching for the right reasons. We have changed the paradigm regarding the leadership and governance model at our "public" schools and applied it to quasi-public schools (charters and vouchered private school tuitions).

The leadership paradigm in charters is "anyone" can be the school leader, especially CEOs. The conservative paradigm of traditional school leadership practice has been presented to the public as a weakness of the public school system. It is actually one of its greatest strength.

Are hospitals better now that they are being run by business leaders rather than former doctors? Did Health Maintenance Organizations improve health care opportunities?

Would we want a police department where the chief never served in the rank and file? Fire chiefs who never fought a fire?

It is time to reflect on what has transpired in the twenty plus years of experimentation with an economic theory of action that originated in the 1960s. We owe it to the teachers who are leaving the profession at an ever-increasing rate to fix the issues in the financial and governance practices exposed in this and other reports. The new paradigm is not attracting people to the profession. It is discouraging them and driving them away.

Politicians calling the current field of teachers illiterate is not helpful. Neither is rhetoric equating all teachers as "liberals." There are just as many perfect SAT scores in the ranks of teachers as there are in any other profession. The truth is there are conservatives, moderates, and liberals in the ranks. The desire to serve their community and children is what they have in common. In 1974, when the author started teaching, all but two of the twenty-two male teachers in the system were veterans of either Korea or Vietnam. They had all volunteered. That trend continues in the teaching ranks.

We want our future citizens exposed to all types of views in a republic. We also want them to be able to work with their fellow citizens no matter what their background is. What we don't want is any type of financial opportunist taking advantage of those teachers.

NOTES

1. Net is revenue minus expenditures.

2. Note on Accounting Practices regarding Distributions: The amounts paid for distributions are listed as negative numbers (−$200,000) on the audits as the money is paid out. As a convention for understanding in this report, all negatives are reported in brackets and with a negative sign.

Chapter 29

Opportunism

Deregulation of charter school finances and the governance structure they operate under has created an opportunity for opportunists. The laws enacted, based on an economic theory of action, present an opportunity for those opportunists to use public money for private gain. Their justification for this is built into the economic theory underlying the "free market" business approach.

> There is one and only one social responsibility of business—to use its resources and engage in activities designed to increase its profits so long as it stays within the rules of the game, which is to say, engages in open and free competition without deception or fraud.
> —Milton Friedman, *New York Times*, September 1970

The rules of the game that Mr. Friedman, an economist, described are the rules (laws) discussed in the previous chapter. *The competition created by those laws is not open nor is it free.*

The practice of what would be normally be called deception and fraud are rampant because of laws that rely on situational ethics and the "good faith" of ownership and its self-appointed corporate governing boards. This is occurring in an ethically and morally neutralized financial market that declares, ""the only social responsibility" of the "public" charter or private school business is to use its resources and engage in activities designed to increase its profits."

Carpetbaggers and scalawags are sacking the public funds used to finance "their" newfound property and assets with impunity. The rules of the game are fixed in their favor by the laws that "free" the charter from most of the rules and regulations. The laws set up the financial and governance vulnerabilities creating an opportunity to profiteer from money meant for educating our children. The laws have been lobbied for by the businesses and individuals who are benefiting from them.

The opportunist target of this financial heist nationally is the estimated sum of $800 billion that U.S. taxpayers spend on educating their children. Public schools' funding sources from federal, state, and eventually the local sources are the target of this hostile business takeover. The "prize" is probably even greater than the estimates indicate.

The financial marketplace experts engaged in this takeover believe the financial prize is closer to a one trillion dollar "market." This figure takes into account ever-increasing revenues once charter market domination takes place. A strategic goal of the industry.

Education was once a locally controlled part of America's public sector. Across the United States that model, locally controlled and operated public schools, is under siege. This is an attack on the democratic principle of locally controlled municipal enterprises. Public schools and the delivery of "educational services" have become the latest private sector corporate takeover target.

The same corporate owners that brought us childcare for $250 per week ($13,000 per year) are players in the next "educational marketplace," elementary and secondary education. The public has been sold an economic theory of action devoid of any of that theory's "rules of the game." The deregulated version of the theory is being applied to a public good. Payment for this economic theory experiment is being made with public funds. The players are held harmless from consequences by laws that protect them from liability for their "good faith" actions.

The carpetbaggers and scalawags in this game are in it for the long haul. These players will explain away most of the failure rate statistics at charter schools by insisting that this is how the free marketplace economic theory works. The market, they claim, will decide winners and losers.

The same cast of characters that created and profited from the mortgage securities crisis (2006–2007), savings and loan collapse of the 1980s, hedge fund disasters of the 1980s, pension heists in the 1990s, and the junk bond backed mortgage crisis that triggered the financial meltdown in 2007 are some of the primary players in this new financial heist. The road to perdition for our public schools runs through Wall Street, Washington, overseas and in our state capitals.

The public outcry for these "reforms" did not originate at the local level. Local school boards did not promote the solution set that has been foisted on the public. Policymakers in Washington and our state capitols decided that the economic theory of action that we are now experimenting with would work. They have trusted these theories but not verified the results.

This work then is a call to trust but verify, as Ronald Reagan would have remind us if he were around today.

The financial demise of the South following the Civil War was followed by a second invasion from the North and from within the Southern communities. During the postbellum period, carpetbaggers descended on the physically and financially devastated South. The Radical Republican Reconstruction Laws, "radical" is a term used in the history books, passed by congress made this land grab possible. The laws were the source documents of the Reconstruction Period's policy decided upon by the policymakers in Congress.

The goal of the carpetbaggers in the newly deregulated areas was land acquisition and quick profits. Aiding and abetting the carpetbaggers were local politicians known "politely" as scalawags. In Arizona, the primary state studied, the carpetbaggers have come from several other countries and at the time of this writing thirteen other states. The numbers are expanding.

"When somebody says, it's not about the money, it's about the money."
—*H.L. Mencken*

THE RADICAL RECONSTRUCTION OF OUR PUBLIC SCHOOLS IS ABOUT THE MONEY

A sanctioned raid on money that once was collected, allocated, spent, and controlled locally is occurring at an ever-increasing pace. Federal and state policymakers have acquiesced to the marketplace solutions posited by the charter, private and voucher lobby. They have legislated charter schools and private school vouchers into existence.

Once a law is passed, the next phase is putting the theory implicit in the law into action. "Policymakers have a theory of action even if they can't articulate it, and they implement plans based on their theory of action, *their guess* about how the world works. Historians are trained to recognize assumptions and theories and to spot their flaws" (Ravitch 2010). The theory of action's results is evidence that the economic theory behind it is fatally flawed. The theorists have "guessed" incorrectly. The deregulated versions of their theories are producing financial and educational failures.

The theories referred to in this research have been articulated in laws. The evidence collected by forensically studying the data points to a verification of the theories in only 23 percent of the cases. History teaches us lessons. We now have twenty plus years of historical information to learn from.

As an educational practitioner, the author was an early promoter of public school choice. The theories regarding public charters were tested by starting charters in the southwestern corner of New Hampshire 1999. Those charters now exist as independent entities in New Hampshire.

A charter model can work effectively and ethically if the policymakers have taken the time to ensure the model has financial and governance integrity. Twenty-three percent or over 100 charters are proof that the model can work.

The current operating model in Arizona and most of the United States lacks financial and governance integrity. That lack of integrity is built into the language of the authorizing legislation.

The governance model rather than acting as a check on oligarchical owners ensures that there is little to no check on the ethically challenged financial schemes that have developed. When governance and leadership are one and the same what else could we expect would occur?

In a 1999, *Cato Policy Report,* Milton Friedman wrote, "There's a common misconception that people who are in favor of a free market are also in favor of everything that big business does. Nothing could be further from the truth.

As a believer in the pursuit of self-interest in a competitive capitalist system, I can't blame a businessman who goes to Washington and tries to get special privileges for his company. He has been hired by the stockholders to make as much money for them as he can within the rules of the game. And if the rules of the game are that you go to Washington to get a special privilege, I can't blame him for doing that. *Blame the rest of us for being so foolish as to let him get away with it.*

I do blame businessmen when, in their political activities, individual businessmen and their organizations take positions that are not in their own self-interest and that have the effect of undermining support for free private enterprise."

Business suicide is being played out in the charter market. The polar opposite of a free market is created when the "free market" is pushing for government assistance and loans to aid and abet its faulty business practices.

This work is a research practitioner's effort to compare what has been promised (the espoused theory of the policymakers and the free market philosophies they have embraced), and what has actually transpired (the theory in use [action]) after twenty-three years. Leadership and change research in the organizational management field is heavily drawn on for this work. Research on theories of action draws heavily from the work of Chris Argyris on organizational behavior. (Argyris and Schèon 1978).

Policymakers have theorized about how the educational world works and what it takes to improve educational outcomes. Their theories of action are driven by the flawed implementation of economic theories about how the educational "marketplace" works. This round of business suicides is being funded with publicly raised capital (taxpayer funded). The results of those flawed theories here in Arizona and across the country have allowed a carpetbagging of the Great American School System to take place.

FOLLOWING THE MONEY OUT OF THE COMMUNITY

The ensuing economic resource shift caused by this flawed economic theory of action has been a blow to the local economies of the towns and cities being taken over by state and federally authorized "educational services providers." The local economy suffers a loss on this transfer of funds to multinational and out of state interests. Microeconomic theory clearly establishes the connection between spending on the local economy and the growth of that local economy. Microeconomics applied to local spending is one economic theory we know is accurate. Is it really the intent of the IDA to lend money to charters to start schools in other states? What stretch of capitalistic market theory allows that political solution to stand?

One unintended result of deregulation is the fact that Arizona's education dollars are flowing to other states and other countries. Millions of dollars of Arizona tax revenues are crossing state and national borders. *The money is not going to improve the lot of the teachers in the local Arizona communities or to providing improved educational services to our children. It is going into the pockets of opportunists. In short, it is about the money.*

This transfer of educational capital is a result of corporate board decisions, many of which are made in other states and countries. The theory posited by promoters of charters stated that CEOs should be running our schools instead of trained professionals from the educational field.

We need to ask, "How did trusting CEOs with a deregulated mortgage market work out in the last financial crisis?" A crisis that was created by the mismanagement of our financial markets by CEOs. What were CEOs doing in their areas of expertise to protect our economy and their client's money during the savings and loan, pension heists, hedge fund, and junk bond market excesses?

Answer, they were doing their CEO jobs. CEOs work for their company and the bottom line, not the public good. Public good and profits are not always mutually exclusive. However, profiteering at the expense of public good is a moral no brainer. We know this. CEOs who are also the owner of the company are even more inclined to work for their own bottom line. These same businesses are now in the public sphere. They are engaging in a "political arena" by lobbying for protectionist policies for their "businesses." The antithesis of a free market.

Natural selection based on faulty business practices in charters is not functioning as they rely on government largesse and loans for their existence. The market cannot self-correct. The failure rate would be double what it is if that were the case.

The retirement and saving and loan heists of the 1980s and 1990s were promulgated by CEOs and endorsed by corporate boards.

What have we lost in this newest deregulated marketplace?

- Local control of publicly raised taxes has been lost.
- This loss of fiscal control of tax revenues applies to the communities *and to the state.*
- We have lost social capital. The ultimate goal for a public school board is to provide an educational opportunity for the citizens of that community. When democratically elected officials are replaced by appointed corporate boards, we can expect what the data indicates.

  - Profit motivates the acquisition process in 77 percent of the cases of charter schools. Natural business failure rates are not occurring because the political via government loans and revenues are propping up the "free market."
  - The motivation for this corporate interest in education in Arizona is the substantive financial gains to be made in the Arizona (and national) educational marketplace. Kentucky, Illinois, Iowa, Nebraska, Michigan, Florida, Tennessee, Nevada, Texas, Wisconsin, Utah, Washington, and New York all have charter footprints in Arizona. They did not spontaneously come here to help our children become better learners.

LOCAL EDUCATIONAL OPPORTUNITIES ARE NO LONGER LOCAL

Arizona mega-charter groups have corporate footprints in other states. These companies spend Arizona generated revenues to establish, advertise, and sell themselves into those footholds in Arizona and in other states and countries. Imagine your local school board operating the same way. Imagine districts using consolidated audits across district lines to hide their financial losses. Consolidated audits and for-profit management companies hide the transfer of Arizona revenues to other states from public eyes.

American Jobs Are Lost in This Transaction

Some charters in Arizona and nationally hire teachers imported from Turkey and other Middle Eastern countries to teach in Arizona schools. The Gulen Schools are one of the largest users of work visas in the United States. They have 106 schools across the United States, 6 are in Arizona (The Daisy Group). Their founder is Fathulah Gulen[1] an Islamic cleric and spiritual leader). Another Arizona charter has its home office in Lebanon. Several of the major "childcare companies" spoken about earlier are now owned by Swiss and Dutch corporations.

The founder and leader of the Gulen school network is an Imam from Turkey who now resides in Pennsylvania. The government of Turkey has been seeking his extradition to Turkey as they believe he was connected to the recent 2015 coup attempt in that country. Our educational tax dollars at work.

Locally owned and operated charters are the 23 percent exception, not the rule.

There is a benefit to the local economy when public schools employ and are owned by local residents. *More importantly,* there is social capital in the model that ties schools to their communities and the values of those communities. Teaching should be a local entry point into the community's middle class. We know this deep in our souls.

There was a reason why public schools in the "good old days" required teachers to be local residents. They wanted the teachers to be members of the community they served. They wanted to encourage their local residents to become the teachers, firefighters, and police personnel in their communities. All three fields used to be the ones children hoped to enter.

NOTE

1. See: http://www.bbc.com/news/world-europe-36855846.

Chapter 30

A Unique Meta-Analysis of the Financial Data

WHY THIS RESEARCH MATTERS

In a paper published by the Grand Canyon Institute for Public Policy, the author has presented a meta-analysis of the financial and governance results of twenty years of "free market" choice in Arizona. This report and the supporting research are the results of an intensive three-year forensic accounting meta-analysis of the financial and governance data from all of the charter schools in the state. The good, the bad, and the ugly of this transformational twenty years were analyzed and reported on. *Thousands of financial documents* were researched, transcribed, and evaluated for this report. Multiple years were analyzed to discern patterns and trends.

The approach to that data analysis was unique.

A RESEARCH PRACTITIONER'S APPROACH

The perspective gained from the data was informed by the author's forty-one-plus years in education. The author has taught all grade levels from kindergarten to graduate school.

- Thirty years (with five years comingled with *establishing public charter schools* in New Hampshire).
- Charter schools (nine years in Arizona).
- Two years running a private educational technology company as its president.
- Financial and governance expertise has been gained through firsthand experience, running three small- and medium-sized businesses, coursework, and

teaching (graduate and undergraduate) in school finance and educational history.
• The author's financial perspective is informed by public and private experiences.

The research looked at the data for specific examples of exemplary practice and examples of the economic theories of action working. Despite the bad news in the data, the author remains a supporter and still believes in well-run ethically managed charter schools.

GETTING IT RIGHT

Twenty-three percent of Arizona's charters *are* providing an educational opportunity while maintaining high ethical and financial standards. The figure should not be a shock. It is close to the figures obtained in psychological research studies that look at factors that influence our decision-making process. That figure is a bellwether on how humans will apply situational ethics when tempted or put to the test. Research data confirms the percentage of people that do the right thing in spite of the situation is usually in the range of 20 percent to 31 percent.

Our laws regarding charter finances and governance are written as if we don't already know that about human behavior. When given unchecked power and leeway around great sums of money, people tend to behave in a self-serving manner. Situational ethics manifest themselves when unchecked by stated behavioral norms. The rules of the game matter.

What is particularly disturbing about the lack of attention to the financial and governance factors is that most of the people who want this type of financial freedom from oversight complained mightily about school administrators, districts, and school boards regarding *their* use of public funds. When confronted with the data several highly placed charter advocates immediately cited district issues. This work debunks those defensive postures.

It is a misdirection of resources to put the regulated and locally governed actions of the districts and their boards under a state microscope. Districts have oversight and regulations that guide their decision-making process. They report directly to their constituents. This is the messy fact of the democratic process. Moves to take more power out of the local communities' hands are a state and federal overreach. That overreach is being pushed by lobbyists from the charter industry and insiders in the state legislature.

We, the citizens, already verify and validate our districts through locally elected bodies, elections, and local input. Charter laws and tuition credits and "scholarships" for private schools expect the public to trust the CEOs and corporate boards without mechanisms for them to verify how the money is being spent.

TRANSPARENCY

The public is being expected to trust charter and private school owners without subjecting them to the same verifying processes that have been imposed on districts. The political and lobbying advocates of "choice" act as if they believe that what matters is not what is true or false regarding "free market" finances and governance but what is believed by the general public.

This lack of verification and a lack of easy public oversight is a formula for fiscal disaster.

IMPLIED AUTHORIZATION TO MANIPULATE THE FINANCIAL SYSTEM FOR PUBLIC EDUCATION

The implied authority to use situational ethics when making financial and governance decisions in charter and private schools comes from the laws cited earlier. The law's authorizations exempting charter owner's from public school financial and governance rules constitute an implicit authorization to bypass the financial safeguards and ethical standards that were built into those operating procedures. The regulations charters sought "freedom" from were written that way on purpose. Fiscal accountability for taxpayer funds matters.

This de facto release from restrictions is the source of a belief system (theory of action) that the owners and corporate boards are free to make any decision they need to ensure financial success for their company. That operational freedom is being abused in 77 percent of the cases.

This theory in use quickly turns into a mind-set: "Since there are no specific rules it is taken on 'good faith' that the state authorizes the owner's use of situational ethics." If the owners are not given rules, then the resulting financial and governance actions they take under that "freedom" from regulation *must* be endorsed and permissible. The financial situation the charter owner and their boards find themselves in dictates the "correct action."

The moral and ethical violations that are identified in this study are not because the people involved in charter schools are inherently dishonest. They are the result of laws that deregulated the finance and governance of a specific educational model, charter and privately owned publicly paid for private school tuitions (via vouchers and tax credits).

THE STINK TEST

There is a simple test one can apply to most situations to determine if it meets Rawls' Theory of Justice. Substitute the word "superintendent" and school board in the statement that follows when you come upon the words owner or corporate board.

In the data set under the heading "Commitments," related party transactions and nonrelated party transactions between the owner and the corporate boards have been delineated and collated from the audits. Built in "rent" or "lease" increases based on either time or student population are noted in these "Commitments"[1] as they are on the audits and were traceable. Leasing from "for-profit" subsidiaries controlled by the owner and corporate board is often accompanied by ever-increasing lease charges. Payments to ownership often occur at a 10 percent markup.

Nonprofit charters plan and set up for-profit subsidiaries to move money around in a private company set up to conceal the transactions. A fee is captured from leases with related parties, leased employees, and management companies. The ownership and corporate boards of the schools are the same people operating subsidiary for-profit firms.

The point of this thought exercise is that the public would be outraged if a superintendent, principal, or school board in their community were operating their schools this way.

MANIFESTATIONS OF THE MIND-SET

This mind-set regarding situational ethics was manifested time and again in audit notes for individual charters dealing with executive pay. Most of the audits had this quote embedded in the discussion about administrative compensation, "the board looked at the administrative salaries at school districts and set their (management's) compensation accordingly." This quote is also found on many of the IRS 990s. The "decision makers" identified were usually comprised of the owners and their friends (or just the owner(s)).

This type of "justification" for executive salaries and distributions is the norm.

The result of this "search method" is telling salaries in the $200,000 ranges for schools that had student bodies in the hundreds of students. The "looked-at" districts (that is, the ones that do pay in that range ($200K)) have thousands of students with multiple schools. There are very few of these types of districts in Arizona. When the use of the term "CEO" for charter owners first was proposed, we should have expected that they would over-compensate themselves. It is, after all, the nature of the beast.

One expects over-compensation to occur in the mega-charter groups where there is a chance that the "CEO" came from a corporate background. However, most of the "CEOs" noted in this study did not have either a corporate or educational pedigree. As they say in Texas, "All hat, no cattle."

SHELL GAMES

Multiple companies with the same ownership and corporate board are gaming the system. There is also substantive evidence that vouchers are being misused due to inadequate oversight.

An incomplete picture is available in the public documentation available. Running multiple for-profit entities doing business with the nonprofit charter schools or private schools established under that entity are deliberate attempts to game the system.

Where's Waldo's Payday

Hidden in the shell companies are distributions, charges for "services," and salaries of the main players in this financial heist. If the owner is paying themselves $290,000 in their for-profit subsidiary company, the public cannot see it. Distributions paid out of these shell companies are also invisible to the public as they are not the same distributions that are shown in the Arizona Charter Board Audits of the charter itself. Payments to the shell companies are visible on the audits. That is, if the audit is delineated into categories regarding where the money was spent. This is normally in the "Expenses" category.

A flaw in the accounting system for audits allows generalized statements, "Charter School Program" and "Administration and Management" as cover items for all of the expenses. This is a poor way to audit any firm. Shills in the media releases and on webpages are used to defend the practices of the firms because of their "academic" results.

When the data shows millions of dollars going to these "private for-profit entities," one can only wonder how they are spending the cash. The practice needs to end. The 23 percent of charters that do not engage in these practices deserve a level playing field, as do our public districts.

The moral and ethical violations cited in this report are the result of laws that deregulated the finance and governance of a specific educational model, charter and privately owned publicly paid for private school tuitions (via vouchers and tax credits).

The laws created an opportunity for financial opportunism. The opportunity was seized. The system for financing and governing our public charter schools encourages, by its lack of rules and consequences for financial failures, a gaming of the system. The gaming for personal benefit extends to the state retirement system when charters participate in that system. Shamefully so.

The resulting ethical and moral problems that are identified in the data will anger the public. It will be a righteous anger. Tempering that anger should be the message of hope in the research. It is hoped that the compelling exceptions to the ethically challenged charter operators will inspire all of us to push for changes to the law. Changes that allow *that type of charter school represented by the 23 percent to thrive*. Those ethical charter operators deserve our support. Tragically, the current system encourages and rewards the mega-charters using the system to game the system at the honest charter operator's expense.

A financial disaster of epic proportion in a "marketplace" that represents billions of our taxpayer-funded dollars is on the horizon. The financial practices creating this dilemma are examples of what Friedman referred to as "business suicide." By playing the political systems, charter advocacy groups and charter owners have taken positions that in the long run are not in their own self-interest. They are undermining support for private free enterprise by gaming the system.

"Red sky in the morning, sailor take warning. Red sky at night, sailor's delight." The current financial picture for 77 percent of charters is a red sky in the morning. Changes need to occur to turn it into a red sky at night. Our publicly financed districts and honest charter and private school owners deserve our vigilance and political will if they are to survive.

The question is can we really regulate poor financial and governance behavior?

NOTE

1. On an audit, commitments are payments that are covered by a rental or lease agreement. A five year guaranteed lease is common. Some for-profit companies lease their own properties, owned by another company with the same owners, back to the schools. The ADM at the school is used as a guarantee for the loan on the property. For links to more information regarding investing in charters, follow the link here. (Link is at Democracy Now.)

Chapter 31

Behavior Can Be Regulated

Barry Goldwater famously stated that we cannot legislate morality. To counter that notion Martin Luther King (1962) said, "It may be true that morality cannot be legislated, but behavior can be regulated."

The regulating of unethical financial and governance behavior should be the role of the State Board for Charter Schools and the Department of Education in each state. Allowing all of the requests to bypass the normal process of bidding services, which has led to a propensity of related party transactions, is not the way to moderate behavior.

The behavior of the bad actors needs to be regulated, not tacitly and implicitly condoned.

This does NOT require massive regulation.

It does require a reframing of the issues rather than a misreading and explaining away of the data that is presenting itself.

What message is it sending to all charters when 90 percent of charters have sought *and received* waivers from the bidding and related party transaction restrictions that public schools operate under? What message are you sending those sincere and ethical charter schools when you open the field of public funding to private placements? Public money should not be used to finance private property acquisition or private schools. Businesses are not entitled to protectionist lending policies.

Private schools, because they are private, have always had this freedom of action. What has changed is the fact that we are using public money designated for a public good to fund these private enterprises. This hurts both the public and private schools. They called themselves private schools for a reason.

ENTITLEMENT ENABLERS

The Republican Legislature in Arizona and other states are in the unenviable position of being one of the biggest promoters of an entitlement mentality in regards to educational spending. A mind-set (entitlement) that they publicly decry in other arenas.

They proclaim that citizens are entitled to choose where they go to school. In April of 2017, the Arizona legislature passed legislation expanding "tuition credits for private placements." The "entitled" users now get to "choose" private placements using a government program providing benefits to members of the private school class. Most of these new "choosers" were going to private schools already, now they become a drag on our educational resources because of "choice" and tax credits.

Now anyone can opt out of what is provided by their community and head to private school. The logic used to justify this "backpacks full of cash" solution, "competition, and choice."

No, it's entitlement.

Where does the conservative logic employed in this kind of thinking end?

Since I don't use those public parks the government can pay for the maintenance fee that my homeowner's fee is charging me.

Don't like your "government police?"

Where's my voucher for my home security system?

How about paying for private guards at my business. Aren't I entitled to that?

TORIES AND MONARCHISTS

The "conservative" mind-set for this entitled mind-set appears more in line with what conservatives were called during the Revolution, "Tories." We forget that the patriots throwing tea into Boston Harbor were the despised "liberals" of the time.

Choice without responsibility for personal payment is a *government-subsidized choice*. While some in the free market and choice community openly state that parents are entitled to the money that would have been spent on a public education privately and in other formats they often speak loudly against entitlements for others.

Going to a private school because you are opting to go to that school as an entitlement is not what a free and appropriate public education was meant to be. We should not be using public funds to pay for our citizens to separate themselves from their fellow citizens into private schools.

The promoters wrap their initial proposals up in language that speaks about handicapped children attending private schools. This "need" ignores that fact that under federal law 94.142 that option is already open to them through a *rigorous special education process*. Districts, the state, and the federal government currently pay for private placements under that law. The laws have been in place since 1977. The federal mandate provided a mechanism for parents to choose out of district placement. *The law did not give carte blanche to the parent to an entitlement.*

It is antithetical to a democratic republic's premise to pay for citizens to opt out of the community's publicly financed and publicly run common schools. Jefferson and Adams both warned against the rise of petty academies after the Revolution. We have common schools because we as citizens are a part of a republic. We are not "consumers of educational services," we are citizens. Our public schools are for educating Americans. They were designed to unite our communities and bring immigrants into the American family.

LOGICAL ANALOGIES

Freedom and Choice in Real Life

Where you live involves freedom and choice. Selecting where you live used to be determined by considering where the best schools were located. Community services were also a primary consideration. A real estate professional will always tell you the three most important items in a real estate sale are, "location, location, location." Devaluing public education does not help your real estate investment.

DOMINO EFFECTS OF THE "CHOICE" LOGIC MODEL

A citizen of Arizona who chooses to live in a "community" developed as such by a contracting company *knows that they will be paying local and county property taxes*. They are listed on the documents signed at closing. Their other choice would have been an apartment, where the taxes on that property are hidden in the rent. Consumer choices lead to fiscal responsibilities for those choices.

What if all of our consumer "choices" came with "entitlements" to tax breaks and credits?

If a 2,000-square-foot home in a community development is paying $2,000 in property taxes, some, not all, of this money goes to the local public district schools. Taxes that the state collects for this and other purposes come out of income, sales taxes, lottery sales, and other taxes.

The money from the property taxes also pays for public services provided by the municipality and the county. The citizen in turn can use the public parks and public spaces they pay for through their taxes. This example leaves out municipal sales taxes and other revenue gathering abilities that the municipalities have.

Water, trash removal, and other city services are billed monthly to the property owner. Approximately: $1,200 per year. The same citizen, by virtue of living in a development, pays a fee for the landscaping and maintenance of the development. A typical amount is $1,000 per year. There are community rules concerning where the citizen's property ends and the community's begins.

In addition, the citizen can either maintain their own property or hire someone to do the work. The charge for this service is $1,500 per year. If the citizen owns a private pool, an additional servicing fee can run up to $1,000 more per year. They have chosen where they live; they expect these charges as part of that contract with their communities.

What's the point of this exercise?

FREEDOM AND CHOICE ARE NOT EQUAL TO ENTITLEMENT

The citizen discussed can use two pools provided for by the homeowners' association. *They are not able to deduct the costs for their private pool from the $1,000 fee paid to the community association.* Likewise, they do not get a tax credit on their town and county taxes for using the parks within the development. Opting out of using the public parks provided by the town you live in is a choice.

The citizen living in a development can't take a state sponsored scholarship (country club opportunity scholarship) to join a country-club of their *choice.*

They do not get a tax credit for the fees paid to the town where water and trash removal comes from. They can't deduct these fees from their income state or federal taxes.

Arizona's municipalities and the state provide superior parks and recreation facilities. The pool in the citizen's backyard is their responsibility. The free citizen has the freedom to decide if they continue to own a pool. They are not entitled to compensation for that choice. Nor are they entitled to a "private pool" tax credit for that choice.

They may not like the "bureaucratic rules" at the community pool but that doesn't lead the citizen to believe that their private choice is the responsibility of the community. The citizen would never dream of asking the state to pay for their country club membership. The right to join a country club is a privilege not an entitlement. You have to apply for membership to these private clubs. As such, they are able to discriminate in their membership selection based on income. In the past, they could segregate by race or religion.

How have we come to a point where the interpretation of "to provide an education" means an entitlement to whatever education that we as private citizens deem fit? The Arizona constitution does not suggest that paying for a religious education was a part of their compact with their citizens. *This is not a conservative approach.*

A PLEA FOR THE WEST

If you are over sixty-five and reading this, you will recall the political rhetoric that baby-boomers lived through when John F. Kennedy faced Richard Nixon in the presidential election of 1960. An issue in that election was the faith of the Democratic candidate. The same issue had been present for Al Smith, a candidate in the 1940s. There was an intense and unrelenting questioning of John F. Kennedy's ability to serve the country before the leader of his faith meaning the Pope. This issue has its roots in anti-Catholicism from the 1840s and beyond.

A Plea for the West (Beecher, 1835) was Lyman Beecher's "conservative" 1835 plea for western states to provide common schools for their immigrant populations. The plea is filled with anti-Catholicism. It is apparent in the writing. Writing that was typical of the time period. The great hope and altruistic purpose in Beecher's plea is that the writer knew that common schools would create American citizens.

The economic, financial, and governance focus of the research in this work questions the reliance on situational ethics inherent in the laws regarding charters and vouchers. These economic and financial issues are cause for alarm.

A bigger issue for our republic is the social capital being lost when we segregate ourselves by "school," schooling alone.

Financial Outrage Is Being Ignored

What will cause the most angst to the general public reading these words is that none of the ethically questionable activities reported on and detailed in this work appear to be illegal under the current laws. Once the players engage in ethically challenging practices it becomes difficult to return to the slow-paced business of making money the old fashioned way, by earning it legitimately.

Most of the over *$26 million (2013–2014) owed to the Arizona Department of Education for overpayments to charter schools was owed by online schools*. Those online schools sued the state to make sure they did not have to pay back the sum all at once. They argued that the state made the mistake and they were entitled to the money for students who had registered and dropped out of their programs. The overcharges are ongoing as of 2017 as the "accounting" for online student attendance is still not up to the task. The problem is present in all states.

For a period of two years, online schools were able to collect 1.5 times the normal rate. This was the infamous TAPBI Program. They did this by claiming students that were in other programs, including districts, and operating online courses for those students. The legislature closed this loophole as the cost of the program skyrocketed without any discernable academic benefits.

The online schools that got used to the 1.5 times payments for their programs have had difficulty dealing with this "loss of revenue." This is mainly because most of the operators who continued to behave as if those payments were still a part of their revenue stream. Ethically challenged financials are the result.

Alexander Hamilton recognized the ethical issues of gaming the system as he created the financial systems for the United States and dealt with financial speculators in that market. This is one reason that he wanted the federal government to hold a controlling interest in the National Banks.

> The spirit of gaming, once it has seized a subject, is incurable. The tailor who has made thousands in one day, though he has lost them the next, can never again be content with the slow and moderate earnings of his needle.
>
> —Alexander Hamilton

We have given up our interest in our public schools when we have given full control of the assets and property of those privately held schools to the whims of the financial marketplace and the players in that real estate marketplace. The owners of charter properties are emulating Ray Kroc's practice of owning the land under McDonald's franchise's buildings. Speculation and over-leveraging of existing property is the result. Mr. Kroc engaged in this practice at his own financial risk.

In stark contrast to the "McDonald's" business practice, charters are engaging in the practice using government-backed loans with an implicit "get out of debt free" card written into law. A spirit of gaming the system is implicit in the law. Local, state, and federal government agencies did not finance Mr. Kroc's ventures with quasi-taxpayer-funded loan programs.

THE PRICE OF GAMING

An online school financial disaster is swept under the rug. Like the tailor in Hamilton's tale, the owners of the online schools got used to the added revenue streams. They have reacted by creating different ways of claiming payment for students. These techniques game the state's ADM accounting system. They have also branched out to other charters and district schools by offering "credit recovery" to those students. Effectively removing the graduation rate ding[1] that those schools would have received from the "partner" charter. Districts have not been blameless in this graduation rate statistic shuffle.

Are students learning?

"Are the students learning, we are looking at that first?"

This type of reply was the standard reply given by the charter association and charter board leadership to inquiries regarding charter school finances and governance over the past decade. What are the online credit recovery results?

Credit Recovery: No Credible Results

This ploy, credit recovery, has had limited effect on the stated goal of credit recovery programs. The goal is helping students graduate from high school. As noted previously, it also allows other charters and districts to game the graduation rate statistics as schools move students into these programs taking them "off" of their student data counts.

The premise of credit recovery is that if you take the students who are far behind in their attainment of high school credits and put them into one online course at time they will finish the course sooner. After obtaining success on one course, they take another and another one by one and catch up. Another way of saying it, "Put the students who are having the worst academic results with an online teacher who is monitoring hundreds of students and assign them to do their work on their own."

How did that idea work out?

Just like you would imagine, it didn't. On top of that dire high school graduation rate college graduation rates for all charters are marginal at best. The gaming of the high school graduation results shows up in the statistics for college success. Charter students nationally have a *25 percent* college[2] completion rate. The schools *did not prepare their graduates for college success*.

The National Student Clearinghouse reported that 55 percent of first-time undergraduates who matriculated in the fall of 2008 finished a degree within six years, versus 56.1 percent of those who began in fall 2007. The charter rate is 25 percent or a 75 percent college dropout rate.

The charter and virtual schools studied for the 2016 Building a Grad Nation Report, Progress and Challenge in Raising High School Graduation Rates suggest that virtual schools are particularly vulnerable to low graduation rates and charters as a whole have a lower graduation rate than public district schools.

> Though alternative, charter, and virtual schools collectively account for 14 percent of high schools and 8 percent of high school students, they make up 52 percent of low-graduation-rate high schools nationwide and produce 20 percent of non-graduates. Regular district high schools account for 41 percent of low-graduation-rate high schools and are where the majority of students who do not graduate on time can be found.
>
> —DePauli 2016

We are judging these programs by intent rather than results.

> "One of the great mistakes is to judge policies and programs by their intentions rather than their results."
>
> —Milton Friedman

The essential questions asked of the research on the charter and voucher programs in this country for this work looks at results and how they correlate with the *stated intentions* regarding charters and vouchers.

It asked "Essential Questions." The subject of the next chapter.

NOTES

1. A "ding" is a negative graduation rate rating. Graduation rates are measured based on the cohort moving through the system. An online student pulled from the normal accounting system for graduation becomes a "transferred" student and no longer impacts the graduation rate for the sending agency. They then "count" against the online schools graduation rate. The accounting system there indicates that graduation is a major issue.

2. A generally unknown phenomenon is the college dropout rate.

Chapter 32

The Essential Questions

What have the promoters of Charter Schools done with the "freedom over their budgets, staffing, curricula and other operations?"

What is the result of eliminating the substantial conformity of governance and finance rules for operating schools (financed from taxpayers' dollars) on the governance and finance of these "free" entities?

THE ANSWERS

The research paper associated with this book asked and answered the essential questions asked above. The report also provided detailed analysis of the financial and governance issues present in the charter and private school tuition credits educational marketplaces in Arizona.

The current laissez faire oversight of charters and tuition credits to private schools has created a marketplace where situational ethics drive the financial and governance practices of 77 percent of the charters studies. Sound fiscal practices have been replaced by practices that game the public funding that is being used to pay for the facility acquisitions, materials, leases, purchased services and related party transactions in charters. Like the tailor in Hamilton's story the practice has become rampant as unscrupulous monopolistic business practices go unchecked by an overstretched authorizing agency.

The laws were intentionally designed to allow this "freedom" and choice by deregulating these quasi-public entities. This freedom of action was supposed to lead to "free market" approaches controlling the marketplace by weeding out nonperforming (academically) schools. There is no evidence that this weeding out is the case. The consequences of this, "Great Freedom" without the attendant, "Great Responsibility" are detailed here.

THE ISSUES IDENTIFIED

- The *Charter School Failure Rate* stands at 43 percent (of all charters opened 1994 through 2016). This figure is a symptom of the issues identified in the report. This calculated percentage does not include district, university, or government agency authorized charters. The addition of that data would skew the number of failures higher. Failures are reported as financial, academic closings (initiated by the charter board, and charters voluntarily leaving the marketplace in Arizona.) The bulk of the failures studied were caused by financial issues.
- *Over-leveraging* of privately owned and held assets (paid for using public funds) are a major factor in the financial failures.
  - Properties and assets are being sold to parties related to the owners (which maximizes the owner's take when those closed sales take place.) Insider trading during transfers of assets and properties are problematic.
  - Those overpayments create a debt load that is unsustainable.
  - Money designated for students is captured using intercepts. Intercepts are a garnishment of equalization payments from the state by finance companies. Intercepts are designed to pay the debt holder first, programs for children come second. This practice is good for the debt holders, bad for students.
  - Massive *property losses* to bankruptcies and business failures estimated at $400,000,000 to date in the state studied are another symptom of the issue. That is, the properties are lost to the taxpayers whose money was used to pay for them.
  - The "free market" of charters is not a true free market. Cronyism and nepotism are present and exploited in the majority of the charters and tuition organizations reviewed. Many charters are oligarchies run by one or two families.
  - Governance issues abound: Governance at the governing board level can include one board member who is the owner; owners can be members of the board and chairs of the board. Related parties are the norm on corporate boards.
- *Net losses* (expenditures exceeding revenues) were reported in the audits of 153 of the charters studied. Fully one-third of the charters studied had net losses in fiscal 2014–2015. This type of loss is not tolerated in districts. When it occurs, Roosevelt District in Phoenix is an example, it is exposed and corrected.
- *Negative net assets (deficits)* for the year were reported in eighty-three charters. This statistic means the assets of the company are less than the liabilities.

- *Distributions that exceed the net for the fiscal year* are being paid to investors (owners), in "for profits."

  ○ Normal stock owned business don't distribute dividends in losing years.
  ○ Distributions from "for-profit" subsidiary companies and salaries paid in those companies *are not available for public scrutiny.*

- The *flawed financial reporting systems* for charters are not tracking all of the administrative (management) costs of the charters accurately.

  ○ Gaming of the reporting system includes under reports of debt to income, overpayments of ADM, manipulation of data to create a positive "fluidity" report from AZCB, etc.
  ○ There is not enough attention to *cash flow issues* at the majority of charters. While *139 charters studied did not meet the Arizona State Board for Charter Schools Financial Performance Review, another 90 did not pass the CASH FLOW element in their passing reports.*

- *Related Party Expenses* are out of control and they are not cost effective. That is, savings is secondary to profit driven, self-serving, related party dealings that profit relatives and business partners. These types of transactions are the norm.

  ○ Related party expenditures constitute the bulk of the expenditures at 77 percent of charters. Related party transactions are by their very nature tainted transactions.

- *Employee practices* that include gaming the Arizona State Retirement System, substandard wages, and the leasing of teachers using subsidiary companies (usually at 10 percent of that payroll cost) are unacceptable.
- *Excessive executive compensation* packages based on student body size and comparable positions in similarly sized districts.
- *Excessive travel expenses* are noted for questionable travel (i.e., to other countries and states).
- *Questionable vehicle purchases* by executives were noted.
- Salary payments to executives are unavailable at "for profits" and subsidiary companies (for profits) controlled by the same corporate board as the charter.

RECOMMENDATIONS FOR ACTION

Charters can be a positive part of public education. The fact that 23 percent of charter owners are operating their schools in ethical, educationally sound ways is cause for hope. The recommendations here are designed to "modify behavior" while leaving great operational freedom intact.

- Additional auditing staff is needed at the state board for charter schools and at the Department of Education at the state and federal levels.

  ◦ The current use of auditing firms by charters in Arizona encompasses 38 auditing firms. This figure includes 6 out of state companies. The auditors should be reviewed and a list of recommended auditors generated. This list should be approved by the state charter board in each state.

- *State Departments of Education need to be able to impose sanctions* on payment to schools that do not provide *timely and accurate* Annual Financial Reviews. The data required is often late. *A fourth pass in December of 2016 discovered changes in reports that were supposed to be in by October 31, 2015*. Unacceptable.
- *Unethical business practices need to be corrected* using the tools currently available for this purpose. The AFRs and Arizona Charter Board Audits.

  ◦ Tampering with self-calculating (a high percentage of tampering was noted) tools built into AZDOE or AZCB documents should have consequences. This is easily detectable and can be done automatically with an algorithm.

- *The comingling of funds between subsidiaries, religious and social organizations, and related ventures of the charter owner need better monitoring.* Audits of related for-profit subsidiary companies with the same boards and owners need to be a required auditing components. The funds financing these ventures are all coming from public sources. The records need to be public.
- *Financial responsibility for losses of public property and assets need to be established.* A revisiting of the laws specifically subsections related to AZ 15–183 Sections O, P, S, and T should be considered. *Private businesses do not get this type of free passes on financial liability.*

  ◦ These laws currently give carte blanche to private individuals to obtain assets and properties without the consequence (responsibility) for the misuse of this freedom.

- While business can operate as LLCs in free markets the owners have some responsibility for their financial practices. This is not the case in charter law which holds owners, their corporate board and officers harmless.

  ◦ The Arizona State Board for Charter Schools should be a party to any transactions related to the sale of charter property and assets. This would give the charter board some degree of control to eliminate rigged sales at exorbitant prices. All sales should be at "Fair Market Value." The sale needs to reflect the true state of the school's enrollment rather than speculative enrollment figures.

○ The Arizona State Board for Charter Schools needs to be given copies of any Memorandums of Understanding that establish payments for properties, transfers of properties, or deferred compensation schemes for former owners. This includes multiyear consulting agreements with payments to former owners or related parties.

Arizona's regulations on charter schools are relatively lax. Laxity is an issue that has been identified by pro and anti-charter publications and research studies. New Hampshire is at the other end of the spectrum with charter laws that protect the taxpayers' investments in public education.

An Arizona Example: The state allows charters to seek exemptions from state laws that require schools to obtain competitive bids for goods services.

Result of the Laxity: Nearly 90 percent of the state's charter holders have gotten permanent exemptions from the state Board for Charter Schools, according to the state's own database.

If local school districts were doing the same thing, there would be an uproar regarding cronyism and nepotism. This is a double standard for services provided by differently classified systems (Charter vs. Public District) *from the same pool of public money.*

The current marketplace is not providing open or free competition.

Chapter 33

Money Talks

Local control of locally raised revenue sources (taxes) and the disbursement of those funds is one of the founding principles of public school financing in this republic. The long and tedious process of creating viable public schools in this country, schools that were the envy of the world, was well documented and analyzed in Lawrence Cremin's four volume, *American Schools* (Cremin 1961, 1965, 1970, 1980). Common Schools in this country were an uncommon asset that unified our citizenry. Public schools as they currently exist are another gift from this country's greatest generation. A little respect for their wisdom is due.

We have been here before. The teaching profession and education in general have been consistently assailed during our national experience with education (Goldstein, 2015). Offering choice and separate educational experiences for different population groups has been tried many times. *It did not work.* The rules for public education financing and governance were established for a reason. That reason was national unity and to provide equal opportunity under the law.

The duty to educate our future citizens was entrusted to the states but more importantly to the local community with governance located in those communities. That democratic process is being undermined by state and federal laws bypassing the local school boards. A de facto takeover of local control. Convenience and expediency are no substitute for democratic process.

Recent school board elections in key cities have been funded by dark money. A danger to our democracy. This political takeover is a part of the hostile takeover of our public schools.

Vouchers are a form of entitlement. They represent a rejection of our local communities' role in education offerings and a removal of our children from learning with their fellow citizens. This has always been a fundamental right when parents choose to pay for their own choice. It has not been, nor should it be, a fundamental entitlement.

POWER OF THE PURSE

In Arizona, the state provides the bulk of the money used for education, albeit at one of the lowest rates in the United States (currently forty-eight). Additional funding comes from county and municipal sources through property taxes, overrides, and local sales taxes. This is not the case in many of the states where the bulk of the funding for schools comes from local property taxes. In districts with great economic power (property value) to raise their own funds for education, less money comes from the state's equalization formula. This factor gives the state of Arizona a great deal of leverage regarding how money from income, sales taxes and gaming sources (lotteries and gambling) will be disbursed.

The tool used is the Arizona Equalized Payments, which is comprised of funds collected by the state through taxation. The policymaking regarding charter finances and governance and private school tuition tax credits have been instigated and directed by the state of Arizona, *not the local communities*.

Charter school funding is the total of the state *Base Support Level* (BSL) and an additional funding category entitled *Additional Assistance*.

The BSL is computed in the same way as traditional public schools— weighted student count times the statutory base level. *Additional Assistance* is a per-pupil dollar amount set by the legislature and multiplied by the simple, non-weighted student count. *Additional Assistance is intended to fund capital* and transportation costs for charter schools. However, charter schools can use this money flexibly and are not limited to using it for capital or transportation expenditures.

Charters do not receive additional funds for teacher experience or some of the performance-based compensation systems districts have. Charters also do not qualify as isolated schools when computing their weighted student count, though they did qualify as small schools (under 600 students) when weighting the student count. That was changed when abuses of the small school weights (i.e., limiting enrollments) were discovered.

The additional assistance rate is currently $1,700. There is little evidence that any serious tracking of this additional money is being required. Operations and Maintenance came in at 14.8 percent of total expenditures in the data. Data on property and assets and their relationship to debt was provided in earlier chapters.

In the data set, a rate of 1.69 percent of overall spending at charters was designated for transportation. The majority of operators do not provide transportation to their schools. As a result, charters are not accessible to all students.

FINANCES OF PUBLIC SCHOOLS 101

Following the financial transactions in public district schools is easy and transparent. The same search is a difficult and obtuse process in the charter world. The reporting systems twist and turn leading the researcher down rabbit holes.

Charters are allowed to use consolidated audits. This means that they can list all of their charters on one audit. It also means that charters in multiple business (i.e., housing, youth clubs, churches etc.) tend to comingle their building funds. The reports generated for this book cut through these obstacles by using forensic accounting methods to analyze the data.

Charters can and do set up private "for-profit" subsidiaries that do not get audited as part of the auditing process. This is done through related party transactions with the subsidiary for-profit companies. We would not tolerate a school board of superintendent in a district with this kind of arrangement. The correct term for this in the business world would be money laundering.

GOVERNANCE IN PUBLIC SCHOOLS

In its most simplistic terms, governance of public schools requires the superintendent, the de facto CEO. The job of this type of CEO is to act as the *agent* of the local school board. This fundamental fact, that the superintendent is the agent of a publicly elected school board is constantly reinforced by graduate schools preparing administrators in the public school system. Boards set policies, superintendents manage the schools based on those policies. The superintendent does not oversee the board. He or she is not a member of that board. A CEO in a charter is there to ensure the company and by default themselves make a profit.

The governance of public district schools demands an easily accessible financial reporting system that is regulated and monitored by the state. The board signs off on those reports. It is a locally elected body of local residents who receive minimal compensation for their efforts. In Arizona, that compensation is restricted to $500 per year. (Source: Article H of HB 2277, Amending Section 15–321, and Arizona Revised Statutes).

The antithesis of this frugal reimbursement for a community service exists in some charters where corporate board members, when they are paid, can be paid $100,000 and more. IRS filings pointed to one parliamentarian/owner/board member took compensation of $276,000 for a school with 300 students in FY 2013–2014.[1] Parliamentarian was how the owner described his position.

At that same charter, the form 990 for the following two years reflected a change downward on these salary payments. *However, they still were $160,000.* This was in an organization that paid *$125,000 to another board member for curriculum. A subsidiary company known as Five Star Educational Research.* Total revenue of the organization for the year in question: $1,935,301. Total Expenses in 2014–2015: $2,011,622. A net loss of (−$76,321). The salaries paid do not reflect the "market factor" of a net loss of money on the year.

This *is* consistent with what is seen in the current state of the unregulated charter business world. Management is protected from financial loss in winning and losing years. This skimming of nonexistent net revenue in CEO compensation passes as free market capitalism. Like the CEOs during the last financial crises in this country, the new CEOs are profiteering whether the "market" is up or down.

Corporate boards in charters and at private schools are appointed. The president of the board is often the owner of the company. Checks and balances are nonexistent.

Local School Boards Have Democratically Elected Members

The elected school board members at districts select the officers of the board at the first meeting of the board. This occurs after an open local election where the local voters select their board members.

The superintendent (CEO) *is not, nor can they be,* the board chair. He or she is a highly trained professional educator with a minimum of a masters' degree and, as is most often the case, a doctorate. The degrees carry requirements in school finances, law, and school history.

A superintendent is an agent[2] of the school board. The board is an elected body charged with designing, approving and establishing policies. These are policies that are debated and approved in public sessions. These policies are the standard operating procedures for a public enterprise. It is the superintendent's job to carry out the will of the board. Policymaking is local in a school district. Policies cannot be in conflict with state or federal laws and regulations.

State law is now trumping those policies. This has been accomplished by passing new deregulated school law for one niche of the "free" market. Federal agencies are also making policy designed to take the local community's role in education away from that community. These "new rules" are for the newly created charter and private entities. Districts need not apply. Lobbyist for the charter and choice industry has had a hand in designing the new rules.

State, county, and local taxpayers are underwriting charter debt through quasi-governmental and now (2017) direct taxpayer backed loans. This type of lending is enabling the over-extended and over-leveraged charter market.

The marketplace is not controlling the compensation packages of charter owners.

Superintendents' salaries and compensation packages are set by the board in negotiations with the superintendent elect. When districts hire a new super-intendent, the candidates are usually obtained through a lengthy highly vetted selection process involving many constituencies.

Owners at charter schools, normally the CEO, purchase a charter. There are no requirements to poll the community or local government when setting up a charter school other than zoning requirements. Communities are not allowed to block charter companies through zoning. CEOs are appointed.

Local elected school board members negotiate the salary and benefits pack-age for the superintendent. The salary is made public when the superintendent is hired. Information on the superintendent's salary is public information.

Charters set the CEOs salary. Usually the CEO is the one doing the setting. Data from 990 indicates year-to-year increases are a part of that compensa-tion. Raises of 10 percent to 25 percent were not uncommon in the data. Teachers were experiencing 1 percent raises at the time noted. One percent of a much smaller salary number. The same pattern was seen in "nonprofit" Arizona Opportunity Scholarship companies.

No Competitive Bids

There is a bidding process for property and asset acquisition in local public schools.

There are even more stringent policies and processes in place when a school district decides to add schools or buy property. To ensure fiscal responsibility the reports that school districts post to the Department of Education must be in on time and accurate. District audits go to the Arizona Auditor General for monitoring.

PUBLIC PROPERTY REMAINS PUBLIC IN A LOCAL SCHOOL DISTRICT

The superintendent and the board *do not* own the property accumulated by the district. That property remains the property of the district and the residents of that political entity and in some cases the state. The assets belong to the tax-payers who elect their representatives to the school board and the legislature. These are the same taxpayers who fund the schools through their income, property, and sales taxes. This is taxation with representation as the founders would have put it.

Taxation and distribution of state revenues without representation on the governing corporate boards of charter schools is only one of the governance items that should concern the citizens of any state, county, or locale in a democratic republic. This type of funding has been ruled on in other states. Washington State's Supreme Court ruled in 2015 that charter school funding and governance structure was unconstitutional. There was a financial reason for that ruling. It had to do with *who owns our schools and how the government was funding private property acquisition.*

TRANSPARENCY

As a taxpayer you can easily follow every dollar of a district's expenditure of public funds through open meetings, postings of budgets, open budget meetings (as the budgets are discussed), and transparent audited filings. You can impact the budgets with your voice at these meetings.

Information regarding the superintendent's compensation is public knowl-edge. Transactions with related parties, relatives of the board or superin-tendent (nepotism), and vested interests are not allowed or highly vetted in public view. Exceptions need board approval. There are not subsidiary for-profit companies paying distributions and salaries to the board or the superintendent.

There is a reason for policies and procedures. That reason is not "bureau-cratic" control, as some would assert, but based on historical precedence (Cremin 1976). There *were* issues in the past with school boards and super-intendents. Like all humans, those early boards and superintendents were not immune to the temptations of unregulated access to public funds. Issues continue to be present as isolated cases.

We know about those cases because they are publicized, not swept under the rug.

Any laws that lack accountability for financial and governance decisions ignore historic evidence at their peril. The oft-quoted value of CEOs running schools ignores known abuses that CEOs perpetrated on their companies by manipulating the financials of those "publicly traded" companies. This type of financial report manipulation persists in the data reporting to different agencies in the study.

PROPERTY OWNERSHIP AND USAGE

If a school district closes a property, it is often used for some other public purpose in the city or town it is located in. In emergencies the local police, fire, and rescue can easily access these public spaces. The public schools are the sites used by the public for access to their property whether it is for sports, classroom spaces, or voting. If a school is sold, the proceeds revert to the community in most states, usually as a reduction in taxes. The data gathered on charters, data that is in the detail on revenue, indicates that most charge the community *substantive fees* to use their property. Some properties take in hundreds of thousands of dollars in fees.

FINANCIAL ACCOUNTABILITY IS NOT A HIGH PRIORITY FOR CHARTER SCHOOLS

An editorial by the editor of the Arizona Republic summed up the issues and the political intrigue that link the legislature, courts, and the charter school movements in Arizona. Mr. Clint Bulick, an attorney and member of two charter school boards (BASIS and Great Hearts), was the subject of the editorial. The excerpt is from Arizona Republic Editorial on the Governor's pick of Clint Bulick for the Arizona Supreme Court. The Institute mentioned in the article is the Goldwater Institute where Mr. Bulick was a Vice President for Litigation.

> Likewise, Bulick is a huge supporter (with a professional interest) in charter schools. Strangely, or perhaps not so, while Bulick and the institute, (Goldwater Institute) have argued often against the secrecy and bureaucracy, he is just fine with the way charter schools get to keep their books fairly secret, and don't have to follow many of the same financial and transparency guidelines of the regular public schools. That might be good for the owners and interest holders of those schools (like Bulick), but for kids?
> —*Arizona Republic Editorial*, January 7, 2016

The system for reporting on charter school finances is oblique in Arizona. *It is readily apparent that most of the mechanisms in place are designed to keep information from the public and not to provide transparent reporting to the public.*

This lack of transparency is especially true of "for-profit" charter schools, which are not required to provide the type of information. "Not-for-Profits" are supposed to provide to the Internal Revenue Service. Example: The salaries paid to executives in "for profits" are not listed. This is also true for subsidiary for profits set up by nonprofit charter groups.

The words "supposed to" in the previous paragraph are used with cause. Locating the IRS Form 990s, a required IRS form for federal nonprofits of all types, and interpreting what has been reported revealed a lot about how this system of checks on nonprofit status is working.

The locating process is often made tedious and time consuming by charters naming themselves with different naming protocols on the 990. The reports are often under-stated, details of this are provided in the data set for this work, with many details being deliberately left out of the federal reporting. The distribution and spending of public funds needs transparent oversight.

The current system of financing and governing charters does not allow for a transparent financial accounting system of taxpayer funds. The governance rules allow, through their silence on the matter, cronyism, and self-dealing practices to exist. The lack of a transparent information system about charter schools makes it difficult to know how widespread the unsavory practices one reads about in the Arizona Republic and National Sources have been in the state's charter schools and nationally. Seventy-seven percent of existing charter organizations is the correct answer.

The report used to inform this book adds to the knowledge base of previous research efforts by drawing on a forensic accounting meta-analysis of the available data. We know the problems exist from this and other well documented reports. The moral courage to correct them is what is needed. To their credit, in the last few years the Arizona State Board for Charter Schools (ASBCS) has been trying to improve on the transparency issue. Though ASBCS is developing better systems, there is still no way to obtain detailed school-by-school information on all charters.

No one is checking whether the required audits the charter board is collecting from their schools matches the information that the same school is

Table 33.1.   Differences in Reports on Net Losses

Charter Name	Net Reported to AZDOE	Net Reported to AZCB	ABS Value of Difference
Hillcrest Academy, Inc.	$105,136	−$4,084,353	$4,189,489
BASIS System Wide Information	−$1,332,911	−$3,074,317	$1,741,406
Edkey Schools	−$658,531	−$1,265,948	$607,417
Imagine Prep Coolidge, Inc.	−$808,488	−$1,129,412	$320,924
Legacy Traditional School—Gilbert	−$543,745	−$1,117,552	$573,807
Bradley Academy of Excellence, Inc.	$211,521	−$1,011,727	$1,223,248
The Odyssey Preparatory Academy, Inc.	−$566,819	−$963,135	$396,316
Juniper Tree Academy	−$442,090	−$818,515	$376,425
StarShine Academy	−$378,015	−$803,397	$425,382

reporting to the Arizona Department of Education on unaudited reports. In most cases, it does not. Sometimes the difference is in the millions of dollars.

The absolute value of the differences in the Net reported to AZDOE and the Net reported to AZCB are given for the top nine net losses reported to AZCB on net in 2014–2015. The complete list has 153 charters on it. Fully one-third of the 407 charters evaluated[3] were operating in the red. Net being the difference between revenues and expenditures.

A CALL TO ACTION

This work is not a call to disband and shut down charter and private schools. The focus on the fiscal and governance improprieties was designed to follow the money. Examples of charter and private schools that are properly managed and fiscally sound were a part of this report. Charters can be a viable part of our educational process.

The questions asked for this analysis were:

What have the promoters of Charter Schools done with the "freedom over their budgets, staffing, curricula and other operations?"

What is the result of eliminating the substantial conformity of governance and finance rules for operating schools (financed from taxpayers' dollars) on the governance and finance of these "free" entities?

In the final chapter, recommendations based on the answers to these questions are provided.

NOTES

1. See Part VII of the Form 990 for FY 2013–14 for detail: http://www.guidestar.org/FinDocuments/2014/861/013/2014-861013916-0a86c89b-9.pdf.
2. As agent, the superintendent is subject to the policies and procedures established by the board. The board makes policy; the superintendent carries it out.
3. Hillcrest Academy went out of business in August of 2016, due to a financial failure. Note they were reporting a positive net to the AZDOE at the end of 2014–2015, keeping their solvency issues away from AZDOE. It is unclear what happened to the Equalized Payments prepaid to Hillcrest at the start of the year, 2016–2017.

Chapter 34

Conclusions and Recommendations for Action

Charters can be a vital part of our educational systems. The public needs to demand that the laws and regulations catch up with what has actually transpired over these twenty plus years. What can be done to ensure the 77 percent meet the same ethical standards as the 23 percent? This segment contains *Conclusions and Recommendations*. It reiterates and adds to some of the points and recommendations made during the presentation part of this report.

Conclusion 1: The over-leveraging of debt and financial distress is at a critical stage. Cash flow, liquidity, bankruptcies, and debt to income issues that this over-leveraging is responsible for are causing charter failure rates.

1. Charter Schools in Arizona and the country are over-leveraged with a financial failure and financial performance rates that are unacceptable.
2. The primary cause of this financial distress is being caused by over-leveraged debt, overspending on overpriced administrative services, and a system that allows too many overpriced related party transactions with for-profit subsidiaries.

   a. These transactions with for-profit subsidiaries are often not in the financial interest of the nonprofit charter schools involved.
   b. Bankruptcies in the charter sector can be traced to these issues.
   c. Charters "surrendering" their charters are typically undertaken in charters in financial distress. No one surrenders a going firm. They sell it.

Conclusion 2: The charter competitive marketplace that was promised and predicted is not reflective of what has developed the existing system, after twenty years, is not an open nor is it a competitive market.

220

1. The current charter "marketplace" is not an open environment.

   a. Multistate organizations have infiltrated and dominated several aspects of the charter market in Arizona (online schools).
   b. Charter organizations control $1.5 billion of what once were public properties. Figures are for Arizona only.
   c. Charters engage in related party activities to enhance profits and management compensation.
   d. Charters create "closed systems" capturing all aspects of the schools operational expenses and profiting from every component that goes to the school. This includes profiting from the "selling" (leasing employees) of teacher services to the schools in the charter.

2. The monopolistic management and governance of charter groups is creating charters that are neither driven by, nor representative of, free or open market economic models. These players are abusing the freedoms given them in the existing charter laws to create monopolistic, family-controlled closed organizations.

   a. An oligarchy or monopoly is an accurate description of the operating and governance mentality of large charter groups.

3. The real estate and asset acquisition markets in charters are neither free, nor open.

   a. Example: Charter building and asset sales are usually closed to market forces. They are closed sales often at inflated prices to a related party.

      i. Inflated, "Goodwill" estimates are used to justify prices, deals, and loans that true market forces would not tolerate.
      ii. The beneficiaries of these sales often maintain either control of the company or payments for consulting fees from the company after they leave. Example Consulting fees of $230 K were found in the data.
      iii. Charter organizations spend inordinate resources on advertising and travel promoting and expanding their market share.
      iv. The advertising in charters is deceptive at best, using cliché naming techniques, that is, academy and deceptive school "attributes" to lure in parents.

Conclusion 3: Management and administrative discrepancies and issues are related to the lack of policies and procedures this in turn leads to a reliance on situational ethics to guide financial and governance at charters and private schools.

1. Result of Issue: Costs at charters do not align with district costs for the same items. Districts are supposed to be competition, in this "Educational

Marketplace." Costs for similar services vary widely at charters. The accounting for these expenses is flawed at best and *deceptive at worst*.

2. Charters cost, on average, double the cost of public school expenditures for the same type of service. Outliers in the top 100 spenders are double and triple this average.

   a. Administrative costs here are averaged using the superintendent's report. They show a 2 to 1 ratio between charters and districts on administrative costs.
   b. The same costs have been shown, in reports cited in the research paper, to be widely divergent from the averages.
   c. The top thirty-three spenders from this study recorded administrative costs that ranged from 38.62 percent to 76.77 percent. The average is almost double the average cost for Administration at districts.

Recommendations for Action:

1. Inconsistent reporting of administrative costs needs to be corrected on the Arizona Financial Reports. Pages 2, 7, and 10 of the AFR need to agree with one another, as they should.
2. Asset and net earnings reporting *should be the same or reasonably close,* on the IRS 990, AZDOE AFR, and in the AZCB monitored audits. This is not the case currently. This practice has the appearance of a fraudulent reporting of Assets to the Arizona Department of Education.
3. For Profits should not be allowed to take "distributions" that drive the net for the year into the red.

   a. An analysis shows this is an issue in too many "for profits."
   b. No data is available to the public regarding subsidiary "for-profits" distributions or salaries paid from those subsidiaries.

4. The "true costs" associated with the ownership of the charter taking payments for leases, services, and related party transactions need to be reflected in the "Administrative" sic management costs of the operation.
5. The relationship of purchased administrative costs to administrative salaries and benefits was cited in this report as an area of concern. Purchased services reflect an amount that usually goes to the management group, not day-to-day administration of the schools.
6. The AZCB should monitor the same information that the AZDOE has regarding reports in the same fiscal years.

   Reason: The majority of the reports studied do not correlate with one another.
   a. This is also true of the IRS 990s studied but to a lesser extent.

    b. The majority of the reports did not correlate well with the AZCB audits from the same year.

Conclusion 4: Retirement, teacher employment, and teacher compensation need to be addressed by the charter board in their policies.

1. The current rate of participation in AZRS is unacceptable and a danger to the financial viability of the Arizona State Retirement System for all teachers and administrators.
2. Dropping AZRS for employees gives charters another method to capture public educational funds that were voted on to support teachers and education. This windfall then is directed to management and profits.

Recommendations for Action:

1. Teachers and administrators in charters need to have access to the Arizona State Retirement System as a contractual part of their employment in schools funded by the Arizona government through funds raised by taxation.

    a. The legislation for charters allows charters to participate. This needs to be a requirement.

    b. Issue: Some charter's status, leasing teachers etc. puts them in a position of being unable to participate in AZRS.

       i. The practice of leasing of teachers needs to be ended. Teachers are not indentured servants of the organization to "sell" to their schools.

       ii. The average cost for this service is 10 percent of the payroll for teachers. The practice is simply a way of capitalizing on your labor costs.

    c. The IRS must approve new charters participating in AZRS. This takes time.

    d. Companies that start a new charter who want to have AZRS for their teachers need to be made aware of this rule.

       i. The approval rate is nearly 100 percent. Charters that are in the approval process should be allowed to put the funds in escrow. This would allow them to buy back the year that was lost while waiting for IRS approval.

       ii. The charter should also hold the employee's contribution in a restricted account during the approval process. Those funds should be labeled, restricted funds, in the audit.

3. Any owner/manager who has the AZRS at the charter they are paid from and does not provide the same benefit at other charters they own needs to either provide the benefit to all parties in their charters or remove

themselves from the system. This practice is shameful and a blatantly unfair labor practice.

4. Once a charter starts in the Arizona State Retirement System, they need to stay in the system. The cost is a cost of doing business in this marketplace. The finances of the charter need to be robust enough for this cost of doing business as an Arizona public school.
5. Managers that have dropped the system after fully vesting themselves and their family members need to be on notice that the charter board and legislature does not approve of this unfair labor practice.
6. The practice of leasing teachers needs to be disavowed by the AZCB and ended. The "Leasing of Teachers" by a Charter's Management Company to their schools is manipulation of the employees' rights. This manipulation is designed to benefit management's profits. The practice needs to be ended.

   a. This practice is rife for abuse and detracts from the amounts available for the classroom and teacher salaries. This report provides evidence that the practice exists (and that it does not result in comparable compensation changes for the teachers).

      Example: A contract for teaching services for $3,000,000 paying 10 percent to the leasing agency takes $300,000 *out of the classroom and into the board room*. This money divided out among the teachers would cover the charter's costs for participating in AZRS (not the teacher's matching contribution).

7. Hiring teachers on work visas should not be an automatic process for filling mathematics and science positions in either charters or districts.

   a. It is not in the interest of the state of Arizona, charter or district schools to encourage the use of work visas for this type of "critical shortage" hiring from abroad. Practitioners should be identified and discouraged from this practice.

Conclusions: The ownership of publicly funded assets need to be public (not private).

1. Public schools (districts or charters) paid for with public funds and financing need to be owned by the public.
2. At a minimum, the sale of these assets needs to be monitored for corruption and rigged sales. A fair market appraisal needs to be done by an independent rating agency.
3. The Arizona Charter Board needs to monitor property transfers and ensure that the property values are reflected in the price charged for the assets being transferred. This is for the protection of the charters as well as

of taxpayers. This includes monitoring Memorandum of Understanding agreements.

4. States and the Federal Government are underwriting the government-backed loans used to finance most charter land and property acquisitions. This is not consistent with free market economics. Taxpayers are on the hook for financial decisions they have no control over.

5. The sale of charter assets needs to be public with open bidding on the assets of the charter school. This is how a free market operates.

6. Excessive payments to related parties for property, leases, or rents need to be noted and stopped.

7. A "takeover" should be possible in a "free charter market" if that is the espoused economic model. That is, the consumers of educational services where a charter is not meeting their needs should be able to organize a new charter group and take over the charter at that location. If the belief is that parents are consumers of educational services then this type of takeover needs to be allowed.

8. Another operator including a school district should be able to make an offer for a charter's assets and buildings if the school is in financial or academic distress. There are currently more "empty" former charters around than there are empty district school spaces.

   Sub-point: Publicly owned buildings should not be given over for private ownership. The communities where the building is located can repurpose the sites.

9. The alternative to an open bidding system for the "assets" of the charter being sold is the current set up where a "friendly" related party takeover occurs instead.

   Reason for Recommendation: In the current "free market," these buy-outs often leave the new owners with a financial distressed, overpriced school because the purchase was based on relationships rather than sound business practices. The examples in the data show this type of transaction is the norm currently.

   a. *Sweetheart Deals are being made rather than sound business practices being allowed to work. This is not how free markets work.*

   b. *Real businesses buy low. That is, letting the property that is distressed go bankrupt prior to purchasing the assets at a reduced price. This was not the case in the data.*

Conclusions: Auditing practices for charters need revamping.

1. Audits need to follow a standard format that requires detail and supporting information on assets and liabilities, revenues and expenditures, and related party expenses.

2. Audits need to be done by auditors with offices located in Arizona with a demonstrated expertise in Arizona law.

3. A list of acceptable auditors needs to be developed using data gleaned from the audits submitted to date to determine which auditors are currently providing acceptable levels of information.

4. Audits need to be done for each charter entity then a Consolidated Audit can be prepared collating that data.

   a. *Example* of Consolidated Audit Issues, a financially and academically failing school can be propped up by sister schools in a large consolidated charter report.

   Consolidated audits for large charters lack detail and confuse the financial status of the individual charters. This gives the appearance to the public eye as a lack of transparency. It is.

   b. *Entities with assets that are not in the school end of the operation, that is, Chicanos Por La Causa's housing units, need to separate the audits for the charter end of the business without regard to the non-charter part of the operation. This applies to properties that belong to religious, civic, and private individuals that have mixed uses for the properties.*

   Comment: This report's data accommodated for this issue.

   i. Travel reporting needs to be detailed and related to operations in the state of Arizona. Transportation expenditures need to be clearly stated especially when cars or vehicles are purchased for management with charter funds.

   ii. All sales and transactions made with public funds needs to be public with open bidding on the purchase of (or sale of) assets for the charter school.

   iii. The audit should detail all of these transactions within the year they take place. This is how a free market operates.

Recommendations 7: Related Party Transactions
Conclusions: Excessive payments to related parties for property, leases, or rents need to be noted and stopped. The percentage and volume of resources going to this practice detracts from and diminishes the education of our children.

Recommendations for Action:

1. *Redundant recommendation here is by Design:* Follow up on previous recommendations as they relate to related parties. A "takeover" should be possible in a "free charter market" if that is the model.

   a. Another operator in the marketplace, including a district, should be able to make an offer for a charter's assets and buildings if the school is in financial or academic distress.
   b. The alternative is the current set up where a "friendly" related party takeover occurs instead.
   c. These buyouts often leave the new owners with a distressed over-priced school because the purchase was based on relationships rather than sound free market business practices (i.e., letting the property go bankrupt.)

2. *Consulting payments to related parties should be spelled out.*

   a. *Reasons for Recommendations:*

      i. Too many of the transactions studied showed consulting fees being paid to former owners or board members.

      ii. There is often no commitment for providing a consulting role spelt out in the Memorandum of Understanding (MOU) legitimizing the fee.
      iii. The consulting fee may be going to product development efforts for the former owner's new businesses. Memorandums of Understanding regarding "consulting fees" need to be available and subject to the approval of the AZCB.

         I. Consulting fee structures can be set up and are sometimes a cover for delayed compensation packages. It is impossible to tell from the audits and 990 reports.
         II. Example: $217 K was reported as a consulting fee for one ex-owner in the data. This was in addition to $1.5 million paid for assets the former owner held.

3. *Related party transactions that utilize taxpayer funds need to follow the same rules as school districts regarding competitive bidding and assignment of contracts for services.*

   a. Recommendations: Charters need to be following the same rules as districts regarding conflicts of interest. Those rules are there for a reason. They safeguard the public's investment in education.

    b. Contracts for overseeing a construction contract need to be awarded to a clerk of the works rather than a related party that overcharges for this service. ($100 to 200 K contracts were noted). Districts *never* spend that amount for this type of service.

    c. Relationships with religious organizations should pass the "separation of church and state" rules that public district schools must follow. If the logic for government funds being used for Catholic schools held up (and still does). That is, they are not allowed. Then, the rules for organizations run by a majority of pastors, imams, rabbis, or "bishops" in their governing boards and ownership should be the same.

4. *Organizations taking and distributing state tax credit funds for religion-specific scholarships are an issue.*

    a. *Logic and Reason:* If a charter school were run by a Catholic Church with a faculty and administration made up of priests, nuns, and brothers, there would be a "problem" declared.

    b. There are charters in the data that have relationships with related religious organizations and taxpayer generated funds that cross over between the various parts of the entity.

    c. An organization raising tuition funds for "Christian Schools" and excluding Catholic Schools from its largesse is neither Christian nor appropriate.

5. *Compensation of Related Parties: When a charter school provides an owner's salary and they are a pastor at the church affiliated with the school (collecting another salary?) that should and does constitute a conflict of interest (i.e., you are either one or the other).*

    a. *Related party transactions involving churches, synagogues or mosques with rental or lease agreements should be detailed and clear in the audits.*

    b. *Too much comingling of funds is apparent in the audits.*

    c. *Related parties "for-profit" schools operating in the same space as the charter need to provide detailed disclosures on how the operations are kept separate.*

6. *Conflict: For-profit K–2 schools tied to three to six charters are questionable.*

    a. *The for-profit school charges full tuition for K–2 then allows the parents to attend the charter school "for free."*

      i. The "tuition" is typically more than the state would have provided for a free and appropriate grade 1 and 2 program.

      ii. The system is being played for greater profits.

    b. Evidence of Issue in the Data: Details in the audit reports show high reporting for tuitions and fees at these types of schools.

7. *Recommendation: Related party transactions should, at a minimum, be limited to 10 percent of all contracts and leases. This is the case in the 23 percent of charters in the data set that are using ethical business practices.*

Recommendations 8: Salaries and Benefits for Owners, Staff, and Board Members

1. *Conclusion:* Salaries for management should reflect the true market value of similar services provided by a similarly sized district school.

    a. *Reason:* There are too many cases of schools paying executives at schools with an ADM of 300 the same salary as superintendents in districts that have 5,000 plus ADMs.

    b. Funding these salaries at excessive levels contributes to the problem of low average salary for teachers at charters. Annual raises of 10–25 percent for management while the teaching staff was experiencing 1 to 3 percent increases were noted.

2. *Conclusion: The information regarding the amounts being paid to teachers (certified or noncertified contractual teachers) and the amount of teachers on staff is suspect.*

    a. The reporting done on page 7 of the AFR needs to be checked for accuracy regarding numbers of staff, qualifications, and compensation.

    b. Currently, charter schools are supposed to maintain a listing of the staff's "highly qualified" status (including resumes and degrees held by the staff).

Conclusion: There is little evidence data is being checked in a consistent way for veracity at either the Department of Education or the Charter Board.

3. *Recommendation: The report regarding these data points (AFR) should be required to have accurate counts.*

    a. Several charters provided no data on their teaching staff. This should be cause for rejection of the AFR.

4. *Conclusion: The freedom given to charters related to the governance of charters is being exploited by payments to board members and related party transactions with board members.*

5. *Recommendation: Board members on charter school corporate boards should follow the same rules as board members on public school boards regarding related party transactions.*

    a. This particular item is especially important as it relates to compensation for board services.

b. The employment of Corporate Board members as employees in the organization is a clear conflict of interest.

> *Issue and Recommendations:* The CEO of the charter company should be an agent of the corporate board not its president or chair even when they are the "owner" of the charter.

c. Corporate Boards need VETO power over the CEO.

    i. *Reason:* The existing set up allows the CEO to have unlimited powers regarding the governance and financing at the charter.
    ii. *Often the CEO is the final arbiter in harassment cases brought against the charter. This is a conflict of interest.*
    iii. *Cases of this conflict have embarrassed the charter movement in the media and the court of public opinion.*

Recommendations 9: Federal, State, and Charter Board Reporting Compliance

1. Federal nonprofits need to post their administrative and management salaries to their 990 report to IRS. All nonprofits in the charter program should be federally registered nonprofits subject to 990 reporting.

   a. Compliance on 990 reporting is limited and inaccurate.
   b. There are vast differences in 990 reports noted in the report.

2. Asset Reporting to AZDOE and AZCB need to match.

   a. Assets reported to the IRS also should agree with the AZCB Audit of the same year. The sum of all AFRs for charters that consolidate their audit should be equal to the consolidated audits total for the organization.
   b. Discrepancies should be noted by the AZDOE and AZCB and followed up on by both agencies.
   c. The auditors need to be informed of the discrepancies noted.
   d. Improprieties need to be checked and monitored by the Arizona Charter School Board.
   e. There is enough data in the audits and AFRs to raise red flags and demand full accounting records for suspicious transactions.

       i. Example from the data: A miscellaneous charge to Administration of $400 K.

3. Annual Financial Reviews are the purview of the AZ Department of Education.

   a. The AZDOE needs authority to send back AFRs where the accounting formulas (summing formulas built into the form) have been turned off by the person filling out the form.

b. AZDOE should be able to impose deadlines for the forms return (one month). The AZ Charter Board should be copied on these requests for information and should vigorously support the AZDOE's request.

c. ALL AFRS need to be completed by the stated deadline with Equalization Payments held up for schools who do not submit the report in a timely or accurate manner.

    i. Reasons: The identified problem was AFRs in the system that were not in to AZDOE at the late stages of this report's data gathering.

    ii. The reports were due for 2013–2014 at the end of October of 2014.

    iii. In late summer of 2014, several reports were still not corrected and posted to the AZDOE site.

    iv. The final corrections for this report were made in November of 2016 and had to be changed as several AFRS were sent in in late October (from the fiscal year 2013–2014 not 2014–2015, which is due October 31 of 2016). In general, the AZDOE needs auditors added to their staff so they can track many of the issues raised in this study.

    v. The same recommendation is made for the AZCB which is trying to solve some of the issues raised in this report with a limited staff.

    vi. This report and the data set associated with it will be shared with AZCB, AZDOE, and the IRS.

1. Members of the Legislature with ties to charter schools or public schools need to recuse themselves from votes that may be perceived as conflicts of interest. By any standard definition those votes are a conflict of interest.

2. Accelerating leases need to be tied to the market for similar spaces in the retail marketplace. Automatic increases of leases tied to ADM and annual automatic increases take funding meant for classrooms and teacher salaries away from the local administrator's budget. Charters should be seeking the best deal for their students, not a related party.

    a. *The practice of leasing schools from companies that "own" the buildings (with the same board as the school) needs to end.* A modification of practice that tied the lease to the debt *being paid by the "for profit"* would suffice. Profiteering from debt that is being guaranteed by the ADM of a school needs to be curtailed.

Addendum A

Access to Source Data

The following is full disclosure regarding the source data. Every effort has been made to make the original documents easily accessible from the data set to allow the reader to see where the information used in this report came from. The data set contains links to the original materials cited in the data. The link locations are noted below.

IRS FORM 990 FOR FYS 2013–2014 AND FY 2014–2015

For this study, the author looked at all of the Form 990s for each nonprofit school. The link to each 990 is in the data set. Example: Legacy Avondale Form 990 FY 2013–2014. Special thanks to Guidestar and Charity Finder for providing the access to this data. Links to the data are in column BA of the data set. For profits do not file a Form 990 and nonprofits that are only registered as such in Arizona are exempt from the filing rules for federal nonprofits.

ARIZONA DEPARTMENT OF EDUCATION ANNUAL FINANCIAL REVIEWS (AFRS)

Arizona School Finance Start Page takes the user to the Arizona School Finance Start Page This is the jumping off point in the AZDOE data set. As of this writing, this page will take you to the starting point for the 2015–2016 Annual Financial Reviews. Moving through the dataset at AZDOE will allow the user to locate the AFRs used in this report. Over 900 AFRs from two fiscal years were used in the creation of this data set. In particular, 2014–2015 is detailed in the data and reported on in this document.

Thanks to the staff at the Department of Education for their patient assistance as the author learned to navigate this information.

Arizona Superintendent of Public Instruction Reports are easily located at the Arizona Department of Education website. The information in this data set was gleaned from Volume One of the Annual Superintendent's Reports for FY 2013–2014, 2014–2015, and 2015–2016 when available. The link is provided here: http://www.azed.gov/superintendent/superintendents-annual-report/.

Arizona State Board for Charter Schools Audits

Arizona State Board for Charter Schools Audits: Each charter has the following link in column BK in the data set. Audits for all of the charters were researched with the 2013–2014 audit used in an analysis of all audit reporting done in that particular year. The years 2014–2015 data (an audit analysis) was performed on all of the charter audits for that year. In all, approximately 1,100 audits were studied for the information in this audit.

A complete listing of the charter school laws in Arizona is provided at the AZCB website here: https://asbcs.az.gov/board-staff-information/statutes-rules-policies.

Access Link for Audits Once there.

Pick Documentation.
Go to Document Management and then Click Charter Holder.
Select Audit Documents and Pick Year; then Download the File.
http://online.asbcs.az.gov/charterholders/view/592/legacy-traditio nal-school-avondale.

Limited Bibliography

Argyris, Chris, and Donald A. Schèon. 1978. *Organizational Learning*. 2 vols. Reading, MA: Addison-Wesley Pub. Co.

Barry, John M. 2004. *The Great Influenza: The Epic Story of the Deadliest Plague in History*. New York: Viking.

Block, Herbert, and George Orwell. 1961. *Animal Farm*. graphic.

Bottari, Mary. 2013. "From Junk Bonds to Junk Schools: Cyber Schools Fleece Taxpayers for Phantom Students and Failing Grades." Last Modified October 2, 2013, accessed March 17, 2017, http://www.prwatch.org/news/2013/10/12257/junk-bonds-junk-schools-cyber-schools-fleece-taxpayers-phantom-students-and-faili.

Consoletti, Alison. 2011. *The State of Charter Schools: What We Know and What We Do Not—about Performance and Accountability*. Washington, D.C.: Center for Educational Reform.

Cremin, Lawrence A. 1961. *The Transformation of the School: Progressivism in American Education, 1876–1957*. 1st ed. New York: Knopf.

Cremin, Lawrence A. 1965. *The Genius of American Education, Horace Mann Lecture*. Pittsburgh: University of Pittsburgh Press.

Cremin, Lawrence A. 1970. *American Education: the Colonial Experience, 1607–1783*. 1st ed. New York: Harper & Row.

Cremin, Lawrence A. 1976. *Public Education, The John Dewey Society Lecture No. 15*. New York: Basic Books.

Cremin, Lawrence A. 1980. *American Education: the National Experience, 1783–1876*. 1st ed. New York: Harper and Row.

Davenport, Debra K. 2016. *Arizona School District Spending (Classroom Dollars) Fiscal Year 2015*. Phoenix, AZ: AZ Auditor General.

DePauli, Jennifer, Balfanz Robert, and Bridgeland, John. 2016. "Building a Grad Nation: Progress and Challenge in Raising High School Graduation Rates." In *GradNation: America's Promise Alliance*. Baltimore, MD: School of Education at Johns Hopkins.

Education, Arizona Department of. 2015. *Annual Report of the Superintendent of Public Instruction*. Arizona: Arizona Department of Education.

Friedman, M. 1999. "Policy Forum: Milton Friedman on business suicide." *CATO Policy Report*. Washington, DC, CATO Institute: 6 and 7.

Hall, J. 2017. The Consequences of Unregulated Charter Schools in Arizona: For Profit American Virtual Academy Nets $10 Million Profit in 2016 After Siphoning $84 Million from Nonprofit Primavera Online, Arizonans for Charter School Accountability.

Heidegger, Martin. 1962. *Being and Time*. New York: Harper.

King, Dr. Martin Luther. 1962. "An Address by the Reverend Dr. Martin Luther King Jr. at Cornell College." Mount Vernon, Iowa, October 15, 1962.

Kuhn, Thomas S. 1996. *The Structure of Scientific Revolutions*. 3rd ed. Chicago, IL: University of Chicago Press.

Lewis, Beth. 2017. "7 Reasons to Become a Teacher." [Website]. ThoughtCo., Last Modified March 2, 2017, accessed March 13, 2017. https://www.thoughtco.com/why-teaching-is-fun-3194716.

Moe, Michael, and Gay, Keith C. 1996. *The Emerging Investment Opportunity in Education*. San Francisco, CA: Montgomery Securities.

Orwell, George. 1971. *Animal Farm: A Fairy Story*. London: Secker and Warburg.

Ravitch, Diane. 2010. *The Death and Life of the Great American School System: How Testing and Choice Are Undermining Education*. New York: Basic Books.

Schultz, Ellen. 2011. *Retirement Heist: How Companies Plunder and Profit from the Nest Eggs of American Workers*. New York: Portfolio/Penguin.

Slivinski, S., Scholmack, Byron, and Dranias, Nick. 2012. Debt and Taxes: Recommendations for Reform. Phoenix, Goldwater Institute.

Staff, AZ Department of Education. 2015. *Annual Report of the Superintendent of Public Instruction*. Phoenix, AZ: Arizona Department of Education.

Index

About the Author

Curtis J. Cardine was superintendent of schools for a large multidistrict supervisory union in southwestern New Hampshire. The supervisory union was comprised of three independent public school districts. Cardine established public charter schools in New Hampshire in 1999 with local private funding and then federal public charter school grant money.

The author opened public charters as lead principal and then as a superintendent in Arizona charter organizations. The New Hampshire charter schools noted have won recognition from the Association for Supervision and Curriculum Development and were featured in Sam Chaltain's *American Schools*. They, and the Arizona charter schools Cardine initiated, are still operating as stand-alone charters.

Prior to becoming a superintendent, Cardine served as an elementary school principal in Troy, New Hampshire (three years), and as a principal (thirteen years) and teacher (eleven years) in Winchester, New Hampshire, two of the least affluent schools in that state. During that time, he created public school options for highly involved multiple handicapped children and a highly recognized program for autistic children. Cardine has instructed at the primary, elementary, high school, and university level. He has expertise in organizational management, leadership and change, gifted education, and school finance law.

He moved to Arizona in 2006 and headed up an educational technology start-up company for two years. Other business experiences include ownership of restaurants and gyms.

From 2008 until 2015, he worked in a leadership role in two of Arizona's larger charter companies. His experience in the business, charter, and public school models informs this work and the philosophy that is evident in the writing.

Cardine left both charter companies for the same reason. Ownership's use of situational business ethics applied to the financial and governance practices of those charter groups. This mismatch created a moral quandary.

Business deals that conflicted with sound ethical business and educational practice were a source of conflict between the educational leadership in the schools and the charter business firms managing those schools. This led to a decision to leave both charter groups. This detachment has been a deliberate stepping away from involvement in the subject being studied.

Since 2012, he has been engaged in a meta-analysis of the data regarding the finances and governance in Arizona's Charter Schools. That report, "A Forensic Accounting Look at Twenty Years of Charter School Finances in Arizona (Data, Observations, Conclusions and Recommendations for Action)," provides the data informing this book.

CPSIA information can be obtained
at www.ICGtesting.com
Printed in the USA
BVHW01*0141091217
502248BV00001B/2/P